Anatomy and Physiology

A Guide for Allied Health Professions

"The book is packed with graphics. One picture does save one-thousand words."

Glen Ledbetter, M.D.

"The book is absolutely great for a coder and other allied health associates who really needs to understand the human body system and its functions."

B. Kandoth, CPC

"There is a drawing on almost every page. Well done!"

Eddie R. Joslin, M.D.

"An excellent book for ICD-10 and CPT. Provides much needed information for allied health professionals, without over-dosing them! Each chapter of this small book is loaded with drawings, Test Your Knowledge and Clinical Correlates, plus a glossary of terms. A perfect reference tool to return to day after day."

Irene Morin, M.D.

AF702622

Since MedBooks 1985

Anatomy and Physiology

For Allied Health Careers

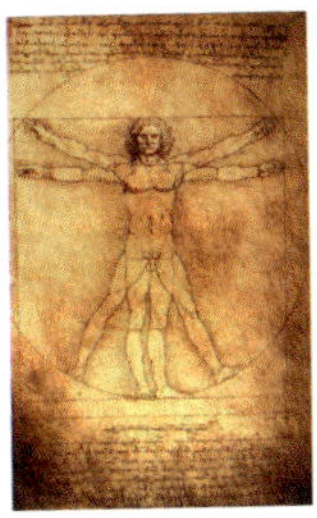

John Brady, MD, PhD

MedBooks, Inc., Richardson, Texas

Published by MedBooks, Inc.
101 West Buckingham Road
Richardson, Tx. 75081
www.medbooks.com

Printed in the United States of America

ISBN: 978-1-937816-01-8

Library of Congress Control Number: 2011942116

Cover design by Mark Lerner

Dedication

I practiced OB-GYN for a number of years before turning to teaching and eventually writing. During that time, I had a medical assistant who worked with me side-by-side from the day I first opened my office to the day I closed it. Shelba was the total package. She was great with patients on and off the phone. She always seemed to know what I was going to need before I did. It was with great respect and admiration for her that I attempted to construct this text, and it is to her that this book is dedicated.

Contents

Illustrations

The Integumentary System

The Musculoskeletal System

The Respiratory System

Figures page #

The Cardiovascular System

Figures page #

The Hemic and Lymphatic System

Figures page #

The Digestive System

Figures page #

The Urinary System

The Reproductive System

The Endocrine System

Figures page #

The Nervous System

Figures page #

The Senses

Figures page #

Preface

When I was asked to write a book on anatomy and physiology for non-majors, I had no illusions regarding the production of a comprehensive and detailed text. My mission was to distill what I felt was the core information and present it in such a way that students pursuing certification in medical assisting, medical coding, or as pharmacy technicians might have a readable, appropriately detailed resource to learn from. Many excellent texts are available, but are simply too detailed and lengthy to be "digested" in the short periods afforded these curricula.

To some, reading this book may seem a bit like "gargling rather than drinking deeply." To those I suggest moving to one of the heavier, more-detailed texts that are available. They will most certainly quench your thirst. For those of you who want never to lose sight of the forest for the trees, this little book may be just what you need.

Note from the Author

Having practiced as a physician for many years and later as a teacher, it became very apparent that health information professionals needed an anatomy and physiology resource that was comprehensive enough, but not "written" for nurses or medical students. What I discovered, both as a physician and teacher, was that current books on the market used in allied health courses were too detailed, and lengthy to be "digested" in the short periods afforded students. The fact that many individuals were not grasping the main concepts was a major concern, and the bottom line was someone that was not .

When the choice became apparent that a book on anatomy and physiology for the health information students needed to be written, I had no illusions regarding the production of a comprehensive and detailed book. The decision to distill what was the core information and present it in such a way that students in allied health fields might have an appropriately detailed resource to learn from was my main objective.

Whether in the classroom, inpatient, office, or outpatient setting, this detailed anatomy and physiology book is a great reference tool that you can return to, time-after-time.

Acknowledgments

Books are never solo projects … not by a long shot!

For planting the idea for this book in my head, I'd like to thank Irby Hunter, M.D. His idea was to create a simple, easy-to-use book that any coder and biller could understand. I believe we have accomplished that within this book. For the idea to separate this text from all the rest of the medical coding and billing material made available through MedBooks, Inc. and make it so that the same book could be used by other students in the medical field (e.g., medical assistants), special thanks goes to Mary Odiase, RHIA, whose powerful recommendation and dedication to the learning of all students encouraged us to make an entirely separate text. There have been many other people along the way who have also made suggestions that have brought this book to being one of the easiest-to-use anatomy and physiology texts available on the market. Among them is Donna Harper, RHIA, whose support, encouragement, and prayers were unconditionally given and very much appreciated, and who brought us to the attention of so many others who helped us. I'd also like to thank Khawar Aizaz, BSc, MB, ChB, FRCSI, who suggested adding the Common Conditions and Diseases sections for each body system. Lashan Washington; Sue Pylant; CCS-P; Chinetta Hall, CCP, AMT; Manual Torres, BESS; Ray Guitierrez, Patty Giles, Holly Ann Smith and Michael K. O'Herron added significant input at each stage of the book's development to make it what you see today.

Additionally, I would like to thank Jenny Grossman, M.D., Lynne Stair, and Julie Smith-Centeno for their final input and review of this publication. Your time and effort have aided me greatly in the development of this book.

Special thanks go to MedBooks and all of the publishing professionals who made this book a reality:

To Trish, whose drive and boundless energy kept me plugging away.
To Mark, whose cover design and desktop creative skills proved essential.
To Randy, who always challenged me with those darn questions of his.
To Heather, for her artistic drawing ability.

Thank you to all of you! Without you, this text would not exist. To those students who purchase this book, may you never lose sight of the big picture.

J. B.

Introduction

This book attempts to present a relatively complicated topic—in this case, human anatomy and physiology—in an understandable, perhaps even entertaining way.

Anatomy is the study of the structure of the human body. This study could be on a microscopic (tiny) level or on a macroscopic (large) one. Physiology is the study of the way the body functions. This too can be addressed at the molecular or "big picture" level.

This book is designed for the non-major and is a simplified discussion of the most basic features. Its purpose is to provide medical coding students, medical assistants, pharmacy techs, and radiology techs with a broad exposure to the structure and function of the human body and to round out their education in their chosen field.

There are a couple of concepts we will build on as we progress through this book.

1. Cell theory places the cell as the central factor on which life is based. A cell is the smallest functioning life form. It is capable of reproducing and maintaining homeostasis (we will cover this term shortly). Cells vary widely in their function as well as their appearance. Thus, there is no "typical" cell. In general, however, they are living "bags of water" whose contents differ markedly from the extracellular fluid in which they lie. The membrane that separates them from their surroundings is selectively permeable to certain substances, and this wall is uniquely equipped to permit the cell to function at its most efficient level.

Contained within the cell are a number of organelles—structures that provide functions such as transport and packaging of materials for release outside the cell, energy storage, or reproductive capabilities. Refer to Figure 1 for a highly stylized drawing of a "typical" cell."

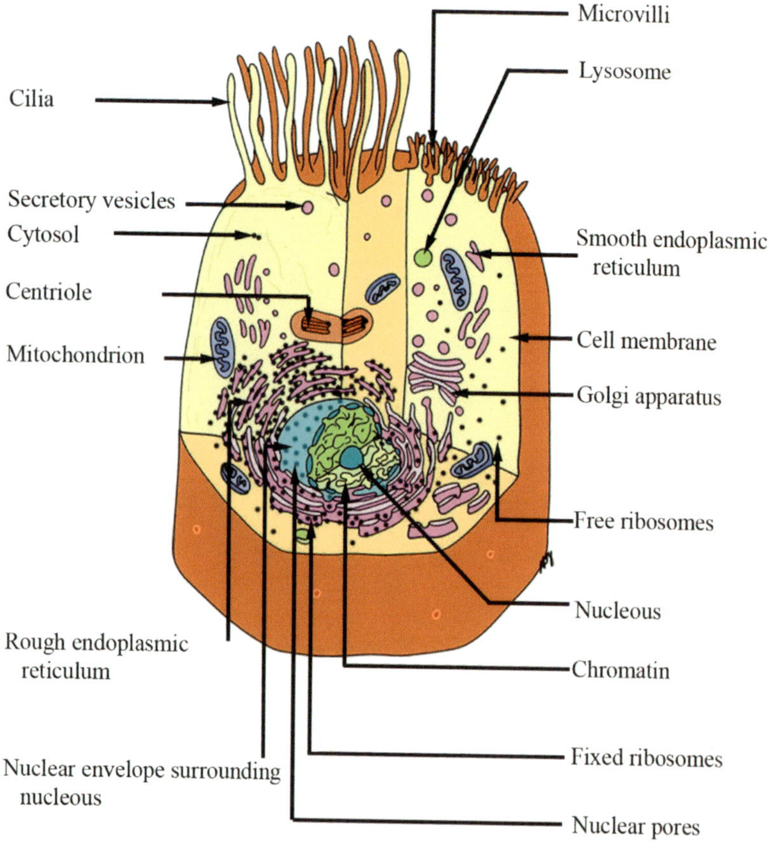

Figure 1. Model cell and associated intracellular structures

2. Homeostasis is a state of balance or equilibrium, regulated by the body, that allows each cell, tissue, or organ to perform at its best.

There are also a few questions you may have:

1. How are you going to deal with those long, complicated medical terms? Easy. You'll learn how to break them down into their component parts. For example, in the term *polycythemia*, *poly* means "excessive" or "many," *cyth* refers to cells, and *emia* refers to blood. Thus, *polycythemia* means an increase in red cells in the blood. Piece of cake!
2. What is the significance of the standard anatomical position? It is shown in Figure 2. When it is used as a reference, everyone can be "on the same page" when discussing the location of a lesion. For example, a mole on the back of the right hand is described as being on the dorsum or the dorsal surface of the right hand. A good way to remember that the dorsal surface is on the back of the body is to think of the big dorsal fin of a shark. It is the fin that is located on the shark's back and shows above the water. Other examples of using anatomical terms for locations are: the elbow is distal (farther away) to the shoulder but proximal (closer) to the wrist, and the umbilicus (belly button) is superior (above) to the pubus but inferior (below) to the thyroid gland. Commit the terms and their definitions to memory as they are discussed in each chapter; they will continue to appear throughout the book.

You will do fine! Take it a day at a time and enjoy learning about your body and how it works.

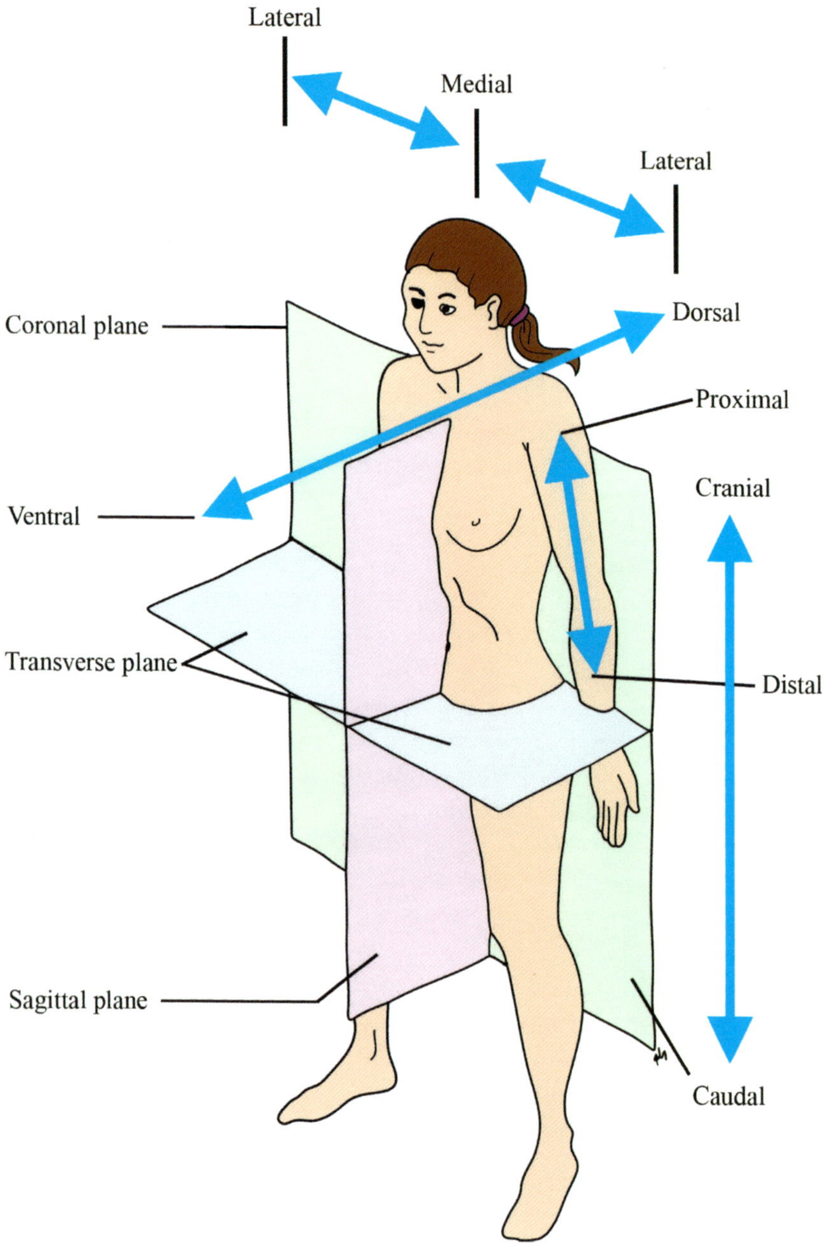

Figure 2. Anatomical positions and body planes

Chapter 1
The Integumentary System

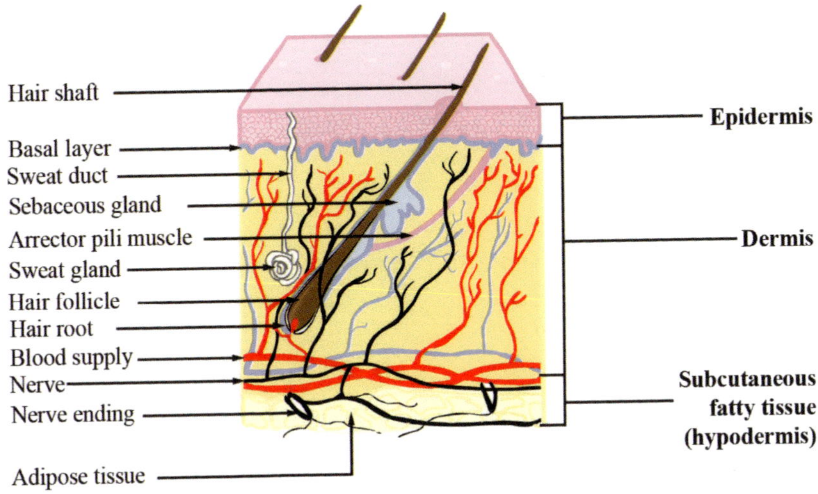

Figure 3. Cross section of skin

For most of us, the appearance of our skin is highly valued and we go to great lengths to ensure it looks good. The word *integumentary* is derived from the Latin root words *integere* and *integumentum*, which mean "to cover." The **integumentary system** comprises the skin, nails, hair, and sweat and oil glands—our entire body surface.

Skin

Aside from providing bodily protection from a host of dangerous external threats such as bacteria, viruses, and toxic chemicals, the skin houses sensory structures (e.g., nerves), provides insulation from cold, offers a flexible tear-resistant covering, and helps regulate body temperature through perspiration. In other words, the skin

- Is the first line of defense in protecting the body's internal organs and tissues;
- Regulates internal body temperature;
- Provides sensory information (e.g., touch, pain, heat, and cold) regarding the surrounding environment; and

- Provides protection from the sun's ultraviolet radiation.

Figure 3 illustrates the layers of the skin and its accessory components.

The Epidermis

Medically speaking, there are two primary layers of skin. The outermost layer is called the **epidermis**. Because of its continual contact with the outside world, new skin cells are constantly being made to replace the ones that our bodies shed. The epidermis consists of a cell layer called **stratified squamous epithelium** that is particularly resistant to tears and injury because the cells are tightly connected. New squamous cells are made at the base of the epidermis, known as the **stratum basale**, and slowly "drift" toward the surface of the skin as the outer cells are lost or destroyed. In fact, it takes about two weeks for a cell to reach the surface after it is created.

The Dermis

Immediately beneath the epidermis lies the **dermis**, a thick layer consisting primarily of **collagen fibers** (Figure 4). It is these fibers that provide much of the skin's strength and resilience. The dermis is home for blood vessels, nerves, and glands (e.g., sweat and oil or sebaceous glands), as well as hair follicles. Waves or ripples in the thickness of the dermal layer produce the valleys and ridges that make up the surface changes responsible for finger prints.

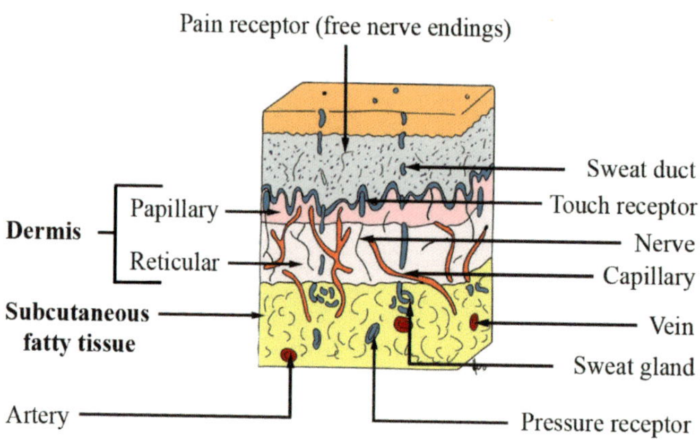

Figure 4. Dermis

The Subcutaneous Layer

Attaching the dermis and epidermis to the underlying structures, the **subcutaneous layer** consists of connective tissue and usually fat (called **adipose tissue**). This fat serves to insulate the body by conserving heat (Figure 5).

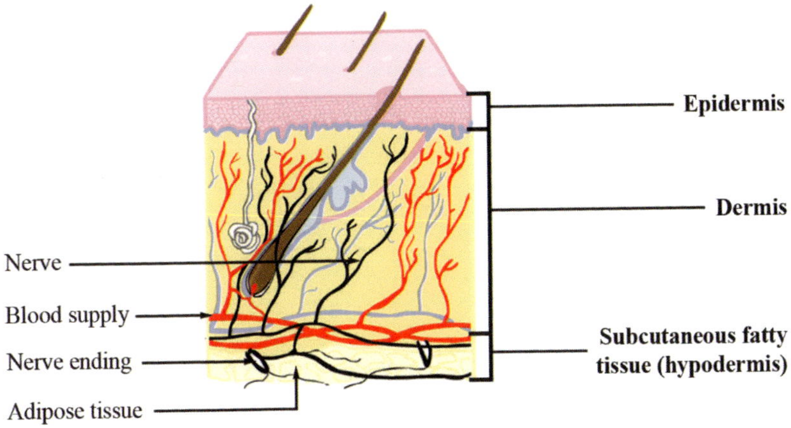

Figure 5. Subcutaneous layer

Skin Color

The color of your skin is largely genetically determined. The darkness of skin varies as a result of the amount of **melanin** present. Melanin is a pigment formed in the deep epidermal layer of the skin. The word *melanin* has Greek roots and means "black." Knowing this will help you when you look at words like *melanoma* (*melan* = black ; *oma* = tumor) that use the same roots. Deep in the epidermal layer are cells that produce granules of melanin. Production of melanin is stimulated by DNA-damaging UVB radiation, and it leads to the development of a tan. Typically, due to the amount of sun located in some areas of the world, people in more tropical areas tend to be darker than people in other areas. Also, among different races of people, skin coloring is determined by the relative kind and amount of melanin made. The **melanocytes** of dark-skinned individuals make both more and darker melanin than those of light-skinned individuals. It is melanin that has protective effects against ultraviolet rays from the sun.

Clinical Correlate

The condition known as ***albinism*** *is caused by an absence of melanin-making cells. Albinos have very fair skin and white hair as well as light-colored eyes.*

Skin Cancers

Skin cancer is relatively common. **Basal cell carcinoma** is the most common and is fairly slow to spread. **Metastasis** (the movement of cancerous cells from their original location to other parts of the body) is quite uncommon if diagnosed early. **Squamous cell carcinoma** is more dangerous and less common than basal cell. **Melanoma** is considerably more perilous with a higher rate of metastasis than either basal cell or squamous cell carcinomas. All types appear related to prolonged sun exposure. Figure 6 illustrates the three types of skin cancer.

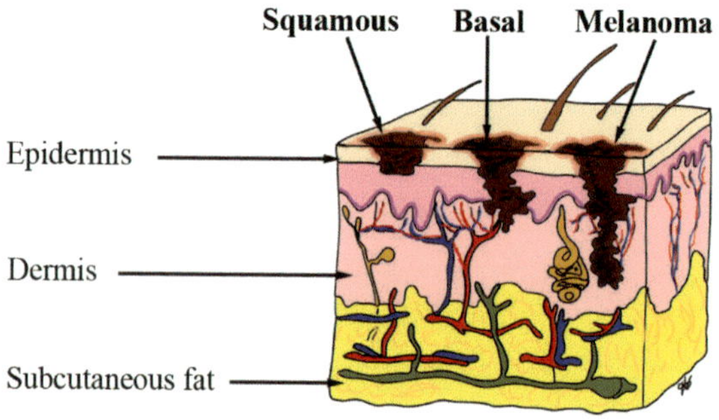

Figure 6. Three common skin cancers

Hair

Hair **follicles** are present in all skin except on the palms of the hands and the soles of the feet. Hair is composed of dead cells. A strand of hair consists of a shaft and a root. The cells of the root eventually die as they move outward in the shaft. Each hair follicle has an associated tiny smooth muscle called an **arrector pili** (Figure 7). Oddly enough, there is a nerve connection to these small muscles that cause them to contract when a kiss from a special person or a cold sensation is felt, resulting in "goose flesh" or "goose bumps." The hair follicle contains **melanin-producing cells**. These cells decrease in quantity as we age and as a result, the hair gets lighter (gray) over time.

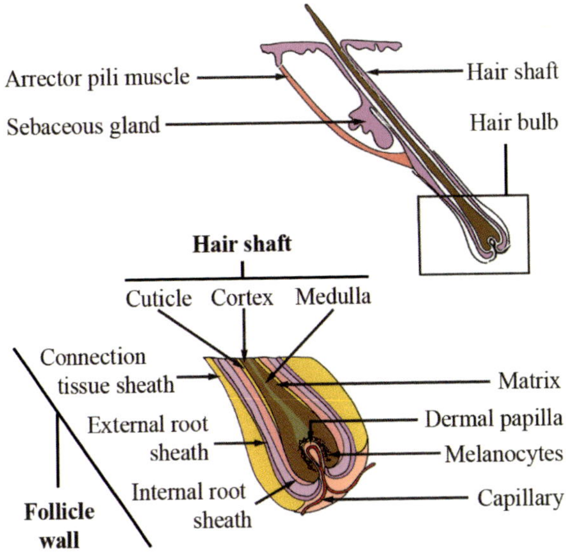

Figure 7. Anatomy of a hair follicle

Glands

Sebaceous glands, which are usually coupled with hair follicles, are oil glands that keep the hair and scalp lubricated by secreting **sebum**, an oily substance with bacteria-suppressive qualities. Puberty leads to increased activity in these glands resulting in acne for some people (Figure 8). **Androgens** (male hormones) increase in both males and females at puberty.

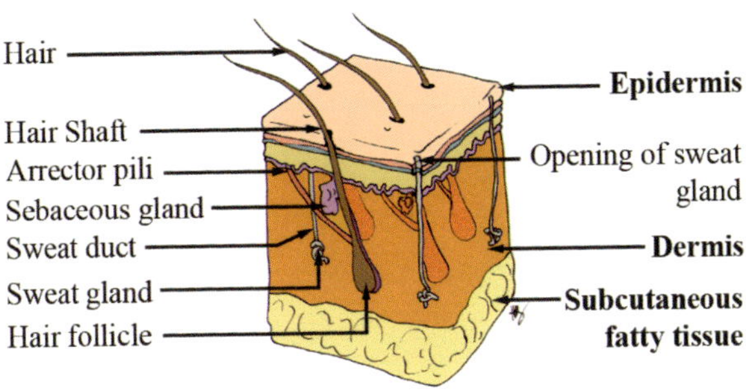

Figure 8. Sebaceous gland and other skin structures

Sweat glands in the dermis become more active when body temperature rises due to external heat or an increase in a person's activity. They are **exocrine glands**, meaning they secrete a watery liquid, which with evaporation has a cooling effect. People routinely lose one quart of water each day through this process, known as perspiration. Sweat glands, also called **sudoriferous glands**, are found under the skin in all mammalian species and are used for body temperature regulation (**thermoregulation**). These glandular structures secrete their products directly to the surface of the body or to a passageway that leads to the body surface.

In humans, **apocrine** and **merocrine sweat glands** form the primary method of cooling. Sweat glands that release their secretions into hair follicles in the armpits (**axillae**), around the nipples (**areolae**), and in the groin are termed **apocrine** sweat glands. Far more numerous and widely distributed than **apocrine sweat glands** are the **merocrine sweat glands**, also known as **eccrine sweat glands**. Merocrine sweat glands are coiled tubular glands that discharge their secretions directly onto the surface of the skin. They are smaller than apocrine sweat glands, and they do not extend as far into the dermis. The adult integument contains around 3 million of these glands. Palms and soles have the highest numbers; estimates are that the palm of the hand has about 500 glands per square centimeter (3,000 glands per square inch).

Nails

Aesthetics aside, a healthy fingernail has the function of protecting the fingertip (the **distal phalanx**) and the surrounding soft tissues from injuries. It also serves to enhance precise delicate movements of the **distal digits** through counter-pressure exerted on the **pulp** of the finger. The nail then acts as a counterforce when the end of the finger touches an object, enhancing the sensitivity of the fingertip even though there are no nerve endings in the nail itself (Figure 9). Finally, the nail functions as a tool, enabling, for instance, a so-called "extended precision grip" (e.g., useful for pulling out a splinter from one's finger).

In humans, nails grow at an average rate of 3 mm (0.12 in) a month. Fingernails require 3 to 6 months to regrow completely, and toenails require 12 to 18 months. Actual growth rate is dependent on age, gender, season, exercise level, diet, and hereditary factors. Nails grow faster in the summer than in any other season. Contrary to popular belief, nails do not continue to grow after death; the skin dehydrates and tightens, making the nails (and hair) appear longer.

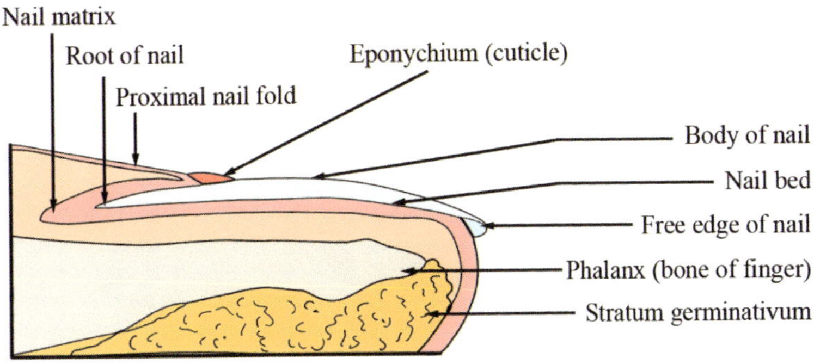

Figure 9. Cross-section of nail anatomy

Common Conditions and Diseases of the Integumentary System

Psoriasis is a life-long disease of an **autoimmune** nature (meaning the body attacks its own tissues). It produces red, flaky lesions frequently found on the elbows, knees, and trunk. It is estimated that 1.5 million Americans suffer from this disease. There is currently no cure.

Nail fungus (subungual onychomycosis), as the name implies, is a fungal infection of the nail and bed (Figure 10). It responds to medications but can require longer than six months to cure.

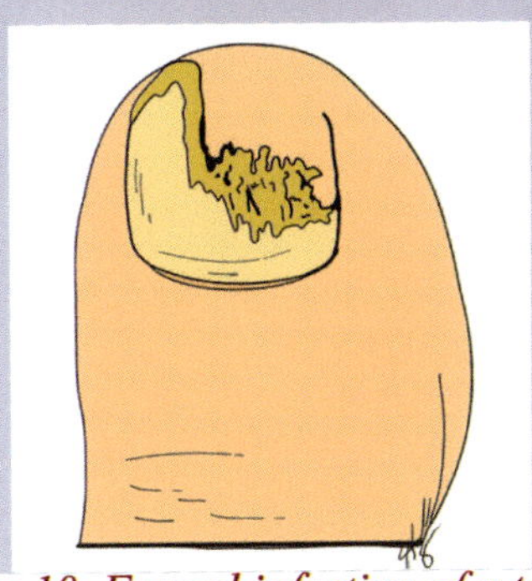

Figure 10. Fungal infection of a toe nail

Pressure sores or **decubitus ulcers** are areas of damaged skin caused by staying in one position too long. They are found commonly in nursing home patients who are not moved about often enough. They can be avoided by the use of padding and changing positions at least every two hours.

Burns of the skin can be caused by heat, electricity, chemicals, or radiation. They are classified by the depth of destruction as first, second, or third degree burns. Since one of the skin's most important functions is to prevent bacterial entry, extensive burns present a challenge to doctors from an infectious disease standpoint.

Integumentary System Glossary

abscess	closed pocket containing pus (white cells and cellular debris) frequently caused bacterial infection
albino	individual with a deficiency of the pigment melanin
alopecia	baldness or loss of hair
cellulitis	diffuse infection of connective tissue
collagen	structural protein in skin & connective tissue
contusion	injury in which the skin is not broken; a bruise
decubitus ulcer	bedsore caused by ischemia (lack of blood flow) caused by pressure points resulting from staying the same position for prolonged periods of time
ecchymosis	irregular area of purplish discoloration that is larger than 10 mm in diameter
epidermis	outermost layer of skin
erythema	redness of skin
hirsutism	abnormal hairiness
impetigo	contagious bacterial skin infection
keloid	abnormally raised or thickened scar that expands beyond the boundaries of the incision (more common in blacks)
keratin	fibrous, water-repellent protein
macule	discolored flat lesion (freckles, tattoo or flat mole)
malodorous	having a bad or foul odor
melanin	substance released in the deep layers of the skin that can result in the darkening of the skin in response to exposure to sunlight (tanning)
necrosis	tissue death
pallor	less color than normal for the skin
papule	small elevation of the skin (pimple)
petechia	small pinpoint hemorrhage
polyp	a raised, mushroom like growth
pruritus	severe itching
psoriasis	common skin disorder characterized by flare-ups in the skin resulting in red papules covered with silvery scales frequently found on the elbows, knees, scalp, back, buttock

<u>purulent</u> producing or containing pus
<u>squamous epithelium</u> flat "fried eggs" appearing cells of the epidermis
<u>stratified</u> arranged in layers
<u>ultraviolet</u> (also known as UV) refers to light that is beyond the visible spectrum at the violet end
<u>urticaria</u> hives

Chapter 2
The Musculoskeletal System

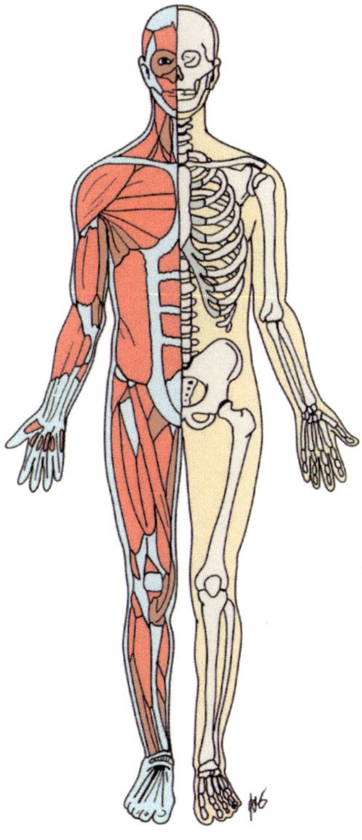

Figure 11. The musculoskeletal system

Some students find this chapter quite challenging at first. "How can we possibly be expected to memorize all the bones and muscles (Figure 11) in the body?" The goal here is not to memorize all of the different bones and muscles but rather to understand how they work to make your body move and function in your normal everyday life. It will also be our goal to explore how bones are built and review important medical terms related to the skeleton that will help you develop a comfortable understanding of this impressive body support system.

The Skeletal System

The bones of the skeleton have a variety of functions beyond supporting the body. They provide storage of calcium, serve as the primary site of red blood cell production (important because red blood cells carry oxygen to different parts of the body), and protect many of the body's vital organs. Together with muscles they also form important lever systems for getting useful work done such as bending, picking up things, and lifting (Figure 12).

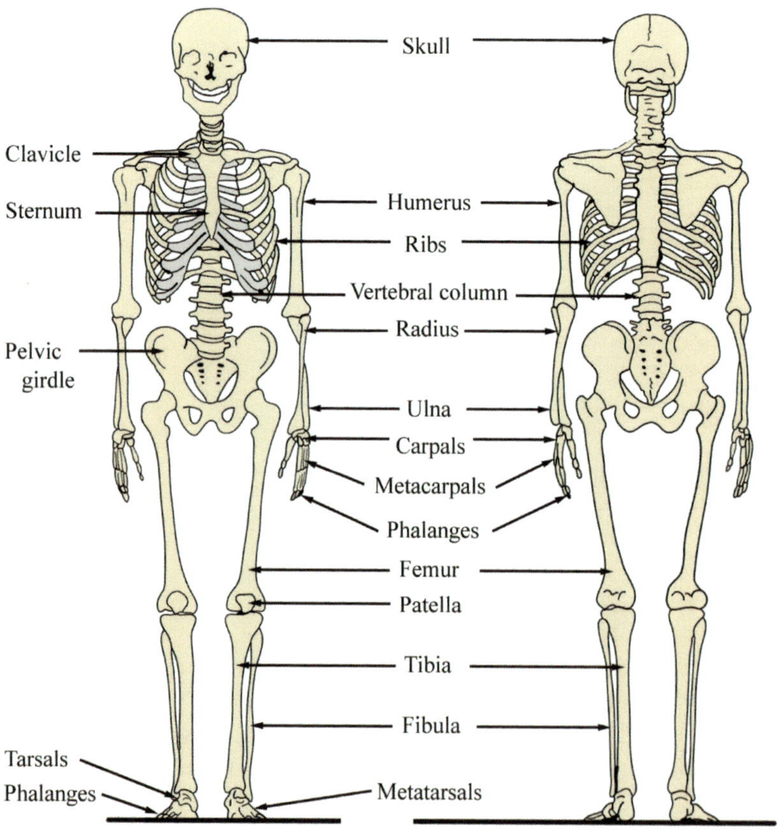

Figure 12. The skeletal system

Bones

Bones are a tissue assembled by highly specialized cells. Their remarkable strength is due in large part to the significant quantity of **calcium phosphate** stored in them. Bone strength has been compared to that of reinforced concrete because it is so strong.

Two types of bone can be readily identified microscopically. The first is **compact bone**, which is a relatively dense, solid form that is typical of the shafts of most long bones in the body. The second is **spongy** or **cancellous** (*cancel* = Latin for "lattice-like") bone, which doesn't have nearly as solid an appearance as compact bone.

Both of these bone types are formed by cells known as **osteocytes** (*osteo* = bone; *cytes* = cells). In compact bone, the osteocytes are arranged in distinct layers around a central canal similar to the rings of a cut tree trunk (Figure 13). Each of these units is called an **osteon**, and they form the functional unit of compact bone. In bone, many of these osteons are like having multiple trees all bound together. It is no wonder why these contribute to the overall strength of the bone. In the case of spongy bone (called such because it resembles sponges from the sea), its microscopic structure is different. Spongy bone has no osteons, and the result is a bone formed of **trabeculae** (meaning "little beams"), a series of rod-like structures (Figure 14).

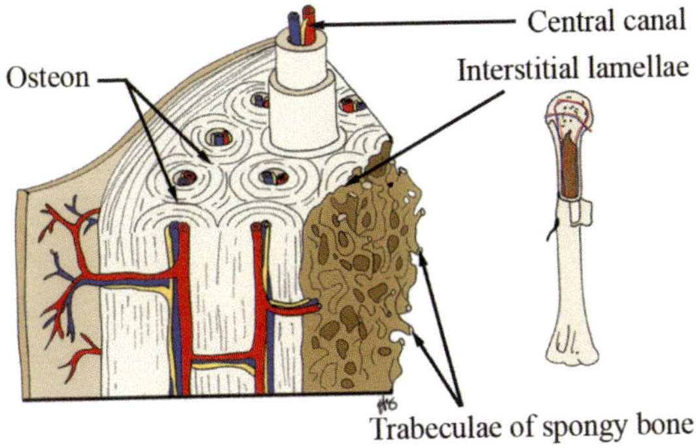

Figure 13. Difference in structure between compact bone and spongy bone. Notice the osteons make up compact bones.

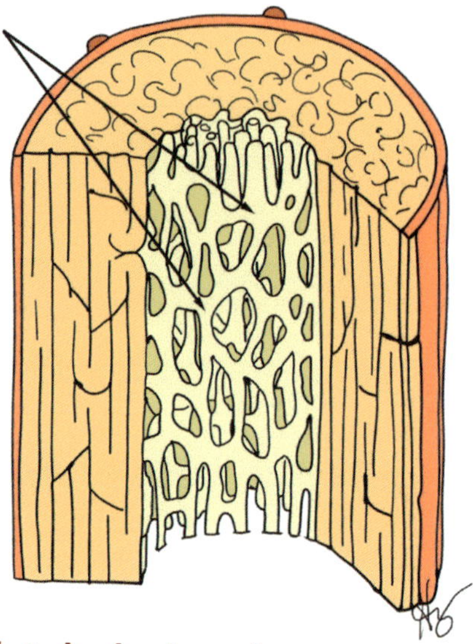

Figure 14. The trabeculae that make up spongy bone

The important thing for you to know is that both types of bone are constantly being remodeled in response to changes in the demands that are placed on them (e.g., weight gain or loss, or an increase or decrease in the amount of one's daily physical activity). This remodeling is conducted by osteoblast and osteoclast cells. It's easy to remember their respective roles. When you see the "**b**" in **osteoblast**, think **build**. In fact, osteoblasts are responsible for making and laying down new bone. **Osteoclasts**, on the other hand, **cut** away existing bone, which accounts for the letter "**c**."

Clinical Correlate

One of the concerns that NASA has had about prolonged space travel is the lack of gravity in space. This lack of gravity reduces the amount of demand (or stress) on the bone and can cause bone to weaken. When exercise regimens are planned and you are told to do weight-bearing exercises, this simply means to place some stress or demand on your bones so that the natural remodeling can take place and you can continue to have strong bones, avoiding the effects of ***osteoporosis*** (*osteo* = bone ; *porosis* = porous).

Skeletal formation begins as early as six weeks after conception. Bone formation, also called **osteogenesis** (*osteo* = bone ; *genesis* = making of), actually refers to two types of **calcification** (also called **ossification**). These are: (1) **intramembranous** (*intra* = inside ; *membranous* = membrane) calcification and (2) **endochondrial** (*endo* = inside ; *condral* = cartilage) calcification.

When **intramembranous calcification** occurs in the early-forming fetus, the osteoblasts (*osteo* = bone ; *blastos* = germ) differentiate from the surrounding connective tissue; that is, the osteoblasts "see" distinctions between the different types of tissue. They form ossification "centers" as they begin to lay down new bone. In **endochondrial ossification** (the most common way bones are created), pre-existing cartilage becomes ossified (Figure 15). Initially, the rate of cartilage formation matches the rate of bone formation. Thus, the bones continue to lengthen. At puberty, however, the increase in sex hormones leads to a significant acceleration of osteoblastic activity, which results in rapid bone growth. (Remember: osteoblasts build bone, and when there is an increase in osteoblastic activity, more bone is created.) During this time, the rate of bone formation overtakes the rate of cartilage formation, and bone growth halts with what is called **epiphyseal closure** (Figure 16). To better understand epiphyseal closure, it is helpful to know that the growth plate is also known as the **epiphyseal plate**. This is the area of growing tissue near the end of the long bones in children and adolescents. Each long bone has at least two growth plates, one at each end. If we were discussing the thigh bone (or femur) we would say that the epiphyseal plate could be found at each end of the femur (where it meets the knee and where it meets the pelvis in the hips). The growth plate determines the future length and shape of the mature bone because closure of the growth plate too early means that the person will be short; later closure could produce a tall individual. When growth is complete—sometime during adolescence—the growth plates close and are replaced by solid bone. You probably remember from your elementary school years that some kids seemed significantly taller than the rest of the class. This was because they had reached puberty and their sex hormones were hard at work producing their growth spurt. Maybe you can also remember seeing them as seniors in high school or later at a class reunion. It may have struck you as odd that these same people that seemed so grown up earlier in your life now seemed not quite so tall. The truth is

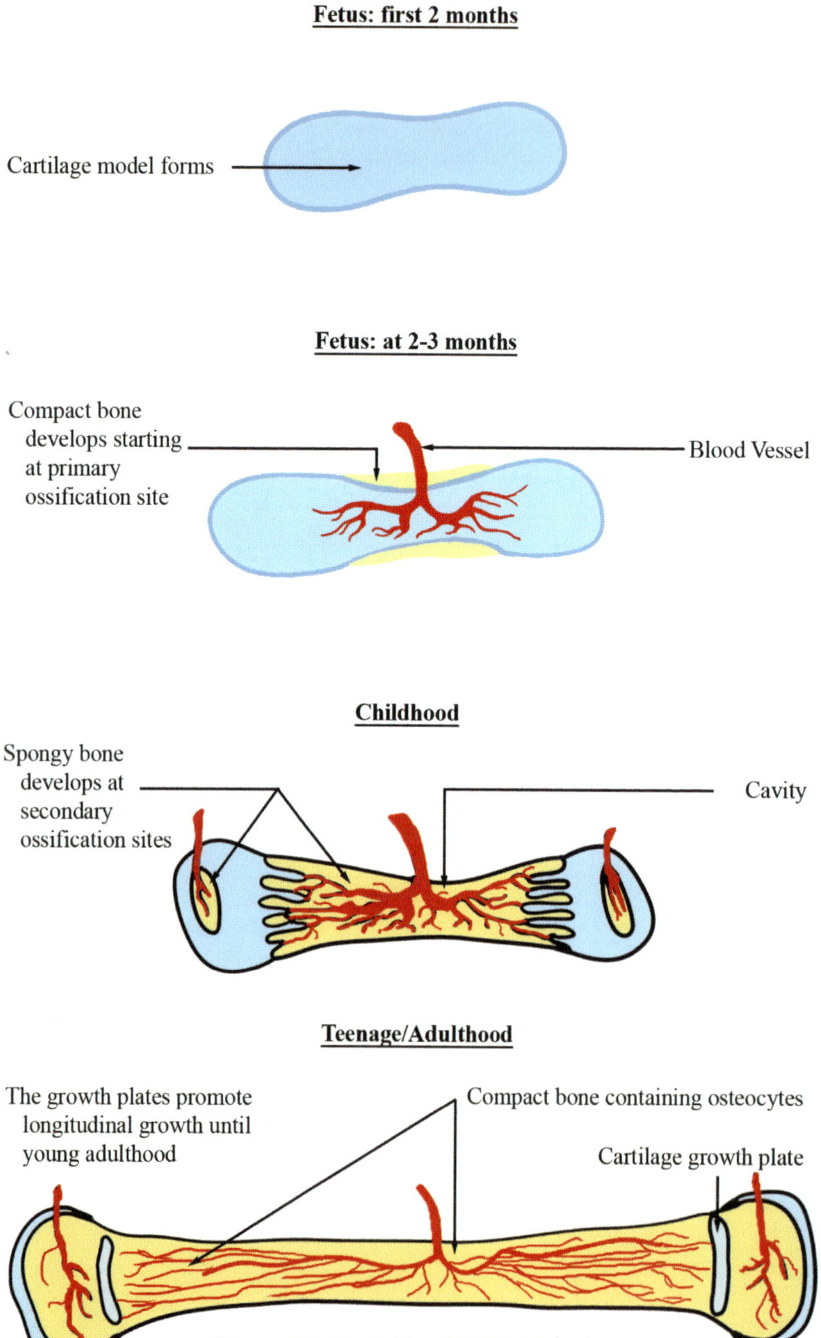

Figure 15. Endochondrial Ossification

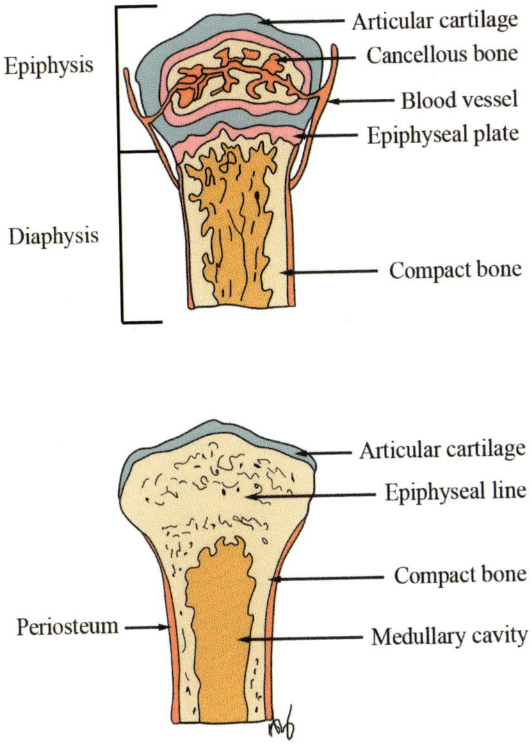

Figure 16. Epiphyseal closure

that these individuals had experienced an earlier puberty and hence also experienced epiphyseal closure much earlier than others in your class.

Bone remodeling in response to changes in stress on various bones is an active, ongoing process. A healthy adult will remove and replace as much as 18% of his or her bony skeleton each year. As you now know, bone changes most often when placed under demand (or lack of it). During **menopause** (from the Greek *men* = month ; *pausis* = cessation), **estrogen** levels drop significantly and bone mass changes because the estrogen levels help maintain the calcium levels in the bone. When the calcium levels drop, the bones can become more brittle, resulting in an increase in fractures.

A number of medications such as Fosamax, Boniva, and Actonel have been developed to counteract bone loss by helping to return the osteoblastic and osteoclastic production to **premenopausal** levels. In addition, close control over calcium levels in the blood are essential if the body's nervous tissue and muscles are to operate at peak efficiency. **Parathyroid hormone** (secreted by the **parathyroid glands**) and calcitriol (available commercially as a form of vitamin D and is made from cholesterol in the human body) tend to raise calcium levels, while **calcitonin** (secreted by the **thyroid gland**) lowers it.

Test Your Knowledge

1. What are the main functions of bone?

 ____

 ____

2. What are the two types of bone? Please describe them.

 ____

 ____

 ____

3. What is the function of osteoblasts?

 ____

 ____

4. What is the function of osteoclasts?

 ____

 ____

5. What happens to bone when someone reaches puberty?

 ____

 ____

The Skeleton

The human skeleton, which consists of some 206 individual bones, is usually distinguished by two divisions: the **axial skeleton** and the **appendicular skeleton**. The axial skeleton is centrally located. It is made up of 80 bones and forms a longitudinal axis on which the appendicular skeleton is attached. (The longitudinal axis is an imaginary straight line that runs through the body's center of gravity, from the head to the space between the feet.) These axial bones primarily run from the head to the **symphysis pubis** in a straight line and provide support and protection for the **brain**, the organs of the thoracic (chest) and **abdominal cavities**, and the **spinal cord** (Figure 17). (The Greek word symphysis means "growing together" or a natural "junction." It is where the **pubic bones** join.)

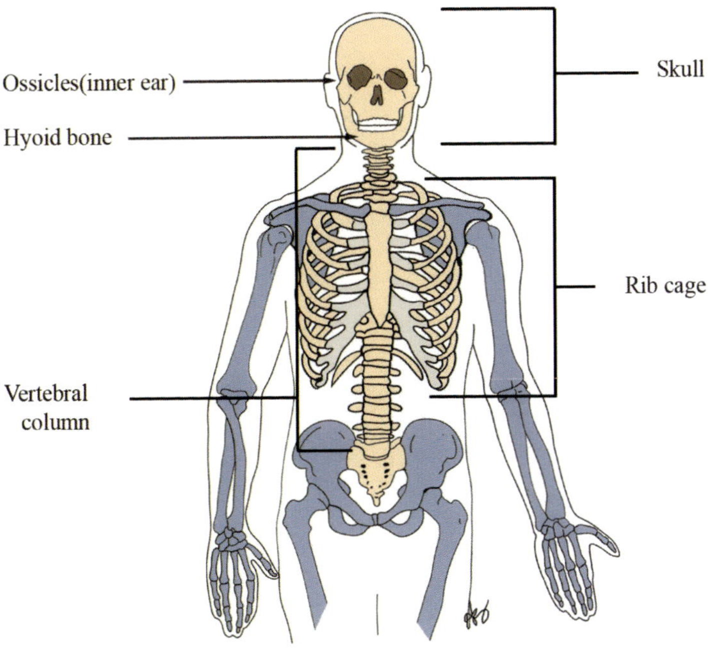

Figure 17. Axial skeleton

The appendicular skeleton is composed of bones of the upper and lower extremities and also the bones that attach them to the axial skeleton at the **pectoral** and **pelvic girdles**. The word appendicular describes a part that is joined to something larger. Functionally, the parts of the appendicular skeleton are involved in **locomotion** (lower limbs) of the axial skeleton and manipulation of objects in the environment (upper limbs). Now let's examine these two divisions in greater detail.

The Axial Skeleton

This part of the skeleton includes the **longitudinal** or **midline bones**—the bones of the **skull**, the **rib cage** (also known as the **thoracic cage**), and the **lower spine** (Figures 18, 19, and 20). The skull and its associated bones number 29 in all.

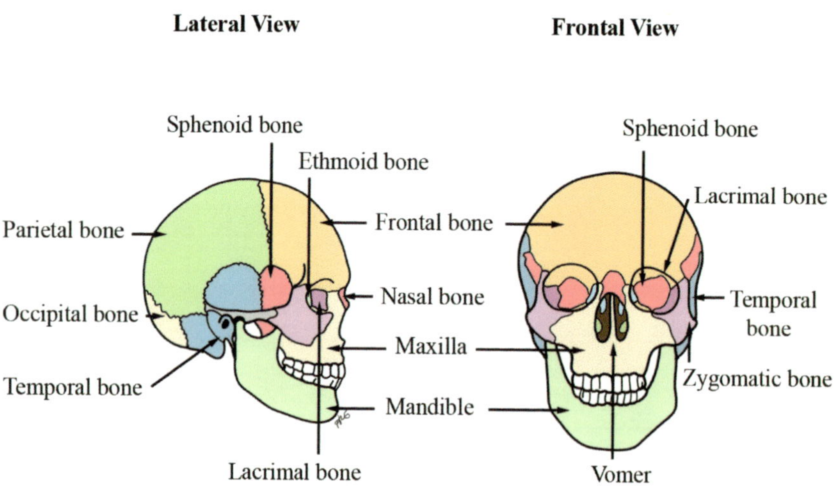

Figure 18. Skull bones

Some important points to note about the skull include the following:

- The **external auditory canal** is located in the **temporal bone**.
- The **occipital bone** protects the portion of the brain's cortex that governs vision.
- The **eye sockets** are actually formed by the merging of several bones in the skull.

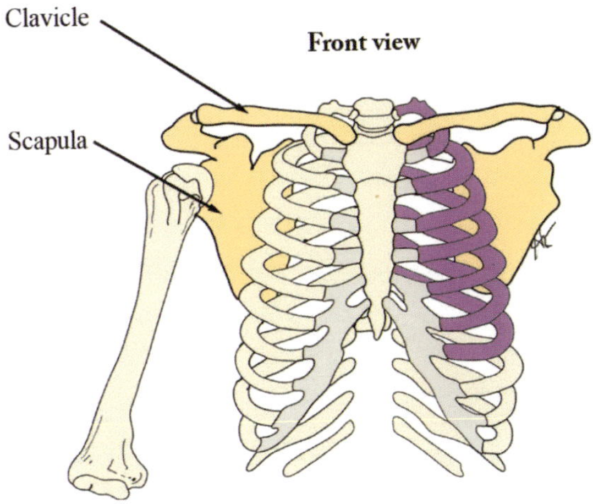

Figure 19. Front view of thoracic cage

- Another name for the "jawbone" is the **mandible**.

Within the facial bones of the skull you will find structures that look like holes in the bone. These are called **sinuses** (Figure 21). These air-filled spaces within the bones reduce the weight of the bones in which they are housed.

Clinical Correlate

***Sinusitis**, or inflammation of these air-filled spaces, is a common clinical diagnosis. At one time or another, all of us have had a case of sinusitis. Sinusitis is commonly treated with decongestants and occasionally antibiotics. Sinusitis can be caused by viral infections, bacteria, fungus that can be ingested with food or inhaled in the air and that aggravates the sinuses, nose blowing, scuba diving, foreign objects (often placed in the nose by small children), side effects of medications, infections caused by the root of a diseased upper tooth, allergies, asthma, the condition of the air that changes quickly causing the sinuses to become irritated, narrow sinuses, poorly functioning mucous membranes, dehydration, anything that reduces the quality of the air, a weak immune system, hormonal imbalances, stress, polyps, and tumors.*

Lateral View of the Vertebral Column

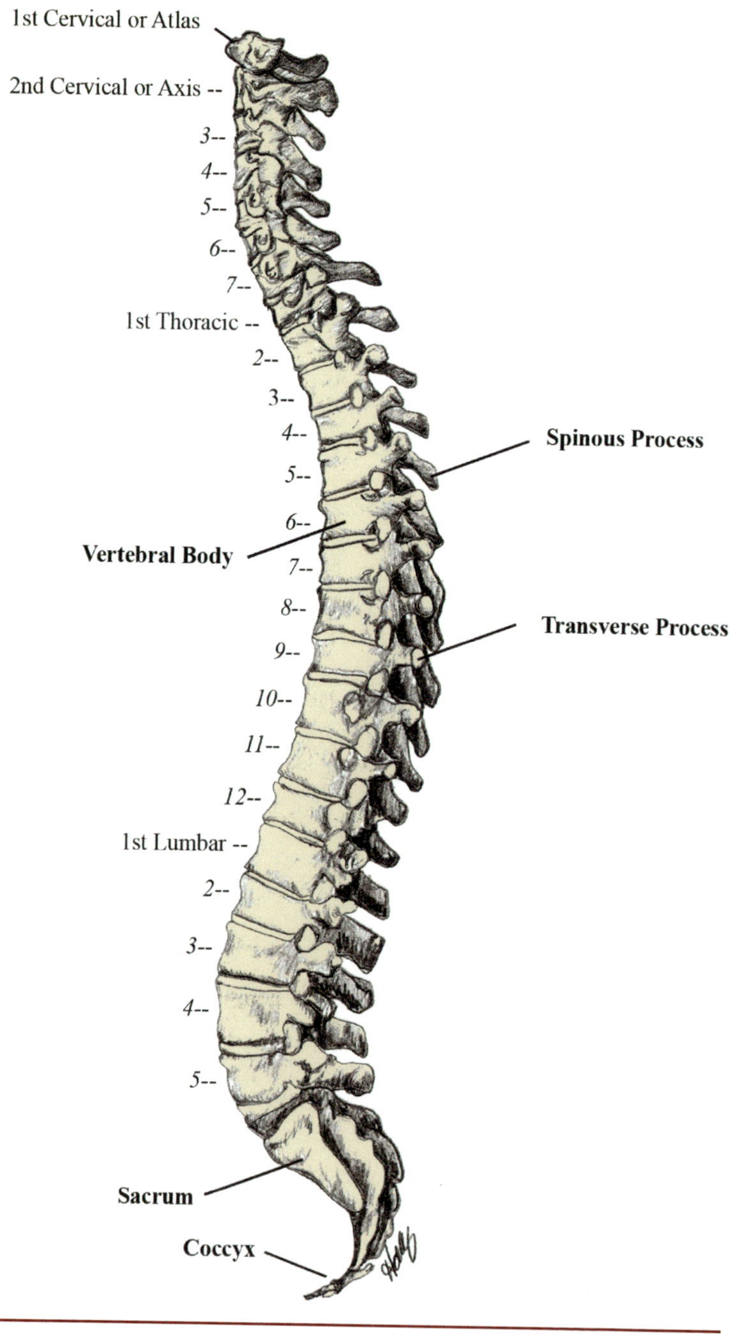

Figure 20. Lateral view of the vertebral column

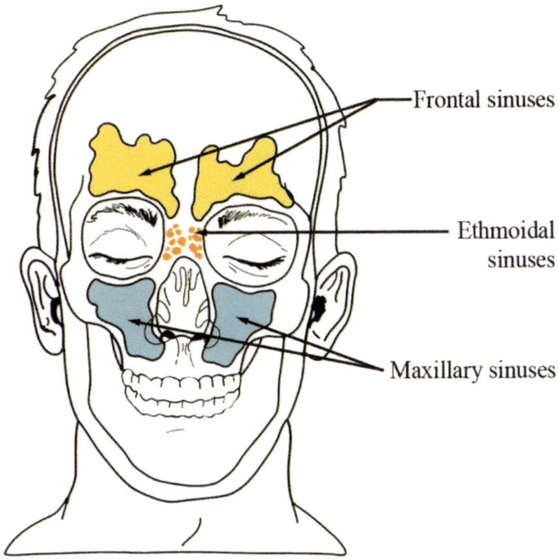

Figure 21. Facial sinuses

Foramen magnum. Beneath the skull is a large opening called the **foramen magnum** (Latin from *foramina* = a natural passage; *magnum* = great) (Figure 22). It's through this opening that the **brain stem** merges with the spinal cord. The **spinal column** is a series of **vertebral bones** that provide support for the body as a whole and also protect the delicate spinal cord, which runs down from the brain inside the **vertebral foramen** (Figure 23). The farther you go from the base of the skull down the spinal column, the bigger and more massive the **vertebrae** become. The reason for this is that the vertebrae must handle more of the body's weight as they extend farther down the back (refer back to Figure 20).

Vertebrae. The vertebrae are subdivided into three sections. Starting with the vertebrae at the top of the spinal column, the first seven, the **cervical vertebrae**, extend from the skull to the thorax (chest); the next twelve, the **thoracic vertebrae**, run down the length of the thoracic (rib) cage; and the five massive **lumbar vertebrae** are at the bottom. These are followed by the **sacrum** and **coccyx** (also called the "tailbone"), where the spinal column ends. In the thoracic cage the twelve pairs of ribs join (or

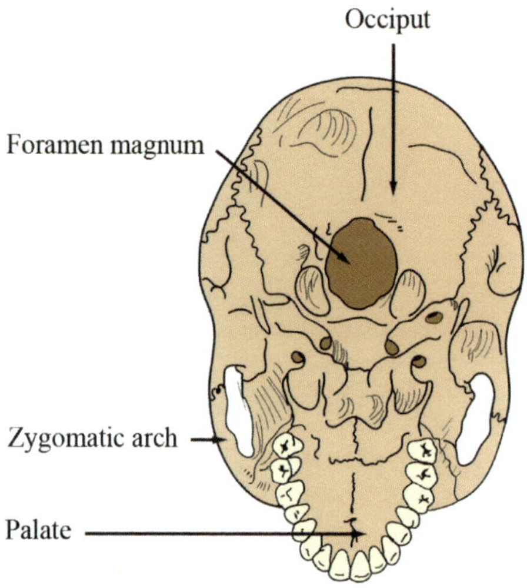

Figure 22. The foramen magnum

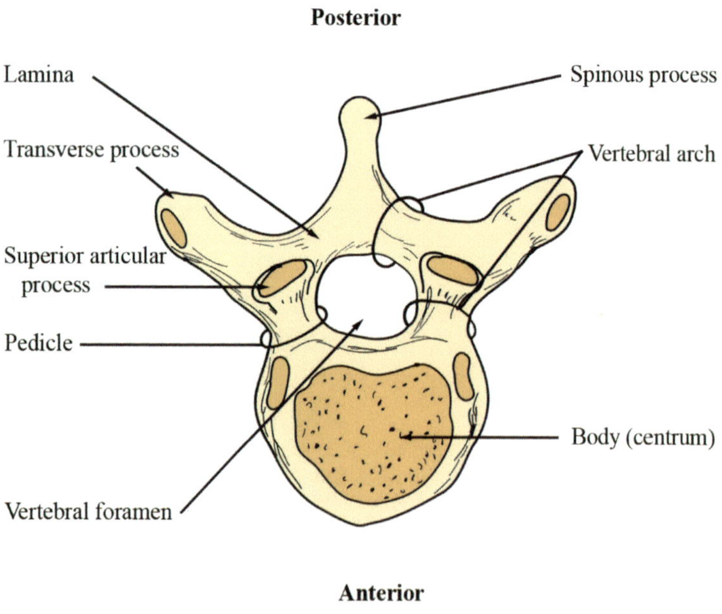

Figure 23. A vertebra of the spinal column

articulate with) the thoracic vertebrae (refer back to Figure 19). The upper seven pairs attach directly to the **sternum** (or breastbone) at the front of the chest and are called "true ribs" because of this attachment. The remaining five pairs are called "false ribs" because they do not attach directly to the sternum. Pairs eight through ten attach to each other and to the seventh pair of ribs by what is called **costal cartilage**. Pairs eleven and twelve are called "floating ribs," since they don't attach to the sternum at all (though all twelve pairs are attached to the thoracic vertebrae at the back).

The Appendicular Skeleton

The appendicular skeleton includes the bones of the upper and lower limbs (arms and legs) as well as the supporting bones that attach them to the axial skeleton. The **pectoral girdle** refers to the area where the upper extremities (arms) attach, whereas the **pelvic girdle** provides the lower extremity (leg) attachments (Figure 24). The joints (or **articulations**) of the skeleton vary from essentially nonmovable (e.g., the bones of the **pelvic cavity**,

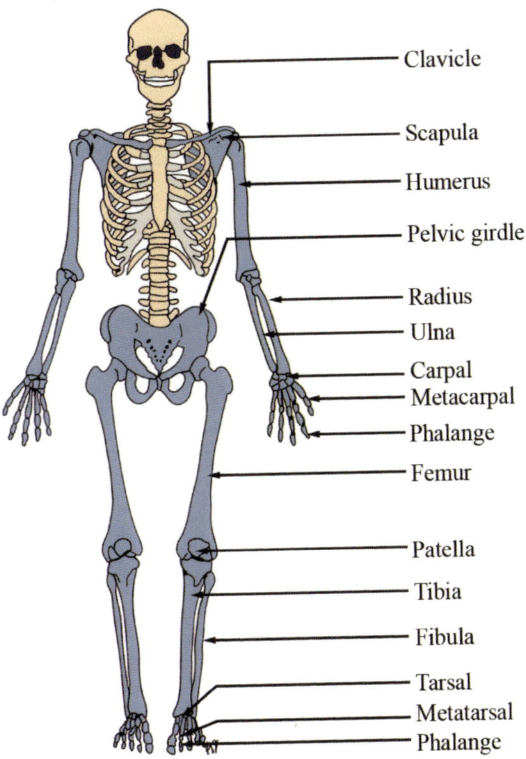

Figure 24. Appendicular skeleton

which is the least movable bony structure) to highly movable (e.g., the **shoulder joint**, which is the most freely movable articulation in the body).

As a general rule, the more mobile the joint is, the more prone to injury it becomes. Not surprisingly, then, joint injuries involving the pelvis are considerably less common than those involving the shoulder or knee.

There are 126 bones in the appendicular skeleton. These are separated into six major areas:

1. **Pectoral girdles** (4 bones)—The pectoral girdle—also called the shoulder girdle—is the set of bones that connects the upper limb to the axial skeleton on each side. It consists of the **clavicle** and **scapula** in humans (Figure 25).

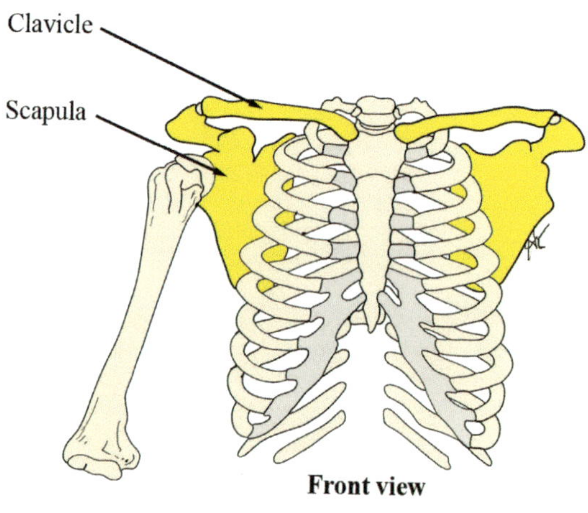

Figure 25. Pectoral girdle

2. **Arm and forearm** (6 bones: left and right humerus [2], ulna [2], and radius [2])—In anatomical usage, the term **arm** refers specifically to that portion located between the shoulder and the elbow. The lower segment between the elbow and wrist is called the **forearm**. The term *forearm* is used in anatomy to describe the lower arm and distinguish it from the arm as

a whole. There is one arm bone on each side. It is called the **humerus**. There are two forearm bones on each side and these are called the **radius** and **ulna**. The radius is the bone that runs in a line continuous with the thumb. You can think of your thumb as a radio antenna to help you remember that the bone that connects there in your forearm is called the radius (Figure 26).

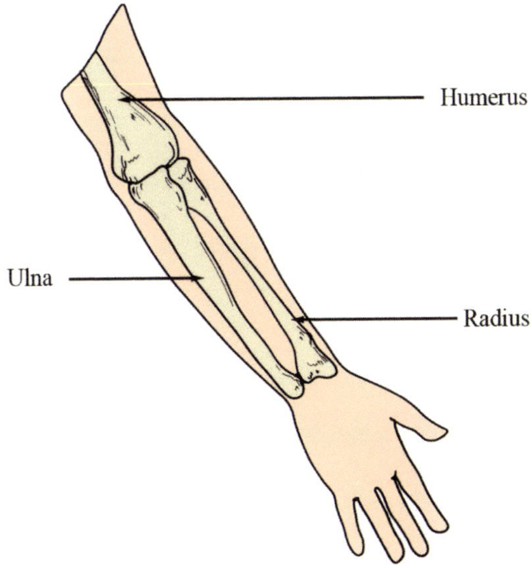

Figure 26. Arm and forearm bones

3. **Hands** (58 bones: left and right carpal [16], metacarpal [10], proximal phalanges [10], middle phalanges [8], distal phalanges [10], and sesamoid [4])—The human hand has 27 bones: the **carpus** or wrist account for 8, the **metacarpals** (palm) number five, and the remaining fourteen are **digital bones** (fingers and thumb). As illustrated in Figure 27, **carpal bones** are found in your wrist. The term *carpal* comes from the Latin word *carpalis* meaning "of or pertaining to the wrist." The term *meta* is a Greek word meaning "after" or "beyond." Thus, the **metacarpal bones** come "after" the carpal bones. The term *phalanges* is the pleural form of the word *phalanx*, which is a Greek term

meaning "a line or array of soldiers." As you can see on the figure, these small bones do line up like soldiers and it makes sense that they would be named **phalanges**. The term *proximal* means "close by." The **proximal phalanges** are closest to the wrist. Moving toward the tips of the fingers, the names of the phalanges change based on how far they are located from the wrist with **intermediate phalanges** being located in between the proximal and the distal phalanges and the **distal phalanges** being located the farthest from the wrist.

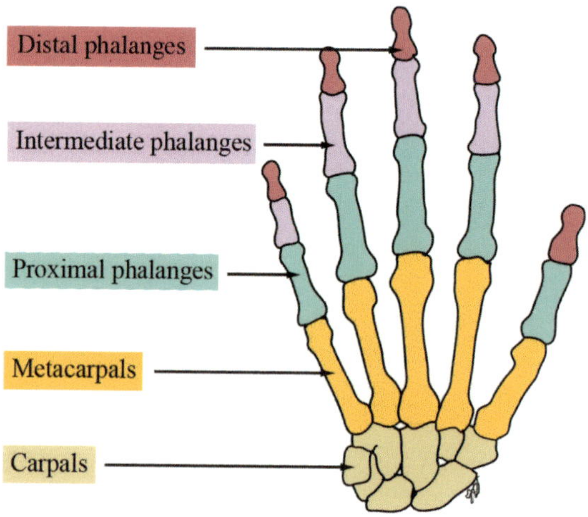

Figure 27. Hand bones

4. **Pelvis** (2 bones: left and right ilium) — The **pelvis** got its name from its shape and it comes from the Latin word for a basin. As you can see in Figure 28, this bony structure appears like a sink or wash basin. The pelvis is also known as **hip girdle** or **coxa girdle**. Before puberty the pelvis can consist of more than ten bones (depending on the composition of the **coccyx**, or tail bone) with each hip bone consisting of three separate bones that have not yet been completely combined — the **ilium**, **ischium**, and **pubis**. In the adult human, the pelvis is part of both the

axial and the appendicular skeletons with its **posterior** dorsal (back) to the **sacrum** and the **coccyx** (the **caudal** or back part of the axial skeleton) and **laterally** and anteriorly to a pair of hip bones (part of the appendicular skeleton or lower extremity). In an adult, the pelvis is thus composed of three large bones plus the coccyx (three to five bones).

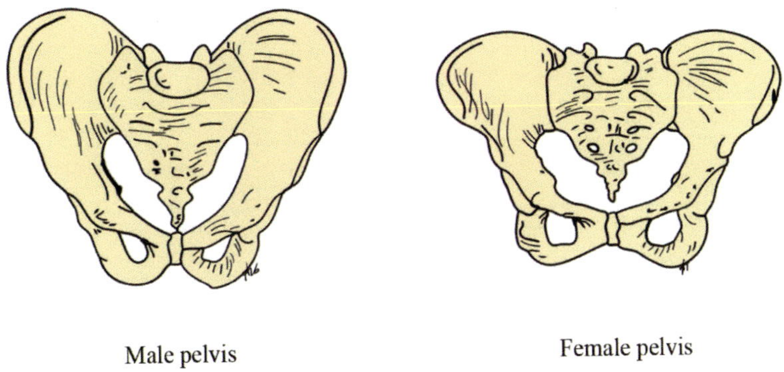

Figure 28. Male and female pelvic bones

It is easy to see the difference between the male and female pelvis. In the female, the opening of the pelvis is much larger to allow for the passage of a baby at childbirth. The opening of the male pelvis is more heart-shaped. A good medical examiner can easily tell the difference between and adult male and adult female skeleton by looking at this opening.

5. **Thigh and leg** (8 bones: femur [2], tibia [2], patella [2], knee, and fibula [2]—Each leg is composed of four bones that help make up the appendicular skeleton:

- **Femur**—the thigh bone
- **Patella**—the knee cap
- **Tibia**—the larger of the two leg bones located below the knee cap

- **Fibula**—the smaller of the two leg bones located below the knee cap

See Figure 29 for an illustration of the thigh and leg bones.

In the human, the **femur** is the longest, largest bone and is one of the two strongest bones in the body. (Another particularly strong bone is the **temporal bone** of the skull). The average adult male femur is almost 19 inches in length and can support up to 30 times the weight of an adult. The femur joins the pelvis to make the hip joint (**acetabulum**). Distally, or in the direction of your feet, the femur also forms part of the knee joint. The femur gradually becomes ossified at puberty when the epiphyseal plates close; this plays a role in determining a person's eventual height.

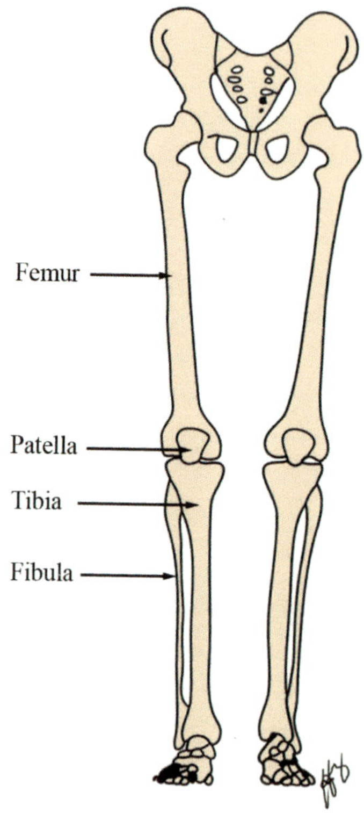

Figure 29. Bones of the leg

The kneecap is also known as the **patella**. You can easily feel this bone. It is a thick, circular-triangular bone that touches and joins with the femur to cover and protect the anterior (front) surface of the knee joint. It is the largest **sesamoid bone** (A sesamoid bone is a bone embedded in a tendon where the tendon crosses a joint. It is found in hands, knees and feet.) in the human body.

The word *tibia* comes from a Latin word meaning "pipe" or "flute." Of the two lower bones of the leg located below the knee, the tibia is both larger and stronger than the fibula. The **tibia** connects the knee with the ankle bones.

The word *fibula* is derived from a Latin word meaning a "pin" or "skewer." It is the long thin bone of the leg. Some dictionaries define fibula as a Latin word meaning "buckle." In Figure 29 you can see that the **fibula** is the most slender and smallest of all the long bones of the leg (so it fits the description of a pin or skewer), and it also joins or "buckles" the knee and the tibia to the ankle. It is located on the lateral side (outside) of the tibia.

6. **Feet** (56 bones: tarsals [14], metatarsals [10], proximal phalanges [10], middle phalanges [8], distal phalanges [10], and sesamoid [4] (Figure 30)—The human foot and ankle is both strong and complex. For most of us the foot contains 26 bones (although some people have more), 33 joints, and more than a hundred **muscles**, **tendons**, and **ligaments**. It is part of the appendicular skeleton. There are three basic parts of the foot. These are the **hindfoot**, the **midfoot**, and the **forefoot**.

   Similar to the hand, the **forefoot** is composed of five toes (phalanges) that connect to five longer bones or metatarsals. In the hand, these similar structures are known as carpals and metacarpals. In the foot, the bones leading to the toes are known as **tarsals** and **metatarsals**. Each toe or phalanx is made up of several small bones. The big toe is called the **hallux**.

   The arch can be found in the **midfoot** and it serves as a shock absorber for the human body. The bones of the midfoot are connected to the forefoot and the **hindfoot** by muscles and the **plantar fascia**. The hindfoot is composed of two tarsal bones, the **talus** (also called **astragalus**), and **calcaneus**, the largest tarsal bone. It is the calcaneus that forms the heel. The top of the talus is connected to the two long bones of the lower leg, the tibia and fibula. It is here that a hinge is formed that allows the foot to move up (**dorsiflex**) and down (**plantar flex**). The bottom of the heel bone is cushioned by a layer of fat. The foot bones are divided longitudinally into the **internal and external sets of toes** (Figure 31). The main weight of the body is transmitted from the tibia through the internal set,

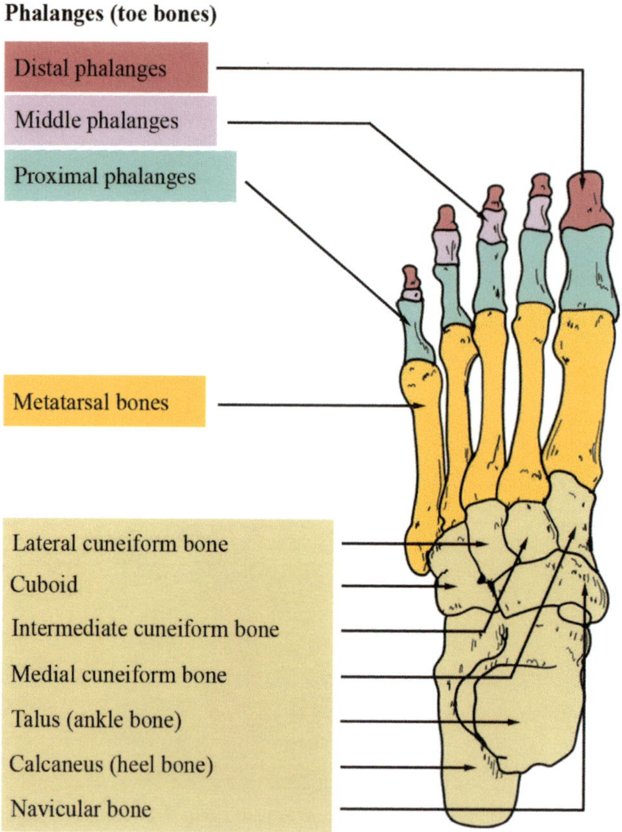

Figure 30. Bones of the foot

which is composed of the big toe (hallux) and the next two toes. The external set is governed by the fibula and is composed of the little toe and the "ring" toe.

Clinical Correlate

If a person jumps from a height and lands on the sole of the foot, the internal part of the foot is more liable to fracture than the external part. Because the arch of the foot is located in the internal area, it is easier for the foot to give way there. The external part of the foot is basically in contact with the ground and less likely to fracture.

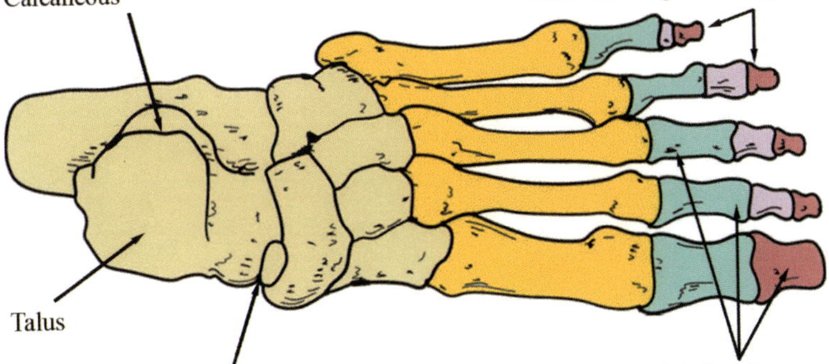

Figure 31. External and internal bones of the foot

Test Your Knowledge

1. What is the axial skeleton?

____

____

2. What is the appendicular skeleton?

____

____

Joints or Articulations

Wherever two or more bones meet, a **joint** is formed. The joints are classified based on either their anatomical structure or their function. The functional categories include

1. Immovable joints or **synarthroses** (Greek *syn* = with, together ; *arthrosis* = joint) like the joints in the skull;
2. Slightly movable joints or **amphiarthroses** (Greek *amphi* = on both sides ; *arthrosis* = joint) like the **sternocostal joint**; and

3. Freely movable joints or **diarthroses** (Greek *dis* = twice, double ; *arthrosis* = joint) like the knee, which joins the femur and tibia (Figure 32).

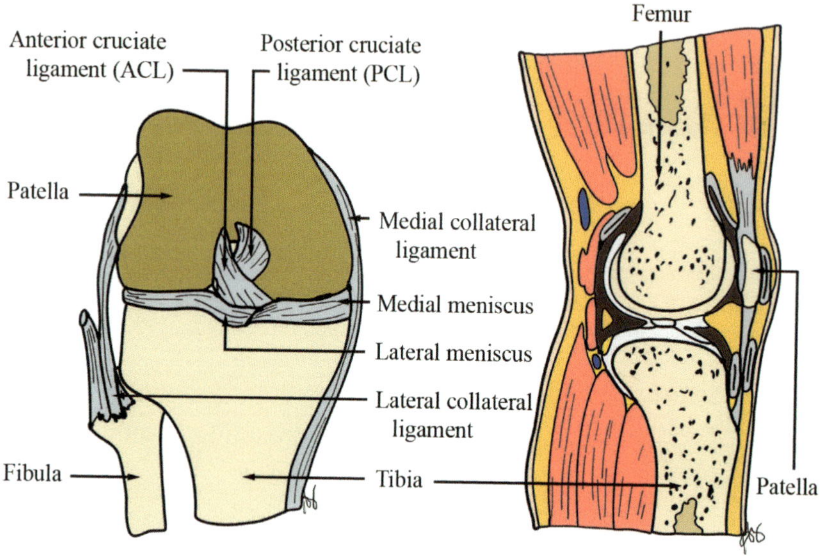

Figure 32. Knee joint (freely movable joints or diarthrosis) and related structures

Various joints are also categorized by the type of movement they permit (Figure 33). Most of the joints that are truly movable are **synovial joints**. Synovial joints have an **articular** covering over portions of the bones where they touch the joints. This produces a joint space in which **synovial fluid** is produced to further lubricate the joint surfaces (refer back to Figure 32).

Additional medical terms to those already covered in this chapter include the following:

- **Flexion**: A position that is made possible by the joint angle decreasing (Figure 34)
- **Extension**: A position that is made possible by the joint angle increasing (Figure 34)

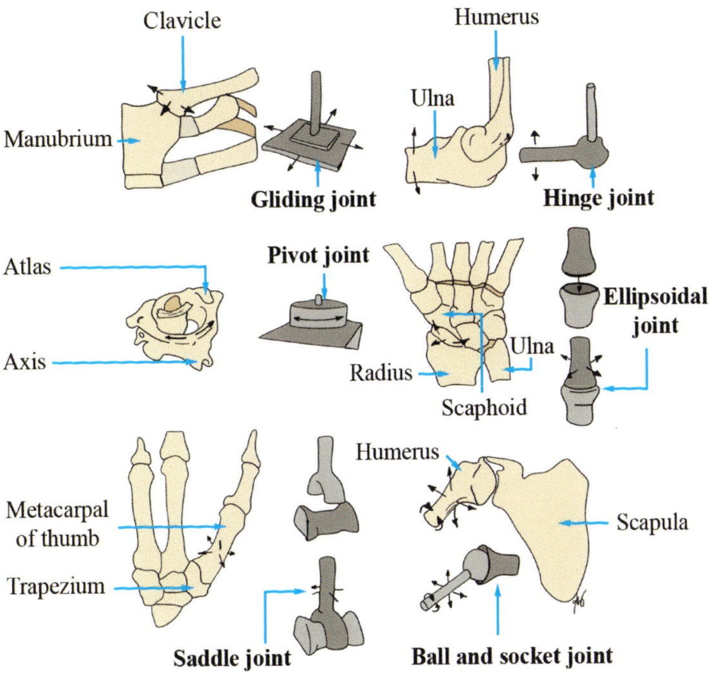

Figure 33. Types of joints

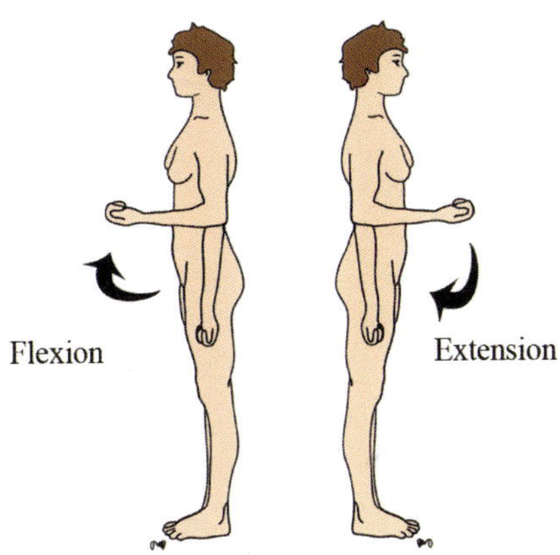

Figure 34. Flexion and extension

- **Abduction**: The movement of an extremity or other body part away from the axis of the body (you can remember this by remembering that when a person is abducted, he is kidnapped and moved away from his home) (Figure 35)
- **Adduction**: The movement that brings a part of the anatomy closer to the **sagittal plane** of the body (you can remember this by noting that the first three letters of the word adduction are "ADD," which in math means to bring together) (Figure 35)

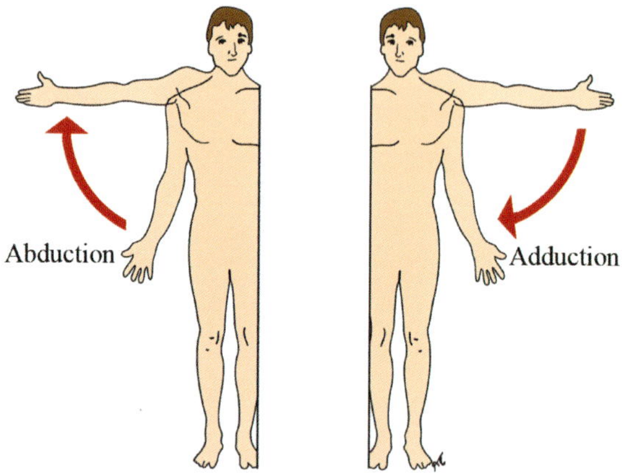

Figure 35. Abduction and adduction of the arm

- **Rotation**: A turning motion like that of a wheel around an axis or a fixed point (Figure 36). An example of this would be moving your palm upward and then turning it down.

Figure 36. Rotation

- **Pronation**: The excessive inward roll of the foot. It can also be rotation of the hand or forearm so that the surface of the palm is facing downward or toward the back (Figures 37 and 38)
- **Supination**: A position of either the forearm or foot; in the forearm when the palm faces anteriorly, or faces up (when the arms are unbent and at the sides) and in the feet when the soles of the feet face up (Figures 37 and 38)

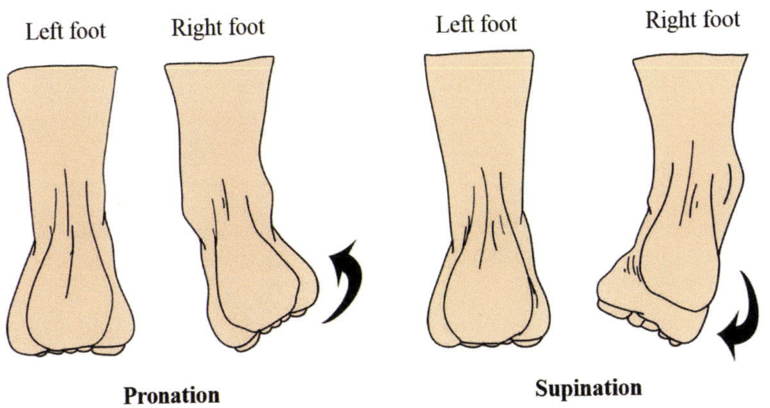

Figure 37. Pronation and supination

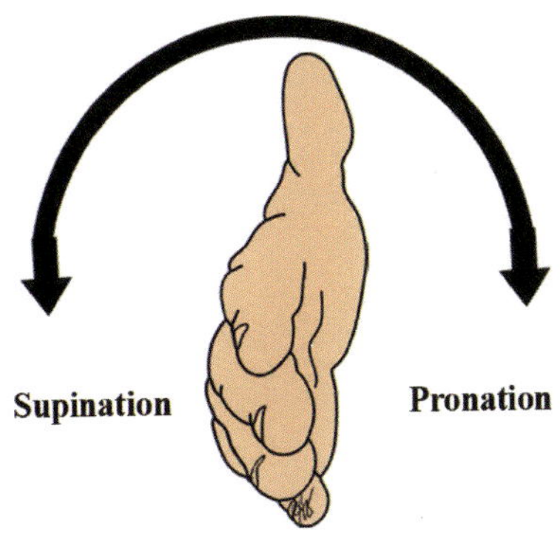

Figure 38. Pronation and supination

- **Circumduction**: A circular movement of a limb or of the eye (like a stirring motion) (Figure 39)

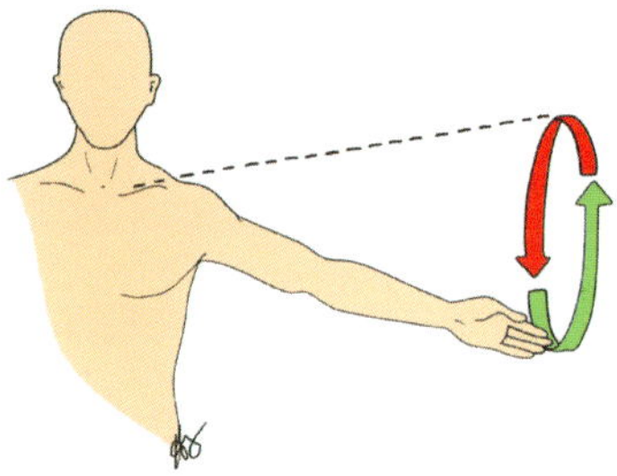

Figure 39. Circumduction

- **Inversion**: A turning inward or other reversal of the normal relation of a part. Typically, a sprained ankle is an inversion of the ankle (Figure 40).
- **Eversion**: The movement of the bottom of the foot away from the median plane (inside) (Figure 40)

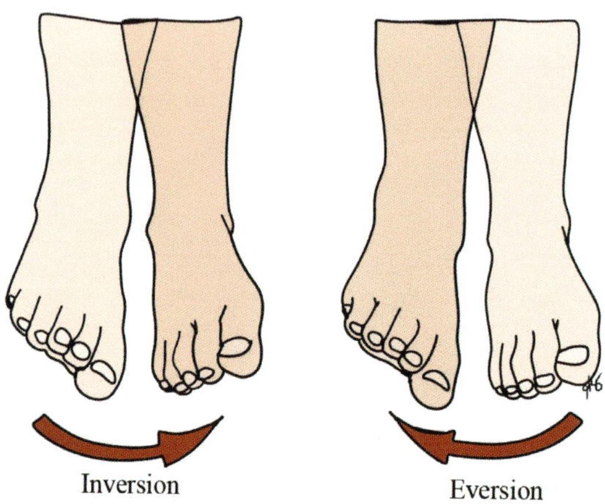

Figure 40. Inversion and eversion

- **Dorsiflexion**: A movement that brings the top of the hand or foot toward the forearm or lower leg (Figure 41)
- **Plantar flexion**: A movement that brings the top of the hand or foot away from the forearm or lower leg (Figure 41)

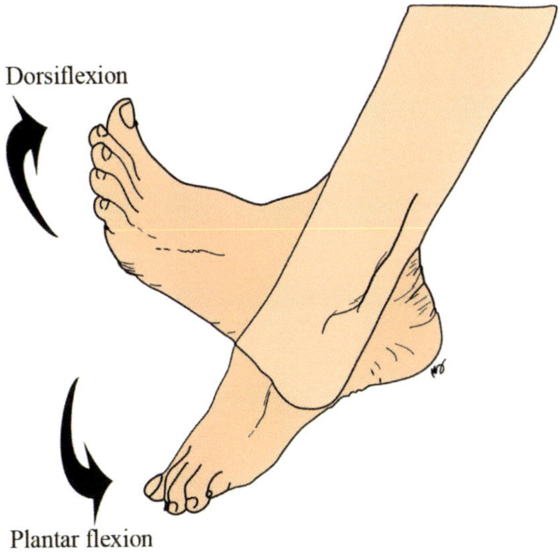

Figure 41. Dorsiflexion and plantar flexion of the foot

Test Your Knowledge

1. Name two kinds of motion that bring parts of your body together.

   ____

   ____

2. What describes an excessive inward roll of the foot?

   ____

3. Which movement brings the top of the hand or foot toward the forearm or lower leg?

   ____

Common Conditions and Diseases of the Skeletal System

A **Colles' fracture** is a distal break in the radius of the forearm. This fracture is typically produced when a person falls forward and attempts to break his fall with outstretched arms. If the bones are **displaced**, an **open reduction** and **internal fixation** may be required. This is a surgical procedure. If the fracture is **nondisplaced**—meaning that the bones are not out of line—a cast alone may suffice.

Osteoporosis is a condition that results from a gradual reduction in bone mass. This thinning of the bone may result in an increase in fractures produced by trauma that might otherwise have yielded no damage. It is more common in females than males and is thought to be due to a drop in estrogen levels. This loss of estrogen accelerates bone loss. The lack of estrogen enhances the ability of osteoclasts to absorb bone. Since the osteoblasts (the cells that produce bone) are not encouraged to lay down more bone, the osteoclasts win and more bone is lost than is produced.

Rickets is a disease primarily produced by inadequate vitamin D in the diet and results in weakened bones causing bow legs, tender bones, and increased fracture risks.

A **bunion** is an abnormal, bony-like bump that forms at the base of the big toe. When the big toe area becomes enlarged it pushes the big toe outward beyond the normal angle of the foot, forcing the crowding of other toes and resulting in pain (Figure 42).

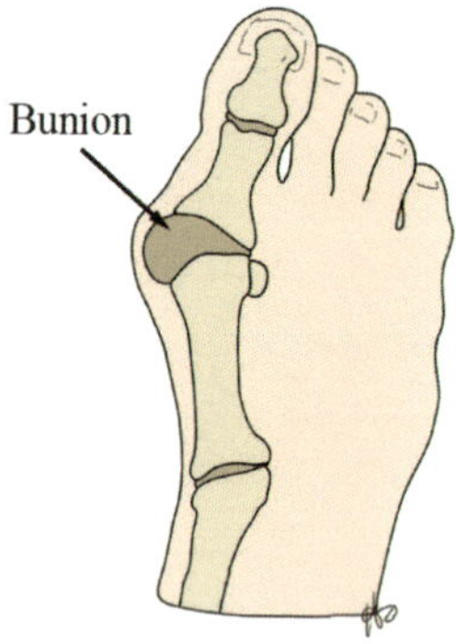

Figure 42. Bunion

Bunions can occur for a number of reasons, but a common cause is wearing shoes that fit too tightly. Bunions can also develop as a result of an inherited structural defect, stress on the foot, or a medical condition, such as **arthritis**. Often, treatment involves conservative steps that may include changing shoes, padding the bunion, and/or wearing shoe inserts. Severe cases of bunions may require surgery.

A **callus** is an especially toughened area of skin that forms in response to repeated friction and pressure. Since repeated contact is required, calluses are most often found on feet because of frequent walking, but they can also be found on the palms of the hands when someone uses a tool or instrument enough to cause such an irritation (Figure 43).

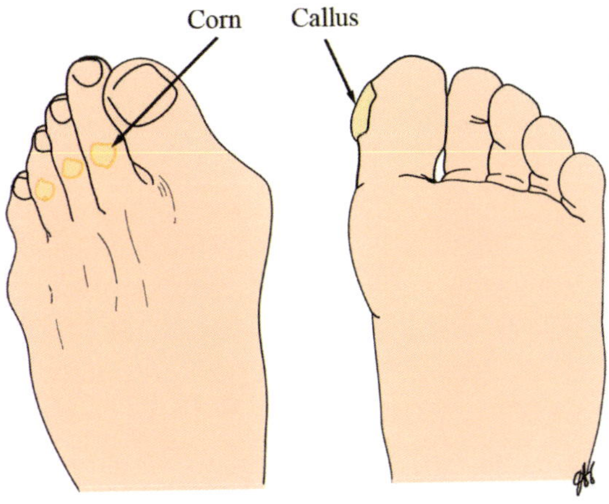

Figure 43. Corn and callus

Plantar warts are skin growths on the soles of the feet caused by the **human papillomavirus (HPV)**, which enters the body

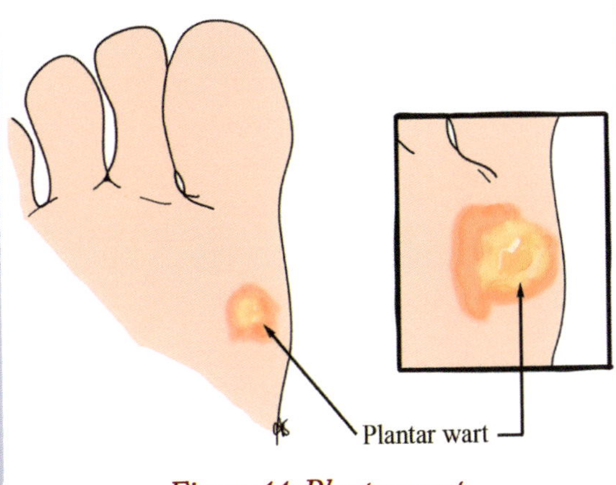

Figure 44. Plantar wart

through tiny cuts or breaks in the skin. These warts often develop beneath pressure points in the feet such as the heels or balls of the feet. Approximately 7–10% of the population of the United States is infected with this virus, which can survive a long time without nourishment from a host. Most people become infected with this virus from walking on moist surfaces such as in shower stalls or around swimming pools (Figure 44).

Complementing the skeletal system, and introducing the characteristic of movement, is the muscular system, described next.

The Muscular System

The body's muscles can be divided into three anatomical and functional categories (Figure 45):

- Skeletal muscle
- Cardiac muscle
- Smooth muscle

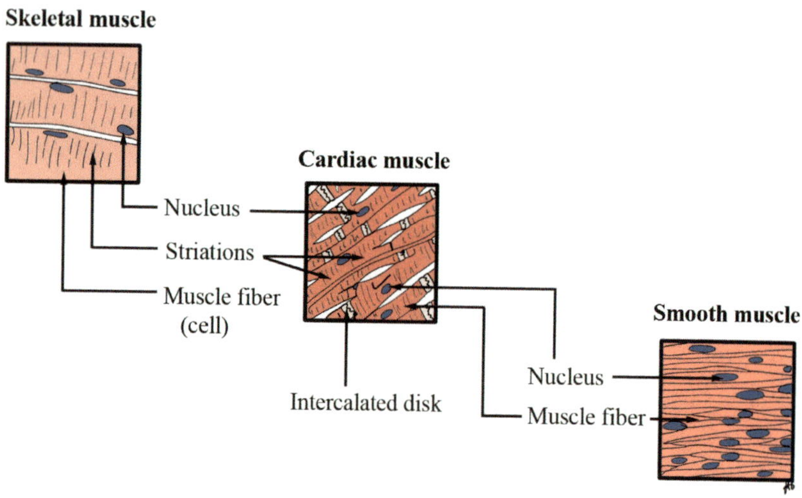

Figure 45. Types of muscles

Skeletal or Voluntary Muscles

Skeletal muscles are under voluntary control, meaning they respond to your will. They have a number of functions, some of which you might not think of immediately. Production of movement and maintenance of body position are two obvious ones, but other functions include maintenance of body temperature, support of soft tissues (like the support of the pelvic floor), and "guarding" of body entrances and exits (e.g., the mouth, anus, and urethra).

To fully appreciate these remarkable structures that most of us take for granted, the **microanatomy** (microscopic structures) must be reviewed. Skeletal muscle cells contain many nuclei and are described as **multi-nucleated**. Within each muscle fiber are **myofibrils** (Figure 46), which are the **contractile units**, which means they contract, or shorten, under

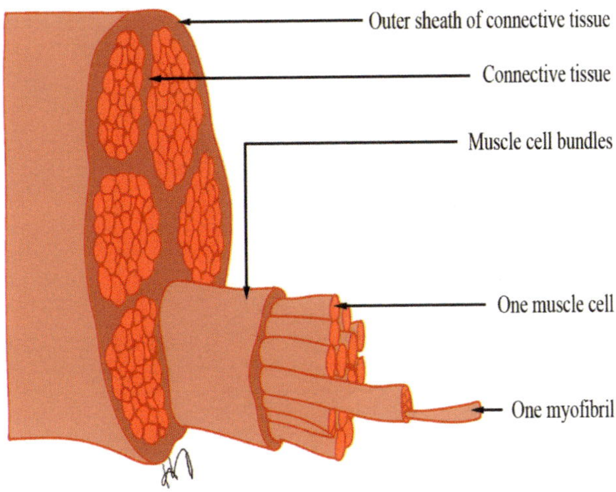

Figure 46. Cross section of skeletal muscle

certain conditions. It is important to remember that muscles only pull or shorten, they don't push. These myofibrils house the **actin** and **myosin proteins** whose molecular interaction produces muscle shortening (Figure 47). These highly organized myofibrals are the reason skeletal muscles appear **striated** (lined) on microscopic exam. This remarkably elegant event

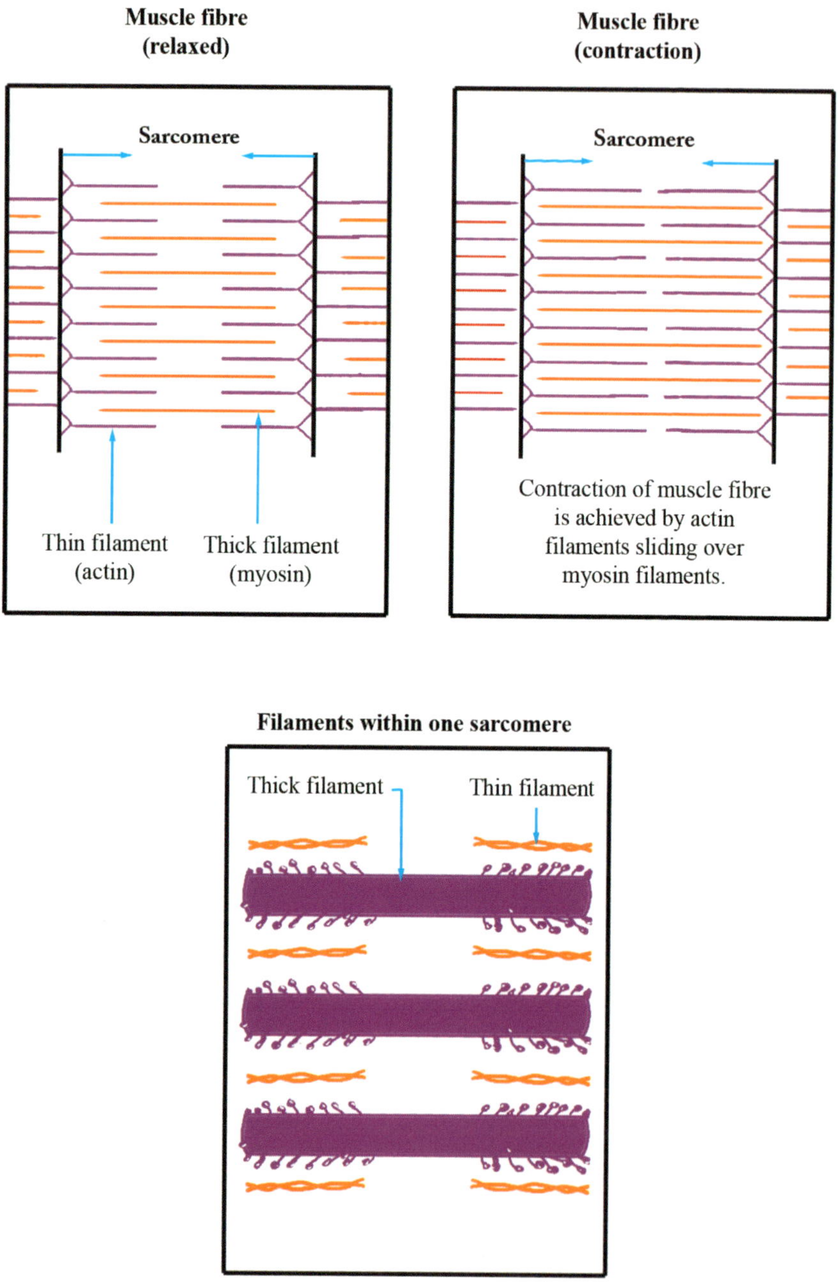

Figure 47. Muscle shortening through use of actin and myosin

involves a bridging or cross-linking of these two proteins and requires the presence of calcium that has been stored in an **intracellular structure** known as the **sarcoplasmic reticulum**.

How is fine motor control achieved? Or for that matter, how is any level of control possible? The nervous system "talks" to the muscle via **neuromuscular junctions** (Figure 48). The neuron releases a **neurotransmitter**, in this case **acetylcholine (Ach)**, which crosses the narrow gap between the **neuron** and the muscle cell and produces an **action potential**; that is, it excites the muscle cell, resulting in an influx of calcium that leads to muscle contraction by the cross-linking of the actin and myosin proteins. Thus, muscle shortening occurs. When this contraction occurs, tension develops, and if this tension is great enough to overcome the resistance, the muscles move. The amount of tension created is solely a function of the number of cross-bridges or links generated between the actin and myosin molecules. On a more global level, the muscular tension in a complete muscle is determined by the frequency in which it is being stimulated by the nervous system and by the number of muscle fibers participating.

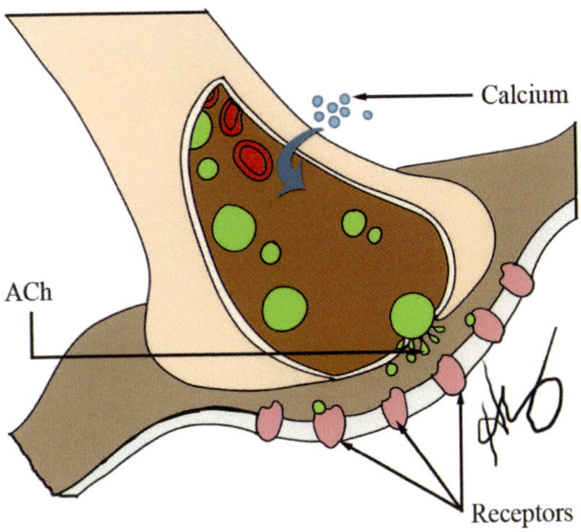

Figure 48. Neuromuscular junction

As the frequency of stimulation increases, the level of tension generated also increases through **summation**, a response that is the result of the repeated and collective actions of the nerves and muscles. At some point the muscle reaches its maximum tension and a condition known as **incomplete tetany** is achieved. In most everyday muscular movements, incomplete tetany is used. In **complete tetany**, there is inadequate time for relaxation between neurostimulations, and a continuous plateau of tension is accomplished with rapid depletion of energy stores followed by muscle fatigue.

The use of the body's muscles requires vast energy expenditures. **ATP**, a molecule that allows energy to be transported around the body, must be generated in enormous quantities if active muscular activity is to be undertaken. ATP is produced through **aerobic** (oxygen requiring) means in the **mitochondria** of the cell, or **anaerobically** (without oxygen) via **glycolysis** (the breakdown of **glucose**), in the **cytoplasm**. When at rest, the majority of the skeletal muscle's energy requirements can be met through **aerobic metabolism**. As such, its limitations are dictated by the quantity of oxygen available. When oxygen demands outstrip the available oxygen, **anaerobic metabolic changes** contribute by converting glucose to **pyruvic acid** in the **cytosol** (a part of the cytoplasm), but this metabolism is much less efficient than its aerobic counterpart. As glycolysis continues, pyruvic acid is converted to **lactic acid**, which begins to accumulate within the muscle cells. The increased acidity causes a lowering of the **pH**, which is a measure of hydrogen ion concentration and indicates the level of acidity or basicity in the cells or tissues. This drop in pH has a variety of effects, not the least of which are detrimental effects on enzyme functions.

When available energy reserves are exhausted, **muscle fatigue** sets in. This means the muscle is no longer capable of contracting even with persistent nervous stimulation. As muscular activity declines, the muscle enters a state of recovery. Lactic acid is recycled and pH levels begin to return to normal. It is the mobilization of those energy reserves and their use that produces the body heat so characteristic of muscular activity.

Cardiac Muscles

Unlike skeletal muscle (and smooth muscle for that matter), **cardiac muscle** is found solely in the heart. It is striated, like the skeletal muscles, but that is where their similarities end. The muscle of the heart has only one **nucleus** per cell and is arrayed in a branching pattern (Figure 49). Each of these cells communicates with its neighboring cardiac cells through

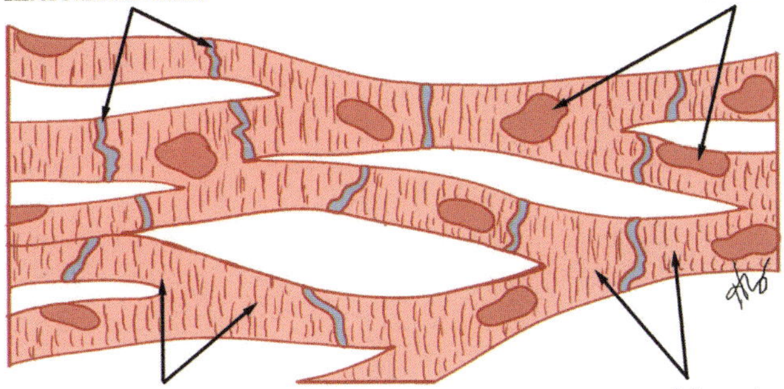

Figure 49. Cardiac muscle

structures known as **intercalated discs**. This facilitates the production of simultaneous contractions. Cardiac muscle cells also have the property of **automaticity**; that is, they can produce contractions without neural input by virtue of **pacemaker cells**.

In addition, these special cells lack the ability to achieve tetany. Avoiding tetanic contractions is essential because a heart "frozen" in tetany would not be able to relax and receive blood to be pumped with the next contraction.

Clinical Correlate

*Disorders such as **coronary artery disease**, **valvular heart disease**, **viral infections**, **diabetes**, **kidney failure**, and a variety of other inflammatory diseases can cause the cardiac muscles to weaken. This is called **cardiomyopathy** (cardio* = heart ; *myo* = muscles ; *pathy* = disease).

During a "heart attack" or **myocardial infarction**, a variety of chemicals is released into the blood stream from the injured muscle; these chemicals are detectable through laboratory evaluation. They are produced at different times following heart injury, and this is why patients seen in the emergency room with chest pain are frequently kept in the hospital for serial blood work (i.e., following blood levels of certain chemicals over time to help determine if a heart attack has occured) to rule in or out a cardiac event.

Smooth Muscle

Smooth muscle tissue is found throughout the body and is nearly as prevalent as skeletal muscle. These muscles are not under voluntary control, have a single nucleus per cell, and lack the striations so characteristic of skeletal and cardiac muscle. These smooth muscle cells (Figure 50) are found in nearly every organ system in the body where they control blood flows to various structures, function as "gates" called **sphincters** that regulate movements along various passages in the body, and respond readily to commands from the **autonomic nervous system**. There are, however, some sphincters that are under voluntary control.

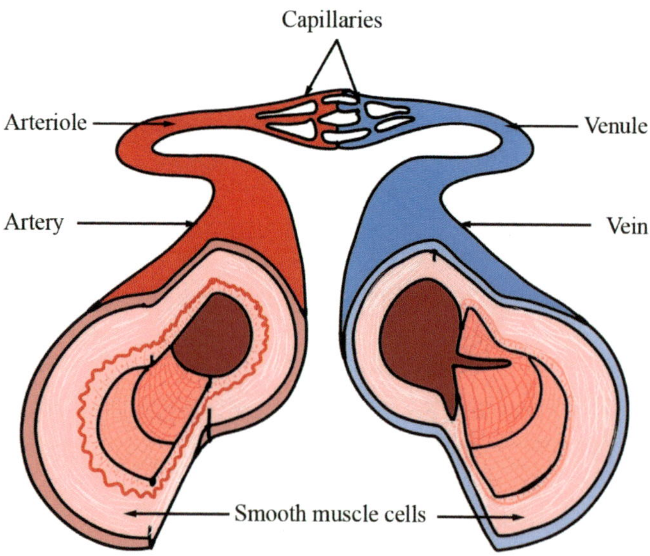

Figure 50. Smooth muscle in blood vessels

Test Your Knowledge

1. What is the purpose of skeletal muscles?

   ____

   ____

   ____

2. What is the purpose of cardiac muscles?

____

____

____

3. What is the purpose of smooth muscles?

____

____

____

Gross Anatomy of the Muscular System

Just as the skeleton was divided into axial and appendicular divisions, so also are the associated muscle groups. The axial group is divided into muscles of the head and neck (Figure 51) including the muscles of facial expression, the muscles of the spine (Figure 52), and the muscles of the trunk and abdomen (Figure 53).

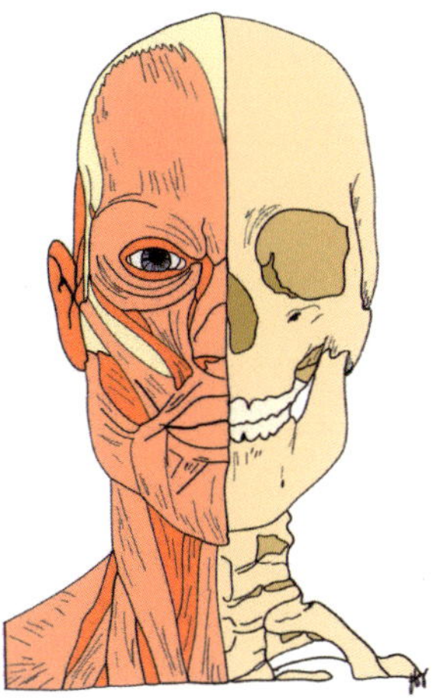

Figure 51. Muscles of the axial group

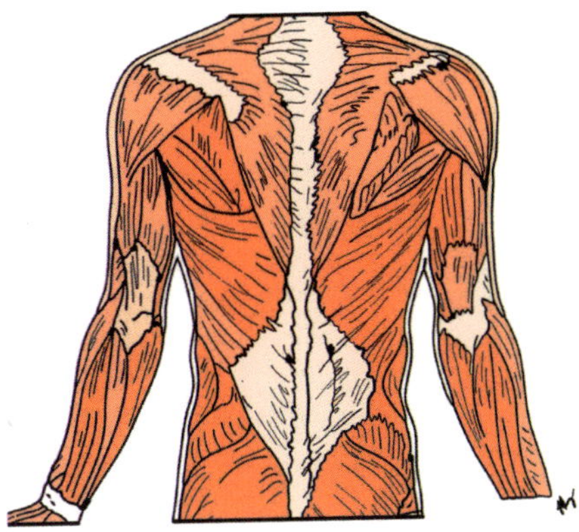

Figure 52. Spine and back muscles

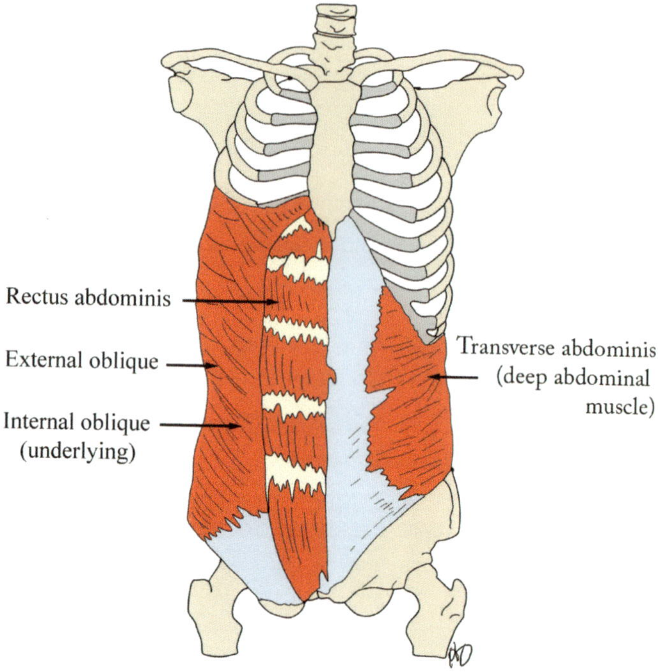

Figure 53. Muscles of the trunk and abdomen

The appendicular muscle group comprises the muscles of the limbs: the shoulders, arms, legs, knees, and hips. The joints near and surrounding these muscle groups are highly mobile and susceptible to injury. They are also quite complex. For example, **carpal tunnel syndrome** can occur when, due to repetitive motions of the hand and wrist, the tendons in the wrist become inflamed and swollen, compressing the median nerve (Figure 54).

Clinical Correlate

*A **hernia** often occurs at a weak spot in the abdominal wall where intra-abdominal pressures are able to push **viscera**, such as the bowel, through the defect. Common locations include the inguinal area, sites of previous incisions, and the diaphragm (Figures 55 and 56).*

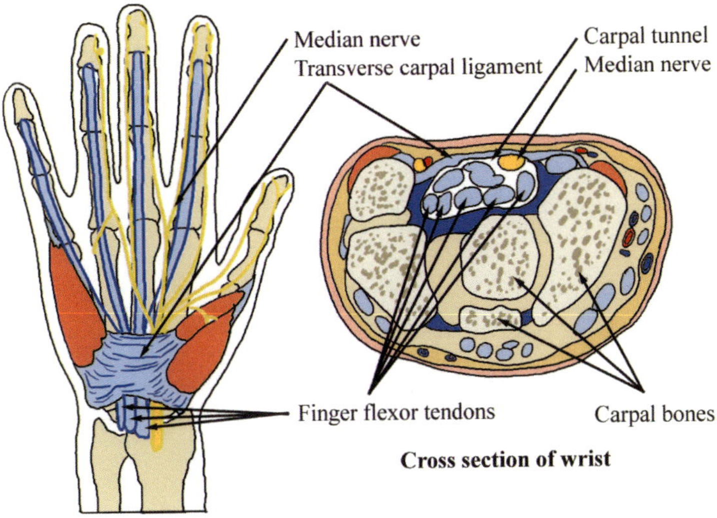

Figure 54. Carpal tunnel syndrome

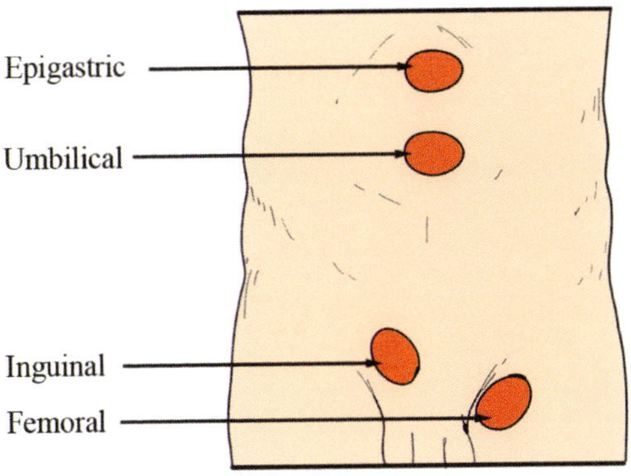

Figure 55. Types of hernias

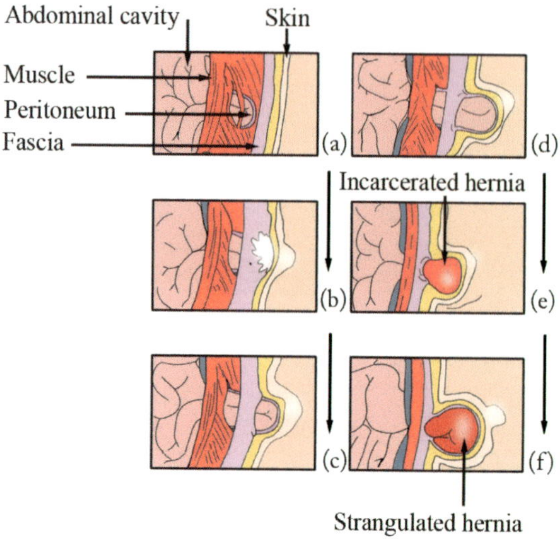

Figure 56. Cross section of hernias

Common Conditions and Diseases of the Muscular System

Myasthenia gravis is a recurring neuromuscular (*neur/o* = nerve ; *muscul/o* = muscle) disease. Characterized by weakness and easy fatigue of the skeletal muscles, it affects females three times more commonly than males. It is typically diagnosed when patients are in their twenties. The disease results from the defective neuromuscular transmission at the motor endplate (where microscopically a nerve "talks" to a muscle via a neurotransmitter). There appears to be a reduction of receptors for the acetylcholine to bind to, and there seems to be an autoimmune component with antibodies directed toward these receptors. Treatment is usually with steroids.

Trichinosis is a disease contracted from eating poorly cooked pork, although other meat sources have also been implicated as culprits. The larvae of the *Trichinella spiralis* get ingested, and they have a predilection for striated muscle. The muscle cells and the invaders live in harmony for a while, then they both die, producing an inflammatory reaction. The first symptoms of this disease often appear between twelve hours to two days after eating infected meat. The waste products excreted by the parasites can cause inflammation with symptoms such as nausea, vomiting, sweating, and diarrhea. Five to seven days after the symptoms appear, patients often develop a fever as well as swelling of the face. After ten days, there is often intense muscle pain, difficulty breathing, and weakening of the pulse and blood pressure. Heart damage can occur and often leads to heart failure, respiratory complications, or kidney malfunction.

Musculoskeletal System Glossary

abduction	moving away from the midline of the body
acetabulum	cup-shaped cavity at the base of the hipbone into which the ball-shaped head of the femur fits
ACL	(also known as anterior cruciate ligament)
adduction	moving toward the midline of the body
arthralgia	pain in the joints
arthritis	inflammation of joints
arthroscopy	examination of interior of joint with arthroscope
atrophy	wasting away; literally without development; causes include mutations (which can destroy the gene to build up the organ), poor nourishment, poor circulation, loss of hormonal support, loss of nerve supply to the target organ, disuse or lack of exercise or disease intrinsic to the tissue itself
bunion	deformity characterized by lateral deviation of the great toe due to the swollen bursal sac and/or an osseous (bony) anomaly on the mesophalangeal joint (where the first metatarsal bone and hallux meet). The larger part of the bump is a normal part of the head of first metatarsal bone that has tilted sideways to stick out at its top;bunion = hallux valgus
bursa	(also known as bursae) sacs filled with synovial fluid which cushion the joint
bursae	(also known as bursa) synovial joints contain bursae or "sacs" filled with synovial fluid which cushions the joint
carpals	bones of wrist
cervical	neck
chondritis	inflammation of cartilage
circumduction	circular (or, more precisely, conical) movement of a body part, such as a ball-and-socket joint or the eye; consists of a combination of flexion, extension, adduction, and abduction; "windmilling" the arms or rotating the hand from the wrist, and rolling the eyes are examples of circumductive movement

closed fracture	simple fracture, break in bone, no open wound in skin
closed reduction fracture	aligning the bone fragments through manual manipulation or traction, without incision
coccyx	(also known as the tailbone) the final segment of the vertebral column
collagen	means glue, tough, yet flexible, fibrous protein material also found in the bone, cartilage, tendons, and ligaments
Colles' fracture	fracture of the distal radius in the forearm with dorsal (posterior) displacement of the wrist and hand; sometimes referred to as a "dinner fork" or "bayonet" deformity due to the shape of the resultant forearm
compact bone	bone consisting of a central Haversian canal surrounded by concentric rings of a hard, virtually solid mass of bony tissue intruded by minute canals called canaliculi; compact bone forms the dense outer shell of bones and has a smooth and homogeneous appearance
complete fracture	break extends through entire thickness of bone
condyle	knuckle-like projection at the end of the bone
dislocation	displacement of a bone from its normal location within a joint, causing loss of function
dorsiflexion	bending the ankle joint so that the foot bends backward (upward); opposite of plantar flexion
epiphysis	the end of the bone
eversion	moving outward from the midline
extension	straightening the extremity at the joint and increasing angle of the joint
false ribs	rib pairs 8 through 10, which connect to the vertebrae in the back but not to the sternum in the front, because they join the seventh rib in the front
fascia	thin sheets of fibrous connective tissue that penetrate and cover the entire muscle, holding the fibers together
flexion	bending the extremity at the joint and decreasing the angle of the joint
floating ribs	rib pairs 11 and 12, which connect to the vertebrae in the back but are free of any attachment in the front
foramen	hole in a bone through which blood vessels or nerves pass
fossa	Hollow or concave depression in a bone

hematopoiesis	normal formation and development of blood cells in the bone marrow
IM, I.M.	intramuscular
insertion	point of attachment of a muscle to a bone it moves
intercostal spaces	spaces between the ribs
inversion	moving inward toward the midline
invertebral disc	flat, circular platelike structure of cartilage that serves as a cushion (shock absorber) between the vertebrae
kyphosis	humpback
ligament	most commonly refers to as a band of tough, fibrous dense regular connective tissue comprising attenuated collagenous fibers; connect bones to other bones to form a joint; they do not connect muscles to bones; that is the job of tendons; can limit the mobility of articulations, or prevent certain movements altogether; function of ligaments: 1) hold bone to bone, 2) promote support, 3) support bone movement
lumbar vertebrae	vertebrae of the lower back, L1 through L5
mandible	jaw
maxilla	upper jaw
metacarpals	join the carpals with the fingers (phalanges)
NSAID's	nonsteroidal anti-inflammatory drugs
open fracture	compound fracture, break in bone with open wound in skin
open reduction of fracture	realigning under direct observation during surgery
ossification	conversion of cartilage and fibrous connective tissue to bone; the formation of bone
osteoarthritis	degenerative joint disease, common form of arthritis and is from wear and tear on the joints
osteoblasts	immature bone cells that actively produce bony tissue
osteoclasts	large cells that absorb or digest old bone tissue
osteocytes	mature bone cells; networked to each other via long cytoplasmic extensions that occupy tiny canals called canaliculi, which are used for exchange of nutrients and waste through gap junctions
osteomalacia	disease in which bones become abnormally soft due to a deficiency of calcium and phosphorous in the blood; disease results in fractures and noticeable deformities of the weight-bearing bones

osteomyelitis	bacterial infection of bone and bone marrow in which the resulting inflammation can lead to a reduction of blood supply to the bone
osteoporosis	porous bones; that is, bones that were once strong become fragile due to loss of bone density
periosteum	thick, white, fibrous membrane that covers the surface of a long bone and contains osteoblasts and blood vessels
phalanges	bones of fingers
plantar flexion	bending the ankle joint so that the foot bends toward the sole of the foot
podiatrist	foot doctor
pronation	turning or facing downward (anatomical perspective), i.e., palms facing floor
prosthesis	artificial substitute for a missing body part
protraction	moving forward; anatomical term of motion for anterior movement of an anatomical part of the body forward (anteriorly); can include the shoulders, jaw, pelvis, etc.
red bone marrow	soft, semifluid substance located in the small spaces of cancellous bone that is the source of blood cell production
resorption	process of removing or digesting old bone tissue
retraction	moving backwards
rheumatoid arthritis	chronic, systemic, inflammatory disease affecting multiple joints of body, mainly small peripheral joints (hands and feet)
rotation	turning head over to the right shoulder, then back to midline; next turning head over to the left shoulder and back to midline
rotator cuff tear	tear in muscles that form a "cuff" over the upper end of the arm or head of the humerous
sacrum	triangular shaped bone that forms part of the hip
sinus	opening or hollow space in a bone; a cavity within a bone
spinal stenosis	narrowing of the vertebral canal, nerve root canals, or intervertebral foramina of the lumbar spinal canal causing pressure on the nerve roots prior to their exit from the foramina

stenosis	abnormal condition characterized by a narrowing or restriction of an opening or passageway in a body structure
supination	turning or facing upward, i.e., palms facing ceiling
sutures	immovable joints, such as those of the cranium
synovial fluid	thick lubricating fluid located in synovial joints
synovial joint	space between the bones which is lined with a synovial membrane
temporal bone	above your ear; situated at the sides and base of the skull, and lateral to the temporal lobes of the cerebrum; supports that part of the face known as the temple
tendons	connect muscle to bone
trochanter	large bony process located below the neck of the femur

Chapter 3
The Respiratory System

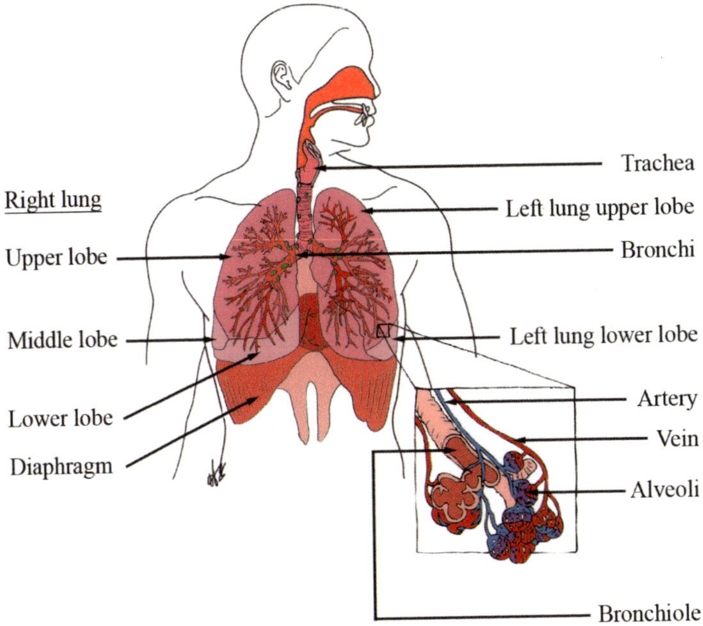

Figure 57. The respiratory tract

To live and experience life as we know it, a process to store and use energy must take place in each and every cell of the body. This process is known as **cellular metabolism** and it refers to the energy movement process. The respiratory and cardiovascular systems work together to provide all of the body's cells with enough oxygen to maintain cell metabolism and to remove cell waste—specifically, carbon dioxide. In this chapter, we will discuss the anatomy and physiology involved in this remarkable process (Figure 57).

The Respiratory Anatomy

Typically, air first enters the body through the nose where it is warmed, humidified, and cleansed of most foreign substances such as dust (Figure 58). This cleansing is assisted by coarse hairs inside the nose as well as the mucous covering of the walls of this upper airway structure. As air is inhaled, it flows around the inside of the nose in a turbulent fashion. The turbulent airflow further assists in the trapping of dust particles that stick to the mucous-covered walls of the airways or are trapped by the hairs in the nose. The inhaled air next passes through the **nasopharynx** located just behind the nose, the **oropharynx** located behind the mouth, and then to the **laryngopharynx**, an extension of the overall pharynx itself, which is located in the throat just before entering the **trachea** (the tube that carries air to the lungs).

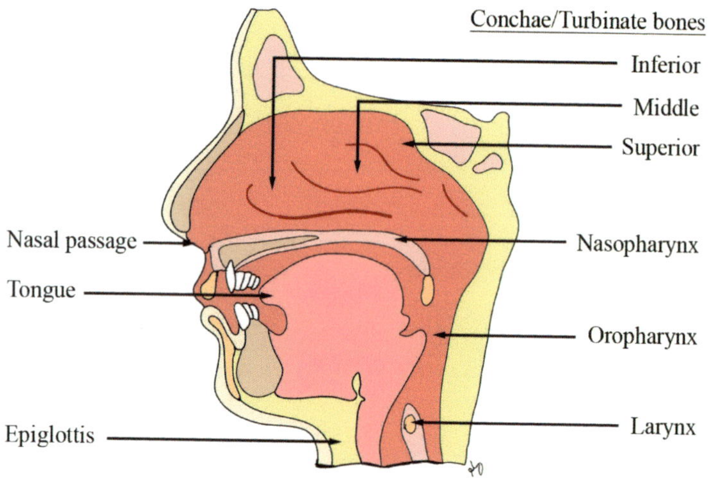

Figure 58. Upper respiratory tract

After passing through the separate subsections of the pharynx, the air reaches the **epiglottis**. The epiglottis is a movable elastic "lid" that prevents swallowed food from entering the trachea. You may have heard or seen someone choking on food and then say, "My food went down the wrong pipe!" Specifically what happened is that rather than swallow their food, the person inadvertently inhaled it. In swallowing, the tongue moves, causing the epiglottis to block the trachea (Figure 59). If the person does not swallow, the epiglottis cannot block the trachea, and the person chokes. (Inflammation of the epiglottis is fortunately uncommon, but it is more common in young children where it can be life-threatening.) As air makes its way down the trachea, the lower respiratory region is entered. Once air passes the epiglottis, it passes through the **larynx**, where its flow over the **vocal cords** can result in the production of sounds.

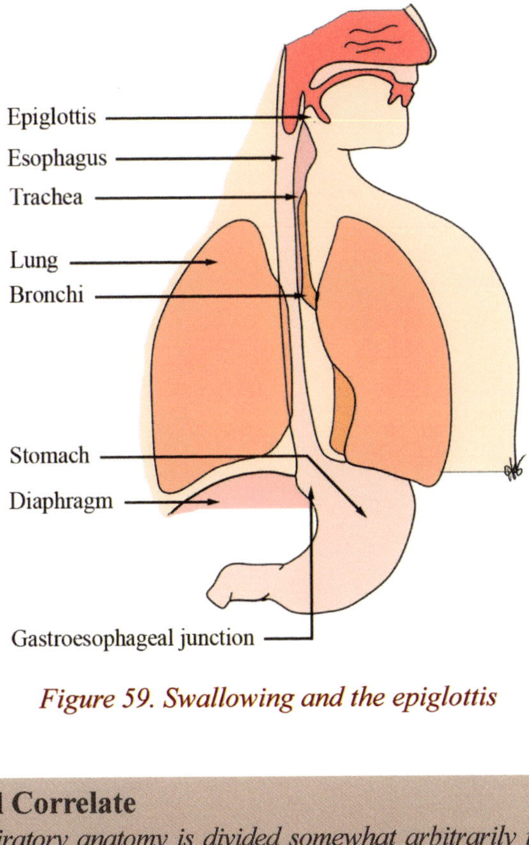

Figure 59. Swallowing and the epiglottis

Clinical Correlate

The respiratory anatomy is divided somewhat arbitrarily into upper and lower parts by using the epiglottis as the dividing point. This division allows medical personnel to distinguish the less dangerous infections of the upper respiratory system from the more significant lower respiratory infections such as ***pneumonia****. Although upper respiratory conditions such as* ***sinusitis****,* ***tonsillitis****, and* ***streptococcal pharyngitis*** *can be quite serious, they are not considered as dangerous as the infections or conditions that occur lower in the respiratory tract.*

Test Your Knowledge

1. What structure does air have to pass over to produce sound?

   ____

2. What happens when someone chokes?

   ____

   ____

The Trachea

Once the inhaled air passes the epiglottis, it heads downward toward the trachea and enters the lower respiratory. Built into the trachea, a tube-like structure, is a series of support rings called **cartilages** (Figure 60).

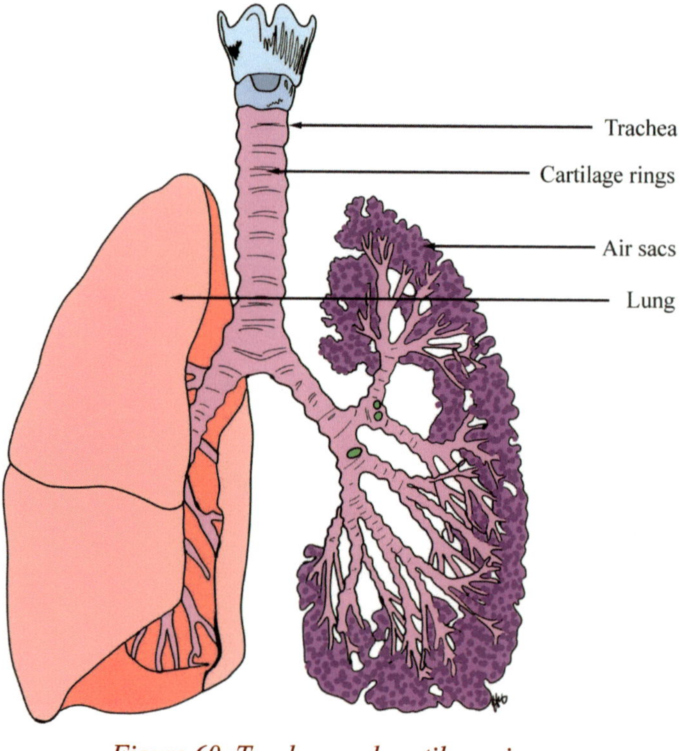

Figure 60. Trachea and cartilage rings

These support rings prevent the collapse of the airway during breathing. Because these rings are not completely round but instead are C-shaped with their open portion facing the back of the trachea toward the esophagus (posteriorly), food can pass down the esophagus unhindered by the trachea. About 12 cm (or approximately 4.8 inches) below its origin, the trachea ends as it divides into the left and right primary **bronchi**, which provide air to the left and right lungs. Much like the trachea, these primary bronchi are supported by rings or cartilages. These primary bronchi further divide into increasingly smaller and smaller tubes, eventually reaching microscopic sizes where they become **alveolar ducts** that eventually terminate into the **alveoli**. It is here—and only here—that the exchange of carbon dioxide (CO_2) for oxygen (O_2) takes place. Figure 61 illustrates the mass of blood vessels surrounding these alveolar sacs to improve gas exchange there. In human beings, the thin walls of these sacs represent a huge surface area, frequently compared to approximately half the size of a tennis court.

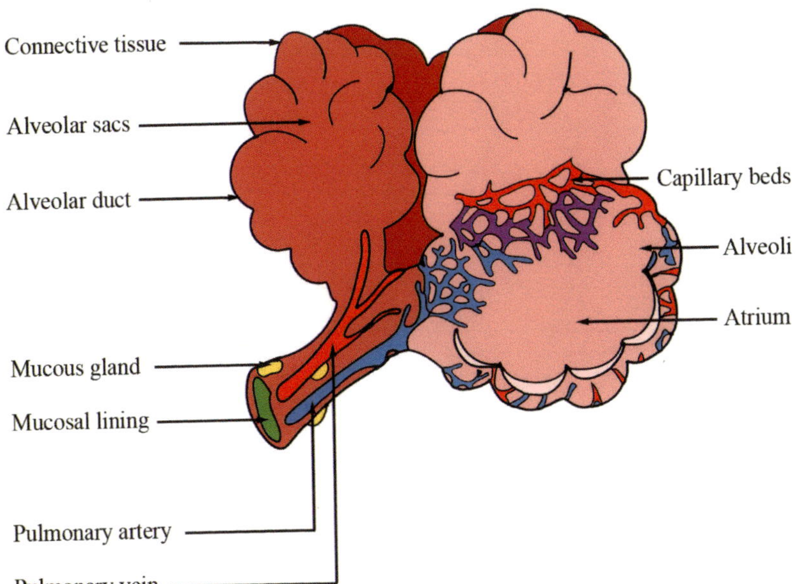

Figure 61. Close-up of microscopic alveoli

The Lungs

A normal individual has two lungs, left and right. The right lung consists of three lobes and the left lung two. An easy way to remember this is to remember that the heart is on the left side of the body and occupies the space where a third lobe could have been. The lungs are suspended within the **pleural cavity**, also called the **thorax**. The word *pleura* comes from a Greek word meaning "rib" or "side." Hence, the pleural cavity is an opening inside the rib cage. A double-layered membrane lies between the lungs and the thorax. The layer closest to the lung is called the **visceral pleura** (from the Latin word *viscus*, denoting a relationship to the organs), and the layer next to the thorax is called the **parietal pleura** (from the Latin word *pariatalis*, which means "of or pertaining to the walls," or for our sake, the ribs). These moist surfaces allow the lung and chest wall to rub against each other during breathing without causing pain (Figure 62). The two pleural surfaces are kept in close proximity by a slight negative pressure between them (called the potential space).

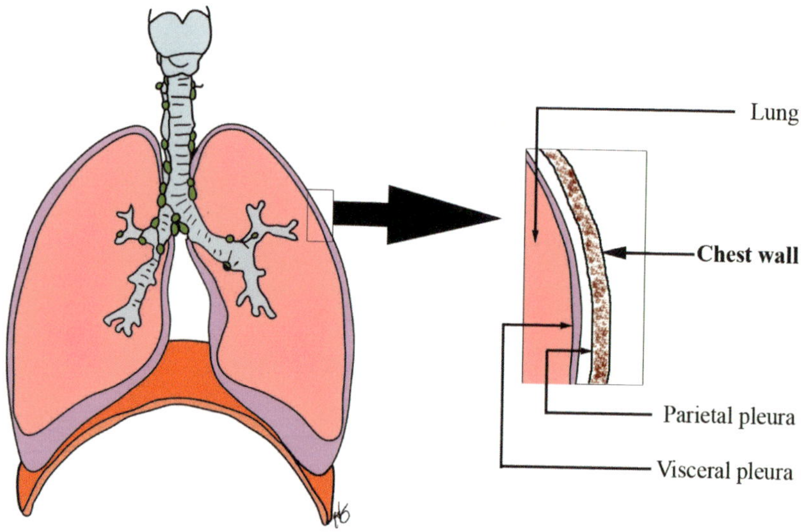

Figure 62. Visceral and parietal pleura

> **Clinical Correlate**
> *A penetrating injury to the lung may cause a loss of the negative pressure in the space between the parietal and visceral pleuras, and the lung on the side of the injury will collapse. This is known as* ***pneumothorax****.*

A great way to remember the structures that air passes through is to remember the following mnemonic: **N NOELL TBA**, pronounced "N" "Noel" "TBA." If you use the mnemonic to put the first letters of the structures together you'll have: nose, nasopharynx, oropharynx, epiglottis, and laryngopharynx (both the epiglottis and laryngopharynx are located at the same level of the body), larynx, trachea, bronchi/bronchioles, and alveoli (located inside the lungs).

The Respiratory Physiology

The process of air flowing into and out of the lungs is known as **pulmonary ventilation** or more simply as "breathing." A complete respiratory cycle consists of one inhalation and one exhalation. When a person inhales, he contracts the **diaphragm** (a sheet of internal muscle that stretches across the bottom of the rib cage) and elevates the ribs by contracting the **intercostal muscles** (groups of muscles that run between the ribs) (Figure 63).

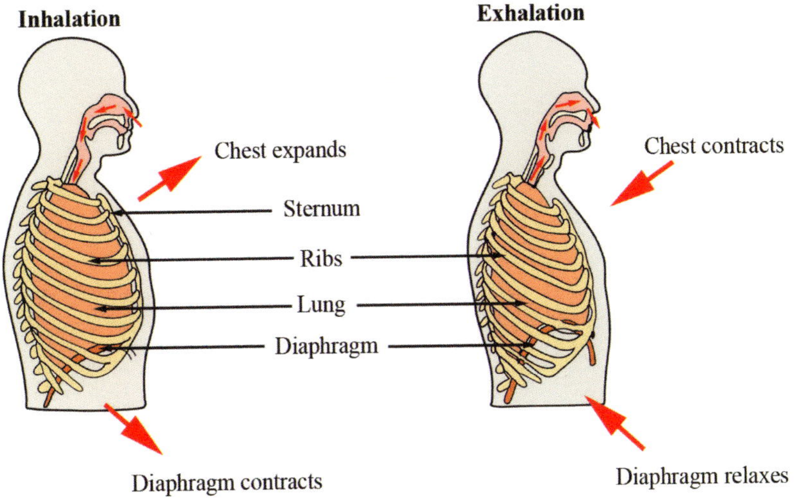

Figure 63. Inhalation and exhalation

This process increases the volume of the chest cavity, which lowers the air pressure there. When the pressure in the chest is less than in the air surrounding us, air rushes into the lungs and equalizes the pressure between the inside and outside. During quiet breathing, exhalation is a completely passive process that is brought about by a concept known as **elastic recoil**. You have seen this concept at work in any item that when stretched and let go, automatically resumes its original, nonstretched state.

Recoil is automatic. When the pressure inside the chest cavity becomes greater than the outside air pressure, the air flows out once again to equalize itself. When the air pressure inside and outside are the same, no air flow occurs.

The air we breathe begins to change as soon as it enters through the nose where it is warmed, humidified, and cleansed of most environmental impurities. When it finally reaches the alveoli, the inhaled air has already mixed with the air we just exhaled. Now it contains less oxygen and more carbon dioxide than the air in the atmosphere. This is because a certain amount of air never fully leaves the lungs. Instead, it occupies what is known as **pulmonary dead space**. It is also warmer than when it first entered the body due to the overall warmth of the body.

Test Your Knowledge

1. Exactly where does the exchange of gas occur in the lungs?

   ____

   ____

2. T or F: When a person inhales, the diaphragm relaxes?

   ____

3. What is included in a complete respiratory cycle?

   ____

   ____

   ____

Gas Transport

Oxygen (O_2) and **carbon dioxide** (CO_2) are transported in the blood by **hemoglobin** contained in the red blood cells, although hemoglobin favors the transport of oxygen rather than carbon dioxide. *Hemoglobin* comes from the words *hem* = blood ; *globin* = protein. It is capable of carrying oxygen, carbon dioxide, and carbon monoxide.

Let's talk about the transport mechanism of oxygen and carbon dioxide. First, remember that red blood cells contain hemoglobin. When these hemoglobin-containing red cells pass through an area low in oxygen content, they release their oxygen into that tissue. Conversely, when these same red cells find areas of high oxygen content, such as the lung, the hemoglobin molecules bind to the available oxygen to transport it to areas of low oxygen content (Figure 64).

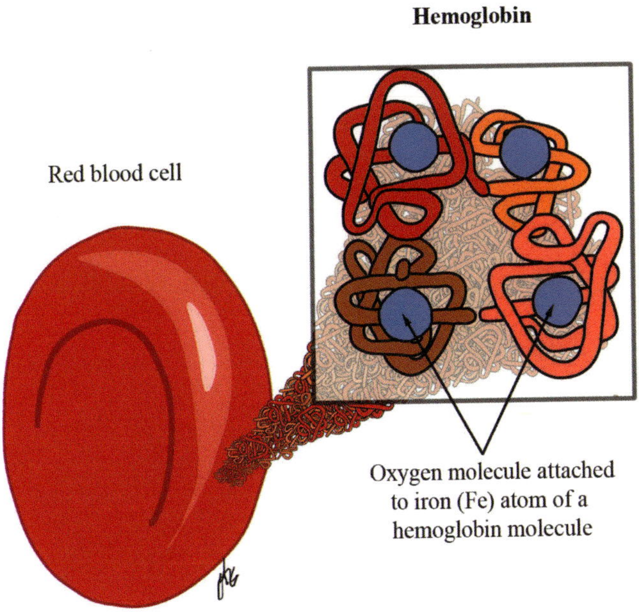

Figure 64. Hemoglobin and oxygen transport

Carbon dioxide is not just "waste." It has important functions in the body. To better understand the role of CO_2 in the body, keep in mind that the fluids and tissues in the human body must stay within a normal acid–base range. The normal pH balance in the human body is 7.35 to 7.45 (which is basically neutral).

If the pH gets too low (**acidosis**) or too high (**alkalosis**), causing a deviation from the norm, many organs can be negatively impacted. Carbon dioxide participates in acid-based balance when it is converted to **carbonic acid**. Carbonic acid is a "weak acid" and as such can be used as a means of transporting CO_2 to the lungs where the carbonic acid can be changed to CO_2 and water. Thus, carbon dioxide is a primary regulator of the acid–base balance of the body.

Role of the Lungs: Respiratory Control Centers

Oxygen delivery rates and carbon dioxide removal rates are controlled to a large extent at the local level. As a tissue's **metabolic rate** (the activity level of a given tissue, a measure of how hard it is working) increases, its need for oxygen rises and its need to reduce carbon dioxide speeds up. The result is the routing of blood to that tissue to provide the needed oxygen and remove the carbon dioxide that is building up. In addition to these local activities, respiratory function is controlled by parts of the **central nervous system**. Respiratory centers are located in the **brain stem**, specifically in the **pons** (a band of nerve fibers that connect different parts of the brain) and the **medulla** (the region of the brain concerned with vital functions like breathing and blood circulation).

Test Your Knowledge

1. How does carbon dioxide leave the body?

    ____

    ____

2. What areas of the brain are considered to be the respiratory center?

    ____

3. Why is carbon dioxide important to the body?

    ____

    ____

Common Conditions and Diseases of the Respiratory System

Pulmonary edema is lung congestion frequently seen with heart failure or injury to the **alveolar capillary membrane**. This condition can be caused by, among other things, **hypervolemia** (too much intravascular volume) and **low oncotic pressure** (not enough proteins in the blood vessels to draw **extravascular fluid** back in to the vessels), which would result in the diminished ability of the **lymphatics** to handle this accumulating fluid. If left untreated, this can lead to **adult respiratory distress syndrome (ARDS).**

Asthma is a common condition frequently seen in doctors' offices and ERs. It is a bronchial constrictive disease characterized by both inflammation and wheezing. Initially treated with bronchodilators, it is now common to add therapy directed toward reducing inflammation.

Lobar pneumonia is an infective condition involving an entire lobe of the lung, usually produced by a highly dangerous **pathogen** like *pneumococci*. In fact, more than 90% of all lobar pneumonias are caused by this organism. Potent intravenous antibiotics are usually successful in providing a cure.

Respiratory System Glossary

alveoli/alveolus	thin walled sac like structures where oxygen and carbon dioxide are exchanged
apex	upper, rounded part of the lung
apnea	inability to breathe
auscultation	to listen; a physical examination method of listening to the sounds within the body with the aid of a stethoscope
bronchiole	continuations of the airway that are 1 mm or less in diameter and lack cartilage
bronchitis	inflammation of the bronchi
diaphragm	muscular partition that separates the thoracic cavity from the abdominal cavity and that moves upward and downward to aid in respiration
epiglottis	lid-like structure that covers the larynx during swallowing to prevent food from entering the airway
larynx	voice-box; cartilaginous chamber about 4 cm long whose primary function is to keep food and drink out of the airway; it has a superior opening called a glottis which is guarded by a flap of tissue called the epiglottis
mediastinum	partition that separates the thorax into two compartments (containing the right and left lungs) and that encloses the heart, esophagus, trachea, and thymus gland
oxyhemoglobin	oxygen-loaded form of hemoglobin
pharynx	(also known as the throat) tube or cavity that connects the mouth and nasal passages with the esophagus
pleura	membranes enclosing the lung (visceral pleura) and lining the thoracic cavity (parietal pleura)
pleural cavities	space in the body where the lungs are located
pneumonia	inflammation in the lung resulting from infection by bacteria, viruses, fungi, or parasites or from aspiration of chemicals
RBCs	(also known as red blood cells) contain hemoglobin which permits them to transport oxygen (and carbon dioxide)

respiratory cycle	includes one inspiration plus the following exhalation
trachea	(also known as windpipe) semi-rigid tube about 12cm long and 2.5 cm in diameter, lying anterior to the esophagus; supported by 16 - 20 c-shaped rings of hyaline cartilage
wheezes	continuous high-pitched whistling sounds heard when air is forced through a narrow space during inspiration or exhalation; frequently associated with asthma

Chapter 4
The Cardiovascular System

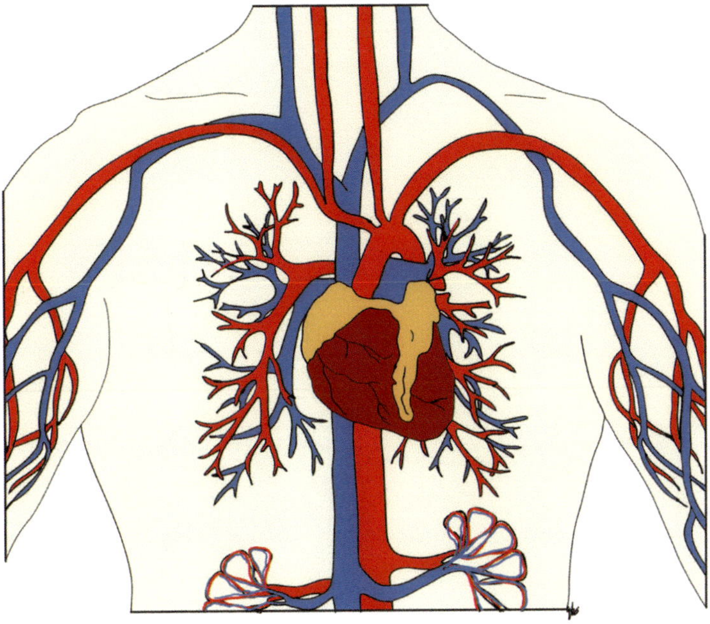

Figure 65. The cardiovascular system

For many centuries, people understood that the red liquid called blood played a significant role in life and death. They could easily see that the loss of blood on the battlefield or from accidental injuries often led to death. It has only been in the past few hundred years, however, that scientists have discovered the many roles and functions of blood.

The Blood

Blood is the transport medium for nearly everything that is carried from one part of the body to another (Figure 65). These substances include oxygen, glucose, hormones, and proteins. For example, **hormones** are transported by the blood from **endocrine organs** to their target tissues. Maintenance of body temperature and pH balance are only two of the many tasks the blood accomplishes.

Blood is a mixture of fluid and cells. It is a liquid made up of living elements (**red cells**, **white cells**, and **platelets**) as well as **plasma**, a liquid that is about 90% water. These blood elements can be seen when the blood is "spun down" in a **centrifuge**, a device that spins a tube of blood so quickly that the heavier elements end up at the bottom of the tube (Figure 66).

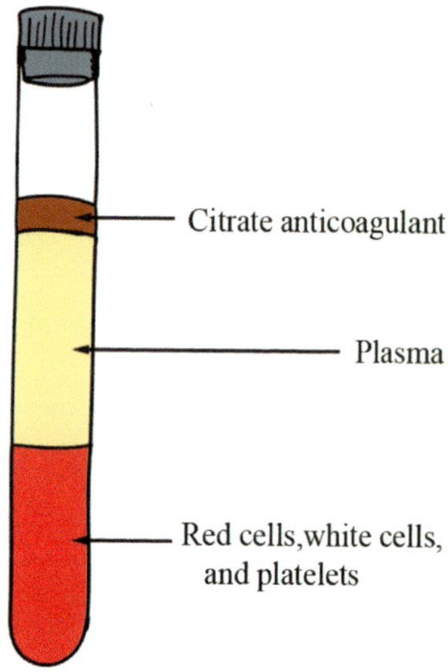

Figure 66. Blood Components after centrifuging

About 99.9% of these formed elements (called such because they are actual cells and not fluid) are red blood cells (RBCs, also known as **erythrocytes** (*erythr* = red ; *cytes* = cells). The other elements are white blood cells (WBCs, also known as **leukocytes** (*leuk/o* = white ; *cytes* = cells), and platelets.

The Hematocrit

When a **hematocrit** (also called a "crit") is performed, a sample of blood is taken and placed in a test tube. This test tube is put in a machine called a centrifuge that spins very quickly. This motion separates blood into two parts: the fluid component of blood (plasma) and its formed elements (red blood cells and white blood cells). When the blood is separated, the technician can determine what proportion of the blood is cells. Typically the red cells outnumber the white cells by about 1000 to 1. Because the number of white cells and platelets is so small in comparison to the red blood cells, the hematocrit effectively measures the red cell volume. This can alert the physician to the presence of a variety of conditions. An example of such a condition is **anemia**, in which the patient has a lower than normal red blood count. Since red blood cells help transport oxygen to the body, anemia is a condition in which the blood's ability to carry oxygen is reduced.

Red Blood Cells

You might think of red blood cells as tiny "delivery trucks." One of their main jobs is to pick up oxygen from the lungs and deliver it to all parts of the body through tubes called **arteries**. Their other main job is to pick up carbon dioxide from all parts of the body and deliver it back to the lungs, to be released into the air through exhalation. For this job, the red cells travel through tubes called **veins**.

The red blood cells (erythrocytes) are shaped like discs (Figure 67). Unlike most other cells, they do not contain **nuclei** (or centers) when they mature. They are usually quite flexible and can travel through the smallest vessels connecting arteries and veins. These vessels are called **capillaries**.

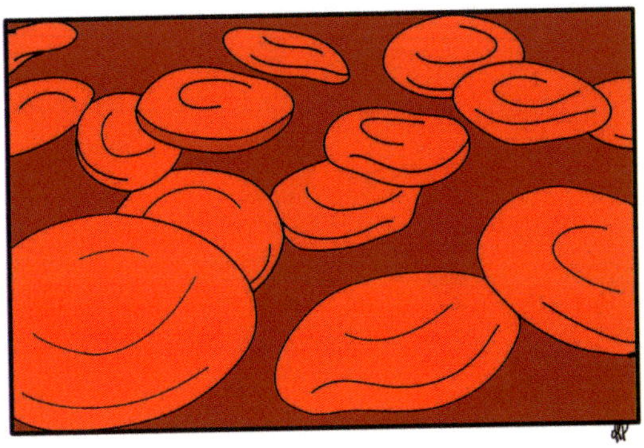

Figure 67. Red blood cells

The red blood cells are especially suited for the task of carrying oxygen because they contain molecules of hemoglobin (Hgb). *Hemoglobin* comes from the Greek word *haima* = blood ; *globin* = protein. It bears repeating that it is the red blood cells that transport most of the oxygen to the body's tissues. The more hemoglobin molecules a red cell contains, the more oxygen that cell can carry. So, in addition to measuring the "crit," another way of testing for the presence of anemia is to measure the level of hemoglobin in the blood through various testing mechanisms like a **complete blood count (CBC)**.

White Blood Cells

You might compare white blood cells (or WBCs) to soldiers, because their job is to protect the body against infections and cancer. These cells make up less than 1% of the blood's volume. However, they serve as powerful "warriors" in the ongoing battle that rages between us and the disease-causing pathogens (germs) that try to invade our bodies every day. Two common examples of pathogens are **bacteria** and **viruses**.

Because their primary job is defense, leukocytes (WBCs) come in several different types (Figure 68), and each type has its own particular job description. Leukocytes can be divided into two major groups: **granulocytes** (literally, cells that contain granules) and **agranulocytes** (cells that contain no visible granules). White blood cells are described this way because of the presence or absence of various colored granules that are visible when the cells are viewed under a microscope.

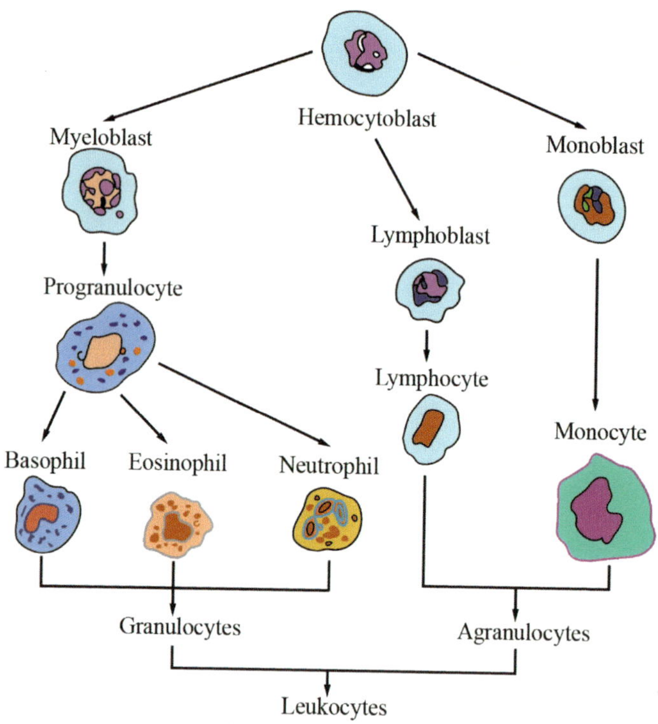

Figure 68. Types of white cells and their origins

Neutrophils are the white cells most commonly seen and are also the most common type of granulocyte. They contain a nucleus with a number of lobes and it is surrounded by **cytoplasm** (the material located outside of the nucleus). The cytoplasm is dotted with fine pink granules. The neutrophil is an active **phagocyte** (from the Greek word *phagein* = to eat ; *cyte* = cell). This is a cell that travels to infected or injured areas of the body, wraps itself around foreign bacteria and fungi, and gobbles them up. Other granulocytes include **eosinophils** (important in cases of parasitic infections and allergic reactions) and **basophils** (the rarest type of WBC and important in producing the inflammatory response).

Agranulocytes consist of lymphocytes and **monocytes**. Lymphocytes are the next most common white cell after neutrophils. The lymphocyte has a large, purple nucleus that takes up most of the room inside the cell. They are only slightly larger than the red cells. Usually, very little cytoplasm is seen when a lymphocyte is viewed under a microscope. These cells play an important role in the body's immune response.

Monocytes are the largest white cells. When activated by the presence of certain chemicals released near an injury or an infection, they become roaming **macrophages** (*macro* = large; *phage* = eat or swallow) that wrap themselves around invading germs and cellular waste and gobble them up.

Platelets

Platelets are an essential component in the blood clotting process and are actually pieces broken off from larger cells called **megakaryocytes**. A megakaryocyte is a large cell in the bone marrow that fragments to produce blood platelets. These pieces or platelets play an important role in the body's clotting process by sticking to injured areas in blood vessels, initiating the clotting process.

Test Your Knowledge

1. Which elements in the blood are responsible for clotting?

   ____

   ____

   ____

2. List two names for the elements in the blood that are responsible for carrying oxygen.

 ____

 ____

3. List two names for the elements in the blood that are responsible for fighting infection.

 ____

 ____

Now let's turn our attention to how blood cells are produced and the factors that influence their production.

Blood Cell Production

The blood cells just discussed are produced in the marrow of certain large bones (e.g., femur, pelvis). The body's day-to-day needs for the different types of blood cells are monitored, and the bone marrow produces these cells to meet those needs. The production of blood cells is referred to as **hematopoiesis** (*hem/o* = blood ; *pooiein* = to make). Bone marrow stem cells called **hemocytoblasts** (*hem/o* = blood ; *cyto* = cells ; *blasts* = build) live within the marrow and produce daughter cells. These daughter cells differentiate into either **lymphoid** or **myeloid** cell lines (refer back to Figure 68).

Red Cell Production

Red blood cells have a life span of about 120 days. The marrow continuously replaces these cells through the division of the bone marrow's stem cells, which are the hemocytoblasts. Once in the blood stream and fully mature, the red cells lose their nuclei as well as the tiny subunits inside them (called **organelles**). In this way, they are turned into mature red cells that carry oxygen to all parts of the body. Red blood cell production is controlled by the release of a hormone called **erythropoietin** (*erythro* = red ; *pooiein* = to make). This substance is released by the kidneys in response to declining oxygen levels in the blood. It regulates the rate at which the bone marrow produces erythrocytes.

White Cell and Platelet Production

In addition to red blood cells, both white blood cells and platelets originate in the bone marrow. Like red blood cells, their production is regulated by hormones. The release of these hormones is not completely understood, but it is probably related to the detection of bacterial toxins (poisons) or other foreign substances in the body.

> **Clinical Correlate**
>
> ***Leukemias*** *are malignancies of the blood-forming tissues. There are actually a variety of types. Most are associated with greatly elevated white blood cell counts, but some simply show elevations of immature white cell forms. Without treatment, most leukemias are fatal.*

Hemostasis and Blood Clots

If damage to an artery wall occurs (for example, through injury or from plaque formation due to high cholesterol), an efficient and speedy response usually follows. You might compare this response to a "construction zone" in the body's arterial "highway." The "construction workers" (platelets) halt any further blood loss and quickly begin the repair work to correct the problem. This process is referred to as **hemostasis** (*hemo* = blood ; *stasis* = to halt). Hemostasis occurs in three general phases:

1. Vascular spasm;
2. Platelet plug formation; and
3. Blood clotting (also called coagulation).

In the first phase (**vascular spasm**), the injured artery wall constricts (narrows). This decreases blood loss while additional repair measures are coordinated. You might compare this process to the reduction of water flow you experience when you're washing your car and the hose gets kinked.

The second phase (**platelet plug formation**) involves the **aggregation** (clumping together) of platelets. During this process, the platelets become "sticky" by exposure to the injured area of the artery wall. Then the platelets attach themselves to the injured area to form the beginnings of a patch, further reducing the flow of blood.

Finally, blood **coagulation** begins when clotting factors present in the plasma are activated. This complex sequence of events results in the deposit of **fibrin** (fiber-like) strands that collect around the injured area to form a more permanent patch.

Test Your Knowledge

1. What is hemostasis?

____

____

____

2. Describe the stages of blood clotting.

____

____

____

3. What is hematopoiesis and where does it occur?

____

____

____

Human Blood Types and Transfusions

Fortunately, most of us will never need a blood transfusion. But for those who experience injuries that result in the loss of 15% or more of their blood volume, transfusions can be life-saving. A working knowledge of human blood types and typing is required in order to transfuse blood safely.

Everyone has a specific red blood cell type. The kind of blood you have, called your **blood type**, is determined by heredity (meaning that it is genetically determined). Blood types are different because different proteins are found on the surface of the red blood cell's membranes. These proteins are called **antigens**.

There are four blood types: A, B, AB, and O. The body's **immune system** is constantly trying to identify "self" from "nonself." It will ignore items it finds that are "us," but attack those that aren't "us." Picture a cell represented as a basketball covered by pictures of your family on its surface. When the body's immune system "looks" at that cell and sees pictures of your family, it knows that the cell is okay. But if it sees members of some other family, it identifies the cell as "foreign" and attacks it. Stated in a more scientific way, when the body recognizes antigens as its own (self), no immune response occurs. But if antigens from another source (someone else's blood) are detected, the body's immune system attacks these cells. The result is destruction of the transfused cells with unfortunate consequences such as allergic reactions and in some cases even kidney failure.

The ABO blood group typing technique (Figure 69), designed to avoid most transfusion reactions, has been around for many years. The ABO group was discovered in 1900 at the University of Vienna by Karl Landsteiner, who was trying to learn why blood transfusions sometimes cause death and at other times save a patient. What he discovered was that depending on a person's blood type and the antigens that appear on the surface membrane of each cell as well as the antibodies that appear in the **blood serum**, only certain types of blood can be transfused into certain blood types.

	Group A	Group B	Group AB	Group O
Red blood cell type	A	B	AB	O
Antibodies present	Anti - B	Anti - A	None	Anti - A & Anti - B
Antigens present	A antigen	B antigen	A and B antigens	None

Figure 69. Characteristics of blood types

As previously explained, the ABO blood groups are based on the presence or absence of two types of antigens, A and B. People with Type A blood have A antigens on their cell surfaces (they have the A group of "family pictures"), and their serum contains **antibodies** to Type B blood. (An antibody is a protein produced by cells in the body in response to the presence of an antigen). In most cases, an antibody is made to fight infection (e.g. a bacterium or virus) and as such is a primary means of fighting disease. In the case of blood, antibodies act by attaching themselves to what they consider to be a foreign cell or antigen (or transfused blood) to weaken or destroy it. Here's how it works. Let's suppose you have Type A blood. The white blood cells (or attackers) of people with Type A blood will mount an assault on Type B blood if exposed to it. And the reverse is true as well: People with Type B blood have B antigens on their cell surfaces, and their serum contains antibodies to Type A blood. The white blood cells of these people will attack Type A blood if exposed to it.

Think of it this way: Since your cells are Type A, the serum around the cells doesn't want any Bs getting to the As on your cells. Therefore, the serum contains B antibodies so that if B does come into your body, the B antibodies will attack it. Taking this reasoning a step further, people with Type AB blood have both A and B antigens on their cell surfaces, and their serum contains no A or B antibodies. Consequently, the antibodies in the serum do not attack either the A or the B antigens. People with Type O blood have no A or B surface antigens, but they have serum that contains both A and B antibodies.

The **Rh blood group** is somewhat different. People with Rh-positive blood (roughly 85% of the population) have D antigens on their cell surfaces, and their serum contains no antibodies related to that antigen. Unlike the ABO system, however, people with Rh-negative blood (the remaining 15%) *have no antibodies to D antigens* in their serum. In order to develop these antibodies, they must be exposed to Rh-positive blood at some point.

The best example is an Rh-negative pregnant woman who has an Rh-positive partner and delivers an Rh-positive infant. The mother may be exposed to the infant's blood toward the end of her pregnancy or during delivery, which causes her to develop antibodies to the D antigen of the infant. This generally has no effect on the first pregnancy, but future pregnancies involving an Rh-positive baby will be affected by the mother's development of the antibodies to the D antigen from the first pregnancy. This happens when the anti-D antibodies cross the **placenta** and attack the baby's Rh-positive red blood cells. The infant develops severe anemia while still inside the mother's **uterus**, and the resulting complications are known as **hemolytic disease of the newborn (HDN)**. Thanks to advances in prenatal care, and the use of RhoGAM (Rh immune globulin shots) over the past few decades, HDN can be prevented in most cases. Today, when a woman with the potential to develop Rh incompatibility becomes pregnant, doctors administer a series of two Rhogam shots during the pregnancy. Typical times for the administration of RhoGAM are around the 28th week of pregnancy and the second within 72 hours after giving birth. Rh immune globulin acts to cloak the Rh antigens so that the mother doesn't make antibodies against them. A dose of Rh immune globulin may also be given if a woman has a miscarriage, an **amniocentesis**, or any bleeding during pregnancy.

If a woman already has Rh antibodies, the pregnancy will be closely monitored to detect any sign of fetal anemia. In rare cases, if the incompatibility is severe and the baby is in danger, a series of exchange transfusions can be performed. Exchange transfusions are needed in fewer than 1% of the Rh-incompatible pregnancies in the United States to replace the baby's blood with red blood cells that are Rh negative. This procedure stabilizes the baby's level of red blood cells and minimizes further damage caused by circulating Rh antibodies already present in the baby's bloodstream.

Those who are Rh negative and also have Type O blood are considered universal donors because they can donate blood to anyone. Since they lack all of the antigens present in people with other blood types, they can create no immune response in a recipient. Conversely, Rh-positive people who also have Type AB blood are considered universal recipients. Since their blood already contains no A, B, and Rh antibodies, no donor with any other blood type poses a threat to the immune responses of these people (refer back to Figure 69).

Test Your Knowledge

1. Which blood type is considered to be the universal donor?

   ____

2. What is the most dangerous combination of blood types that could affect a future pregnancy?

   ____

3. If a person has a blood type of A, what kind of antibodies do they have in their blood serum?

   ____

4. Why do we need to be careful about matching blood types in transfusions?

   ____

   ____

   ____

Organization

Think of the cardiovascular system (CVS) as two streets that go in different directions. These streets are called circuits or pathways and like other streets, they have names: the **pulmonary circuit** and the **systemic circuit** (Figure 70).

The word *pulmonary* comes from the Latin word *pulmo* = lung. In short, it is through the pulmonary circuit that blood goes to the lungs. Specifically, in the pulmonary circuit, blood that is low in oxygen and laden with waste products (such as CO_2 and **lactic acid**) returns to the heart and from there is sent to the lungs, where the CO_2 is released and the O_2 is added.

The systemic circuit, called such because it takes oxygen-rich blood back to the different body systems, distributes this blood to every single cell in the body to provide oxygen for **cellular metabolism** (cellular work). It is the delivery of this freshly oxygenated blood to the body's various capillary beds that defines the primary goal of the CVS. The microscopic, thin-

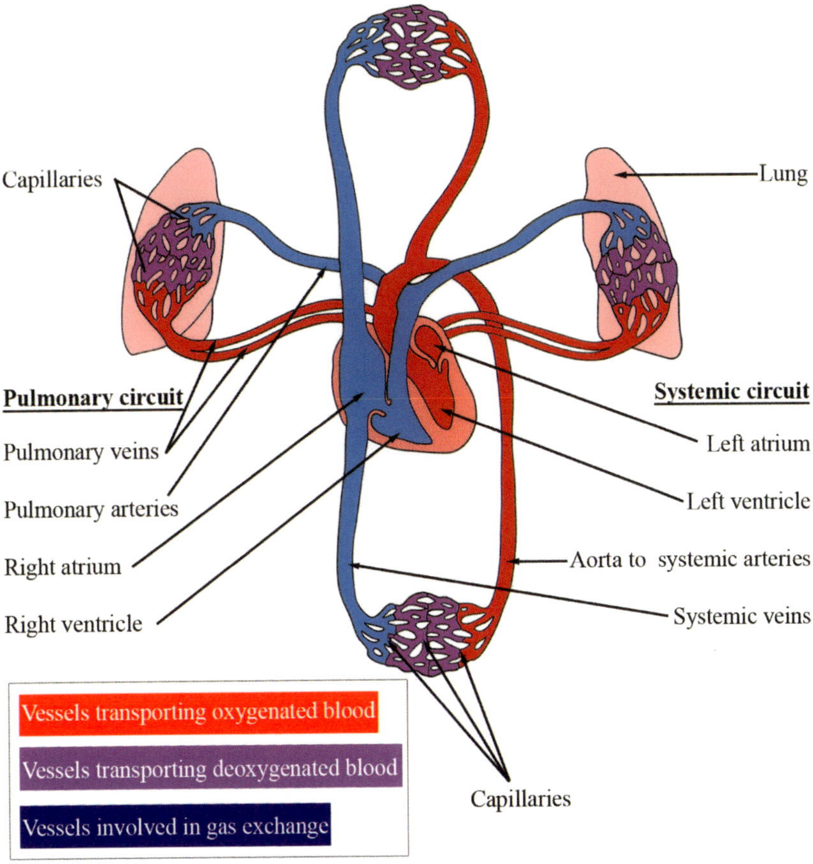

Figure 70. Pulmonary and systemic circuits

walled vessels where the exchange of oxygen, carbon dioxide, and other nutrients takes place are called the capillaries (Figures 71 and 72).

The Heart

The heart makes its home in the thoracic or chest cavity, almost directly behind the sternum (or breastbone). Here it lies, in the **mediastinum**, nestled between two spaces in the thorax called pleural cavities (Figure 73). The mediastinum is the area between the sternum anteriorly (in front of) and the vertebral column posteriorly (behind) and from the thoracic inlet above to the diaphragm below.

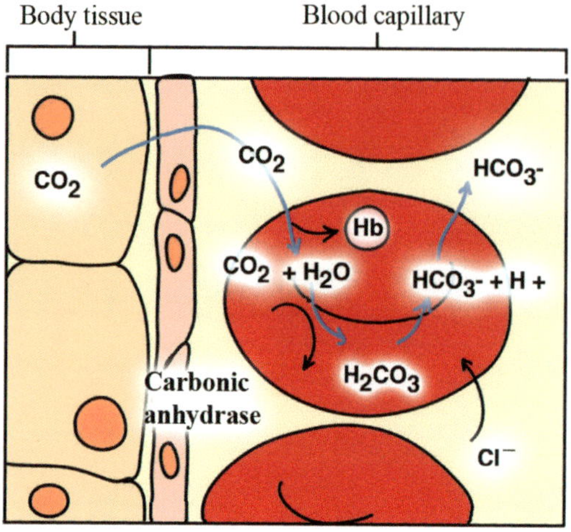

Figure 71. Exchange of O_2 and CO_2 in the capillary bed

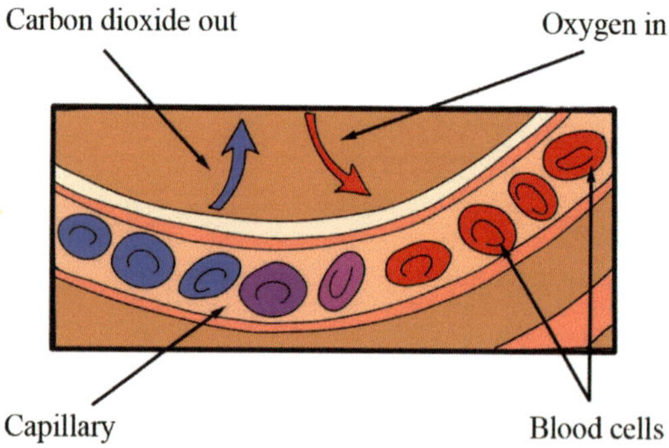

Figure 72. O_2 and CO_2 exchange

The heart serves as a pump that moves blood though a complex system of "pipes" throughout the body. And it stays on the job with amazing efficiency, every single minute of every single day without taking a break, for roughly 80 years in most people. These living "pipes" make up the body's **vascular system**. The heart itself is nestled within a slippery, well-lubricated sac called the **pericardium**, which lies within the mediastinum. This sac provides a near friction-free environment in which the heart can move while it contracts.

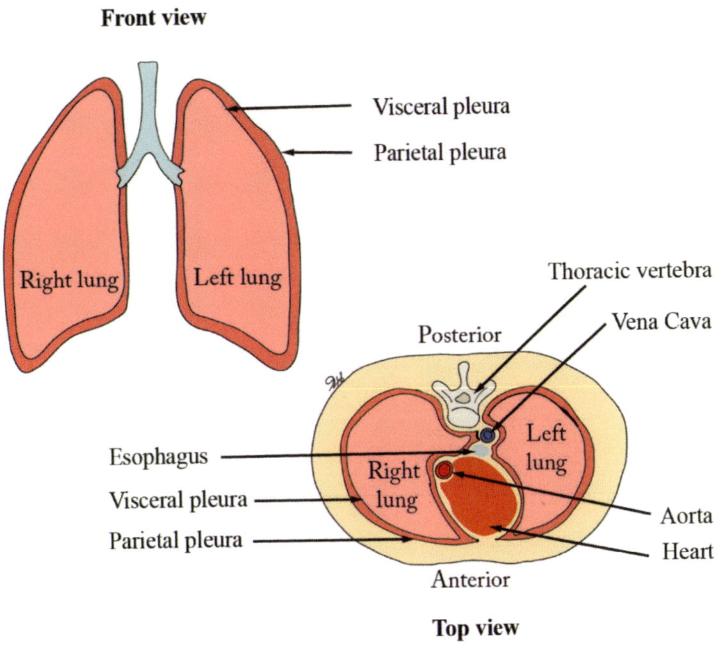

Figure 73. Pleural cavities

About the size of an adult fist, the heart is composed of four chambers or compartments that are connected to each other (Figure 74). These include two **atria** and two **ventricles**. The word *atria* comes from the Latin and Greek word *atrion*, meaning "hall." In anatomical terminology, the word *atrium* designates a chamber that allows entry to another structure or organ. It makes sense then that atria are the hallways that receive blood arriving from outside the heart and the ventricles receive blood that is already directed to them from the atria. The veins are the "pipes" that return blood to the heart. There it passes through the right **atrioventricular valve** (sometimes called the tricuspid valve because it has three leaflets or cusps) and then into the right ventricle. From there blood is pumped to the lungs where it picks up a fresh supply of oxygen. This freshly oxygenated blood then returns by the **pulmonary veins** to the heart by entering the left atrium, passing through the left atrioventricular valve (sometimes called the **mitral** or **bicuspid** valve) and collecting in the left ventricle (Figure 75). There it is pumped out to the rest of the body with each contraction of the heart.

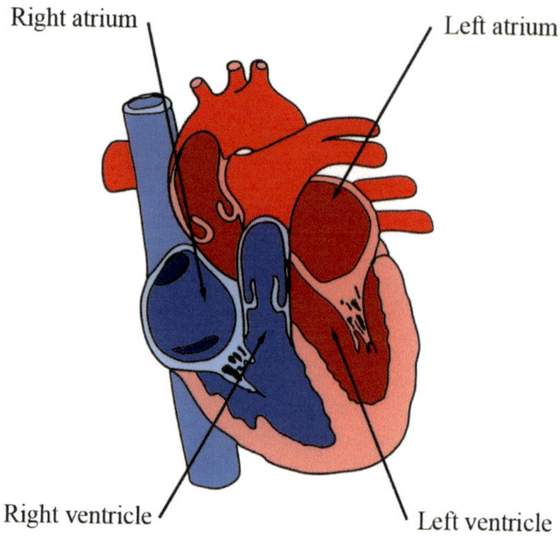

Figure 74. Heart chambers

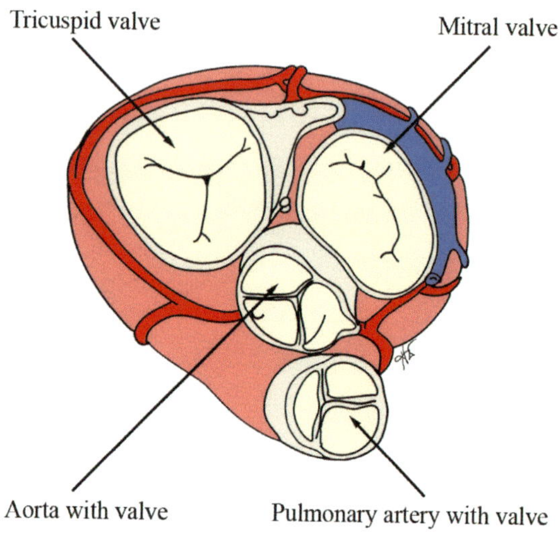

Figure 75. Heart valves

The Vessels

The human body houses two different types of blood vessels: **veins** and **arteries**. Veins are the vessels that carry blood to the heart, and they range in size from very tiny veins that receive blood from the capillaries, to the large veins called the **vena cavas**. These veins connect directly to the heart and can measure more than two centimeters or almost an inch in diameter (Figure 76).

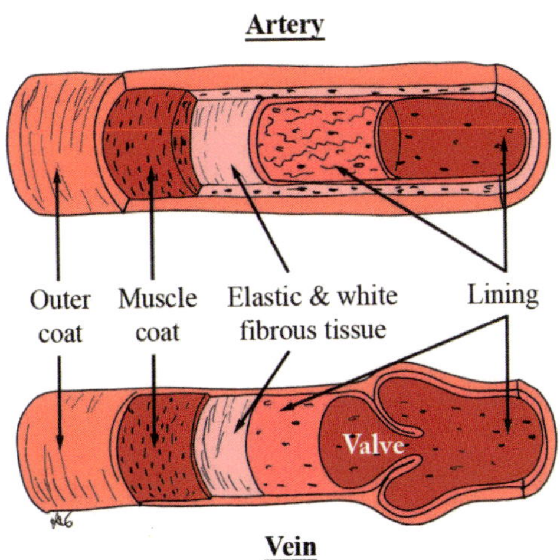

Figure 76. A cross-sectional view of veins and arteries

Arteries are the vessels that direct the blood away from the heart (Figure 77). Their walls tend to be more muscular than the walls of the veins, but both veins and arteries are able to contract and expand. Therefore, they affect blood flow by changing the diameters of their **lumens**, the channels within them. Like veins, arteries vary in size from tiny arterioles that feed the body's capillaries, to the **aorta**, the large artery attached to the heart's powerful left ventricle.

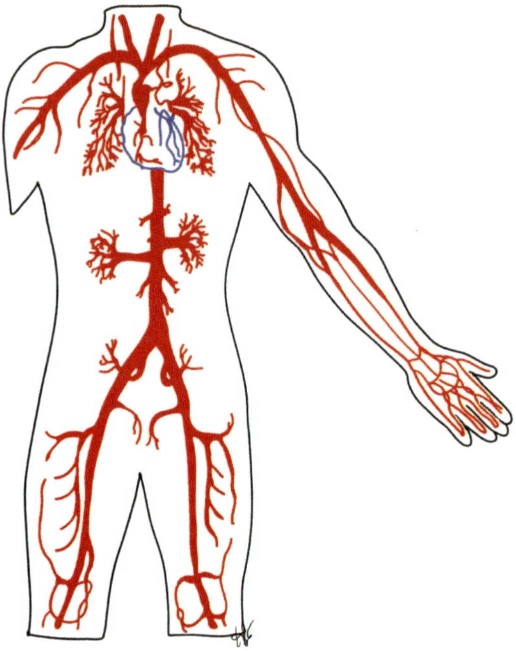

Figure 77. Major arteries

Let's now turn our attention to a more detailed discussion of the anatomy of the heart and vascular system.

Test Your Knowledge

1. Where does the heart reside?

 ____

 ____

2. How many chambers are in the heart?

 ____

 ____

Cardiac Anatomy

Figure 78 illustrates the flow of blood. Arriving from either the superior or inferior vena cavas, **venous** blood enters the right atrium and passes through the right atrioventricular valve where it then enters the right ventricle.

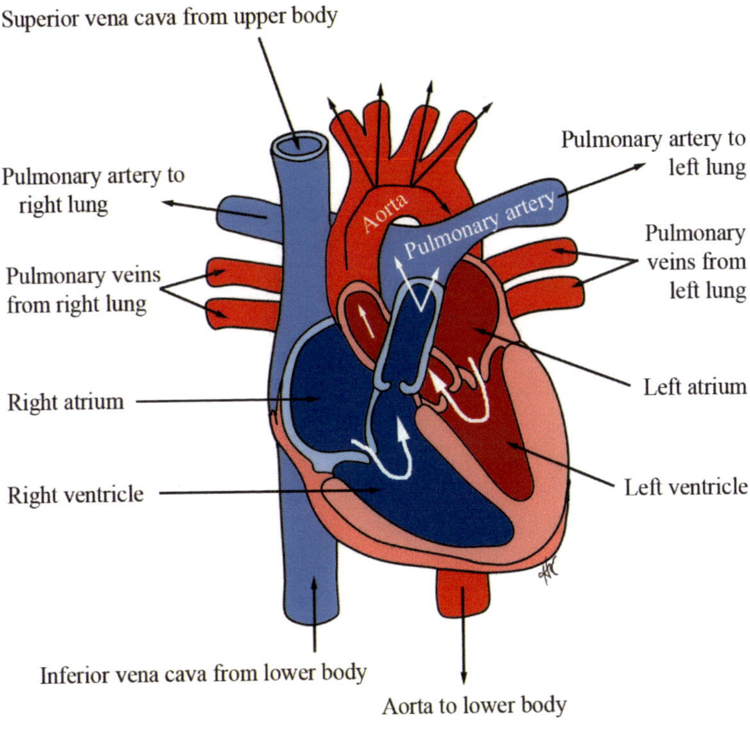

Figure 78. Blood flow within the heart

About 80% of the blood enters the right ventricle passively. That is, it doesn't require an atrial contraction to fill most of the ventricle. When the right atrium does contract, however, it "tops off" the right ventricle, filling it in preparation for ventricular contraction. The reason patients with significant atrial damage are still able to live fairly normal lives is that most of ventricular filling is done passively; that is, the filling does not require any "work" on the part of the heart. The ventricular contraction forces the blood into the **pulmonary artery**, which transports the blood to the lungs for a fresh supply of oxygen. It's important to remember that the pulmonary artery is the only artery in the body that does not carry oxygen-rich blood. However, it is still called an artery because it carries blood away from the heart.

After passing through the lungs, the oxygen-rich blood next enters the **pulmonary vein**, which carries it to the left atrium of the heart. Once again, the left ventricle fills passively as blood passes through the left atrioventricular valve. An atrial contraction is needed only to complete the filling. The left ventricle then contracts, expelling blood out the **aortic valve** into the aorta and on to the rest of the body. The brief time lapse between cardiac contractions is commonly referred to as **diastole**, which refers to the time when the heart is in a brief period of relaxation and expansion. The time during peak contraction pressure is called **systole**.

In Figure 79, notice that the thickness of the muscular walls of the right and left ventricles are considerably different, and that the left ventricle's walls are quite a bit thicker than those of the right. The reason for this is that the right ventricle pumps blood into the relatively low resistance of the pulmonary circuit, whereas the left ventricle must pump blood to the remainder of the body—an exercise that requires much more work. Thus, its thickness is greater. Note that the right and left sides of the heart work in concert with each other. Specifically, the two atria contract at the same time, and the two ventricles follow the atria, again at the same time. Con-

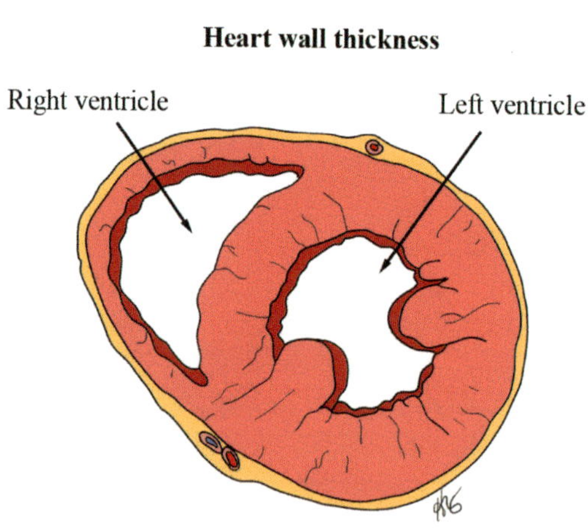

Figure 79. Ventricular wall thickness

sequently, the left and right sides of the heart pump the same volume of blood each time the heart contracts. Specialized cells within the heart's walls are responsible for coordinating the **cardiac rhythm** or heartbeat. These specialized cells are referred to as the heart's **conduction system** (Figure 80).

Cardiac Conduction System

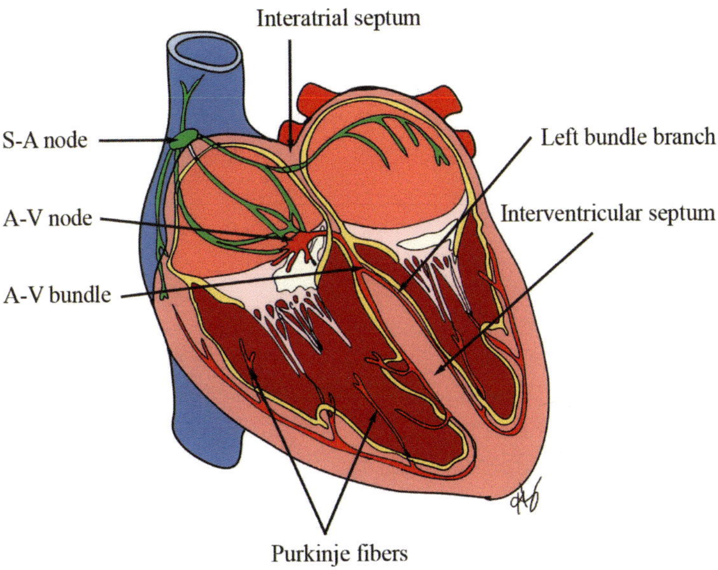

Figure 80. Conduction pathways of the heart

Cardiac Conduction System

In a normal functioning heart, a structure known as the **SA node (sino-atrial node)** establishes a resting heart rate in the range of 80 to 100 beats per minute. The SA node is located in the back (posterior) wall of the right atrium, and its rate is determined by a variety of factors. These include psychological, neurological, hormonal, and pathologic (disease) factors. Conduction fibers transmit electrical signals from the SA node to the **AV node (atrioventricular node)**, which is located near the **atrioventricular septum** (the wall that separates the atria from the ventricles). This process results in contraction of both atria. A slight delay occurs at this node that allows the atria to finish contracting before passing the signal along to the ventricles, both of which contract at the same time.

Damage to this conduction system is common in the case of heart attacks (specifically **myocardial infarctions** or MIs) and can result in abnormal cardiac rhythms that are fatal in many cases. We will discuss MIs shortly in the section on cardiac pathology.

Test Your Knowledge

1. Trace the passage of blood through the heart.

 ____

 ____

 ____

Vascular Anatomy

The primary elements of blood vessel walls are:

1. Endothelial cells that line the inner surface of the vessel;
2. Smooth muscle cells that allow control of the size of the inside of the vessel (vessel lumen); and
3. An extracellular matrix (the part of the tissue that gives the cells their structural support) (Figure 81).

Generally, arteries are thicker than veins and often contain a greater amount of smooth muscle. They are firmer to the touch and tend to hold their hose-like shape even when they are empty. Veins, on the other hand, usually stretch more but are less muscular than arteries. They tend to collapse when nothing is in them. For this reason veins hold a greater amount of the total blood volume than the arteries. In fact, at any given moment, as much as two thirds of the blood's volume is running through the veins. It should come as no surprise that diseases of the vascular system account for more sickness (**morbidity**) and death (**mortality**) than any other system. Vascular diseases include **arteriosclerosis** ("hardening of the arteries") and atherosclerosis (the build-up of **plaque** followed by gradual blockage of the **coronary vessels**). And they can lead to serious problems, including **coronary artery disease** and **stroke** as well as **hypertension** (high blood pressure), which will be discussed a little later.

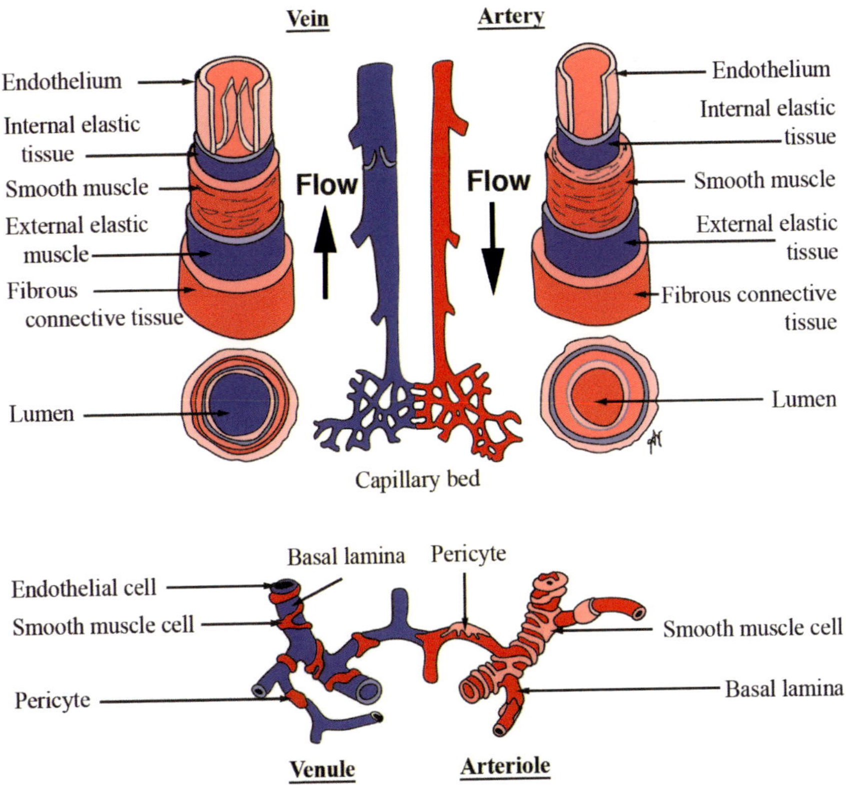

Figure 81. Cross-sectional anatomy of arteries and veins

Selected Pathology of the Cardiovascular System

Pathology is the branch of medical science that studies the causes, the nature, and the effects of disease. The heart muscle receives its blood supply from the coronary vessels, which arise just distal to the aortic valve. Plaque build-up causes these vessels to narrow, which can then result in a less than adequate blood supply to the heart muscle (also called the **myocardium**; Figure 82). What follows are the signs and symptoms of **angina** as well as myocardial infarction where the blood supply to the heart is interrupted or reduced.

Angina

The terms *angina* and *angina pectoris* refer to a choking or suffocating chest pain that comes and goes. This pain is associated with temporary

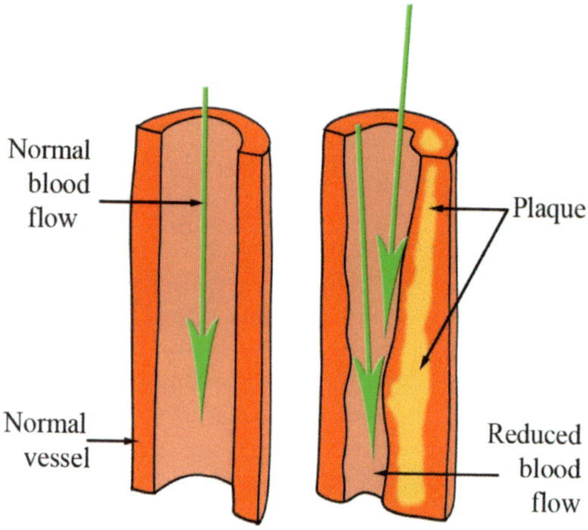

Figure 82. Vascular plaque build up

episodes of **myocardial ischemia** (inadequate blood flow to the heart muscle). A variety of angina types have been described, but the following are three of the most common variations.

First is **typical angina**, chest pain associated with exertion or emotional stress. This kind of pain is usually relieved by rest and often occurs after rigorous exercise. It is a crushing pain that may radiate down the left arm. Typical or "stable" angina is produced by the narrowing of a coronary artery (arteriosclerosis). Blockage of at least 75% of the artery is usually required before this type of angina occurs. Typical angina generally responds to placement of a nitroglycerin tablet placed under the tongue. This medication provides relief by dilating the coronary vessels, which improves blood flow temporarily.

Second is **variant** or **Prinzmetal's angina**. This form of angina is caused by coronary vascular spasms, meaning that the blood vessel contracts spontaneously. This results in narrowing of the inside of the blood vessel and produces angina symptoms. Not necessarily associated with exertion, this type of angina can occur at night.

The third type of angina is **unstable angina**. This condition is associated with increasing frequency of chest pains that are more intense and longer lasting than those of stable angina. This form of angina often occurs prior to a heart attack (myocardial infarction).

The **electrocardiogram (ECG or EKG)** can be useful in diagnosing angina. Since each beat of your heart is caused by an electrical impulse in the upper right chamber of your heart, the doctor can use an electrocardiogram to look for patterns among these heartbeats. These sensitive devices can detect

- Arrhythmias (*a* = without ; *rhythmia* = rhythm);
- Heart defects;
- Problems with the heart's valves;
- Coronary artery disease indicative of blocked or narrowed arteries; and
- In emergency situations, it can pick up on a heart attack as well as previous heart attacks.

Myocardial Infarction

This condition reflects a form of irreversible heart damage called **myocardial necrosis** (*myo* = muscle ; *cardio* = heart ; *necrosis* from the Greek word *nekrosis* = dead). It results from severe ischemia (narrowing) of a major blood vessel. Also referred to as a "heart attack," this condition is the most common cause of death in industrialized countries. Myocardial infarctions (MIs) usually are caused by **coronary thrombosis**, blood clots that result when pieces of plaque break away from the vessel wall and get stuck, preventing the flow of blood (Figure 83). Heart muscle death can begin as quickly as 30 minutes after such a coronary blockage has occurred. However, newer drugs called **thrombolytics** (medications that slow the formation of blood clots or dissolve them) have been developed in recent years. When they are given in time, these drugs can decrease the extent of the heart muscle damage. The degree of destruction depends on which coronary vessel is affected and where it is affected along its course.

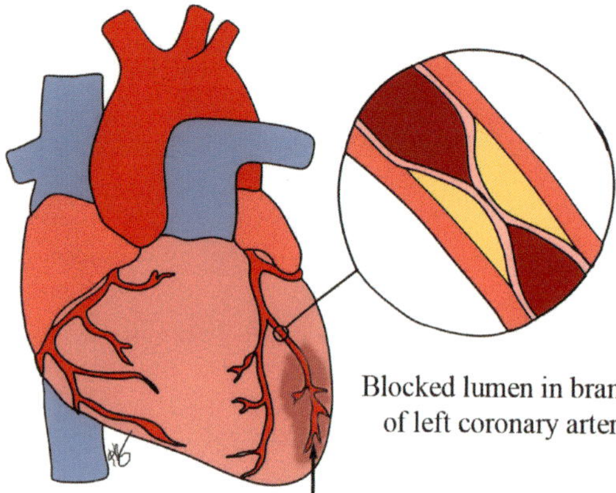

Figure 83. Myocardial infarction

Clinical Correlate

Heart attack (myocardial infarction) is a condition where vessels that carry blood to the heart itself become narrowed or blocked, preventing adequate blood flow to these structures and resulting in insufficient oxygen delivery and permanent damage to the muscle. Chest pain described as a "heaviness" is a common complaint. Several chemicals are released into the blood from this damaged heart muscle and can be measured and followed over several days to rule in or rule out a heart attack.

Hypertensive Cardiac Disease

When we talk about someone's blood pressure, what we are really speaking of is the pressure that the blood produces against the blood vessel walls each time the heart pumps. When the heart contracts, this pressure increases as blood is pushed into the vessels. Conversely, when the heart relaxes, this pressure decreases. Two things determine your blood pressure. The first of these concerns the force the heart exerts as it pumps blood into the arteries and through to the rest of the body, and the second is the amount of resistance the arteries provide to the blood trying to get through them.

Blood pressure is affected by many things from your body temperature, diet, emotional state, posture, medications, gravity, whether or not the valves in your veins are working properly, to the contraction of skeletal muscles that may occur in exercise or rest. During each heartbeat, your blood pressure varies between a maximum amount of pressure called systolic pressure and a minimum amount of pressure called diastolic pressure. When a blood pressure reading is taken with a **sphygmomanometer** (Figure 84) or an automated device, the higher number represents the systolic pressure and the lower number represents the diastolic pressure. For example, 120/80 (120 over 80) means that the systolic pressure is 120 and the diastolic pressure is 80.

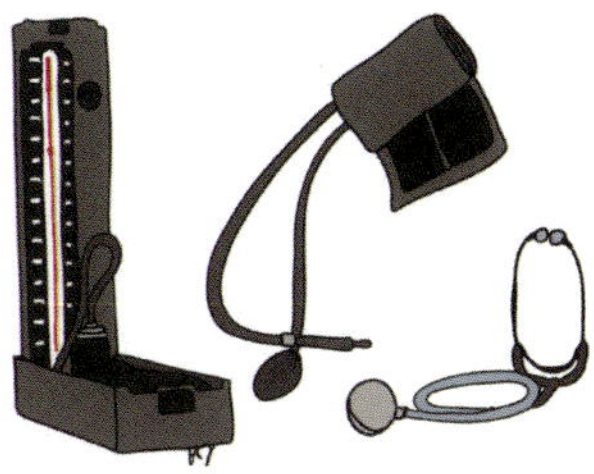

Figure 84 Sphygmomanometer

When someone has high blood pressure, it is a sign that the heart and arteries are working harder than usual and that the blood is powerfully pushing against the walls of your arteries (in an abnormal way) as it moves through your body. This hard work results in a condition known as **hypertension** (*hyper* = over/too much ; *tension* = tension).

Hypertension is medically noted as blood pressures that are routinely higher than 140/90. Hypertension is common and is associated with serious illness. As you might imagine, high blood pressure for prolonged periods of time can damage the blood vessels, heart, and kidneys. These organs are essential for your overall health. Damaged organs cannot function properly and the end result leads to problems like heart attack and stroke, just to name two. High blood pressure usually causes no outward symptoms and so, while your body is being damaged, you may not even know it. This is why it is often referred to as a "silent killer."

When hypertension is present and there is evidence of an enlarged left ventricle (called **left ventricular hypertrophy**), **hypertensive cardiac disease** is present. The suspected cause is the excessive work the left ventricle is forced to do because of the higher than normal pressure against which it must pump to deliver blood to the body's many tissues. Understandably, this enlarged ventricular muscle mass requires more oxygen and nutrients than a muscle of normal size. At some point, its demands outstrip the available blood supply, resulting in injury and damage to the muscle.

Test Your Knowledge

1. What is angina?

   ____

   ____

2. What is the medical term for heart attack?

   ____

3. What is hypertension?

   ____

   ____

   ____

Common Conditions and Diseases of the Cardiovascular System

Other than the diseases of the cardiovascular system that we've already discussed, some other common diseases are as follows:

Mitral stenosis is a condition produced when the valve connecting the left atrium and ventricle becomes narrowed and blood flow is restricted. Often the patient may have no symptoms or only with exercise. When symptoms worsen, blood thinners and valve replacement may be considered.

Congestive heart failure (CHF) occurs when the heart, for a variety of reasons, begins to fail as a pump and inadequate blood is delivered to the systemic circulation. Symptoms may include shortness of breath, cough, and swelling of the extremities.

Cardiovascular System Glossary

ADH — (also known as antidiuretic hormone)

aldosterone — hormone made by the outer portion (cortex) of the adrenal gland that regulates the balance of salt and water (electrolytes) in the body

angina pectoris — chest pain associated with decreased blood flow to the heart (ischemia)

angiotensin II — generated in response to renin released by the kidneys; causes intense vasoconstriction, promoting rapid rise in systemic blood pressure; also stimulates release of aldosterone & ADH

ANH — (also known as atrial natriuretic hormone)

ANP — (also known as atrial natriuretic peptide)

antidiuretic hormone — (antidiuretic hormone ADH) causes intense vasoconstriction in cases of extremely low blood pressure and reduces the amount of urine formation thereby maintaining or increasing blood volume

aorta — largest artery in the body; exists the heart from the left ventricle and provides oxygenated blood to the systemic circulation

aortic valve — heart valve between left ventricle and aorta

arteries — vessels that carry blood away from the heart to the arterioles

arterioles — smallest branches of arteries that carry oxygenated blood into the capillary beds of body organs & tissues; regulates blood flow into capillary beds by vasoconstriction or vasodilation

arteriosclerosis — (also known as narrowing of arteries); thickening, loss of elasticity, and calcification (hardening) of the arterial walls

atrial natriuretic hormone — (also known as ANH) peptide hormone produced by the heart when stretch receptors are stimulated by excessive blood volume or blood pressure that tends to reduce blood volume by increasing urine formation and loss of sodium

atrial natriuretic peptide (also known as ANP) a hormone secreted by cells in the heart in response to atrial stretching that results in lowered blood pressure

atrioventricular node (also known as AV node) neurological tissue in the center of the heart that receives and amplifies the conduction of impulses from the SA node to the bundle of His

atrium the chamber that transports blood to the ventricles located in both the upper right left areas of the heart

AV (also known as atrioventricular node)

blood pressure hydrostatic pressure generated during a cycle of the heart against the walls of the arterial tree

bundle of His structure within the conduction system of the heart

capillaries smallest blood vessels; tiny vessels that join arterioles and venules; role is to exchange materials (gases, nutrients, hormones) between blood and interstitial fluid

CAD (also known as coronary artery disease)

coronary artery disease (also known as CAD) disease of narrowed cardiac vessels in which inadequate oxygen and nutrients are delivered to cardiac muscle

coronary circulation circulation of blood through the coronary blood vessels to deliver oxygen and nutrients to the heart muscle tissue

diastole to expand; brief period during the cardiac cycle when the heart is at rest

diastolic pressure pressure exerted during the brief period when the heart is at rest between heart beats

diuretic any substance that encourages the formation of urine usually resulting in the decrease of blood volume and blood pressure

heart valves structures within the heart that open and close with the heartbeat to regulate the one way flow of blood

HTN (also known as hypertension)

hypertension (also known as HTN) persistently high blood pressure

infarct death of heart muscle distal to a coronary artery occlusion

interatrial septum tissue that separates the two atria

interventricular septum structure(s) that separates the ventricles

<u>ischemia</u> inadequate perfusion (delivery) of oxygen and nutrients to a tissue

<u>lumen</u> cavity or channel within any organ or structure of the body; the space within an artery, vein, intestine, or tube

<u>MI</u> (also known as myocardial infarction)

<u>mitral valve</u> (also known as bicuspid valve) found between the left atrium and left ventricle (cuspis = point)

<u>mitral valve prolapse</u> (also known as MVP) protrusion of one or both cusps of the mitral valve back into left atrium during ventricular contraction; can result in incomplete closure and back flow of blood

<u>muscular arteries</u> (distributing arteries); deliver blood to specific body organs & account for most of the named arteries studied (have thickest media of all vessels); more active in vasoconstriction & less distensible

<u>MVP</u> (also known as mitral valve prolapse)

<u>myocardial infarction</u> (also known as MI) heart attack, death of myocardial tissue (infarction); caused by ischemia (loss of blood flow) as a result of an occlusion (plugging) of a coronary artery; usually caused by atherosclerosis

<u>precapillary sphincter</u> circular smooth muscle structure that can re-direct blood to varying parts of the capillary bed metarteriole & acts as a valve to regulate the flow of blood into the capillary

<u>pulmonary artery</u> artery that exits the right side of the heart carrying deoxygenated blood to the lungs

<u>pulmonary circulation</u> network of arteries, capillaries, air sacs and veins in lungs that allow the uptake of oxygen and the release of carbon dioxide

<u>pulmonary semilunar valve</u> heart valve between the right ventricle and the pulmonary artery (luna = moon)

<u>purkinje fibers</u> network of fibers in the ventricles that transmit impulses to right and left ventricles causing them to contract

<u>renin-angiotensin mechanism</u> hormone system involving the kidneys and lungs that adjust blood pressure and blood volume

<u>resistance</u> in the case of the cardiovascular system, resistance is the measure of the friction between blood and the vessel walls

SA node	(also known as sinoatrial node)
septum	partition that divides the heart into right and left portions
sinoatrial node	(also known as SA node) commonly called the pacemaker of the heart; highly specialized, neurological tissue in the wall of the right atrium; responsible for initiating electrical conduction of the heartbeat, causing the atria to contract and firing conduction of impulses to the AV node
sphygmomanometer	instrument that measures the blood pressure (BP)
stenosis	condition of narrowing of a part of a structure
systole	to contract; period curing the cardiac cycle when the heart is in contraction and blood is ejected through the aorta and the pulmonary artery
systolic pressure	blood pressure during the contraction of the heart
tissue perfusion	delivery of oxygen and nutrients to a tissue
tricuspid valve	heart valve between the right atrium and right ventricle
vasoconstriction	reduction in lumen diameter of blood vessels due to smooth muscle contraction
vasodilation	widening of the lumen of blood vessels due to smooth muscle relaxation
veins	relatively thin walled vessels that carry blood to the heart from the venules
ventricle	lower right or left chamber of the heart

Chapter 5
The Lymphatic System

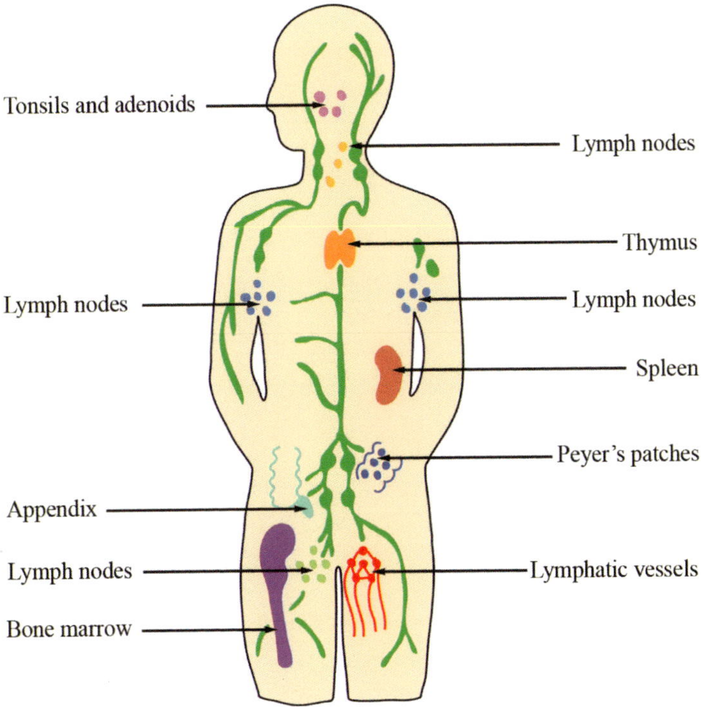

Figure 85. The lymphatic system

Our bodies are constantly being accosted by an enormous variety of potentially harmful bacteria, viruses, fungi, and caustic chemicals. And yet, we are remarkably healthy the vast majority of the time. How can this be? The answer lies in the body's defense system known as the lymphatic system (Figure 85), which

- Produces and transports **lymphocytes** throughout the body;
- Returns fluids that accumulate in the extracellular space to the circulating blood; and
- Resists the spread of disease throughout the body.

The lymphatic system consists of two parts. These are

1. The **lymphatics** themselves including the **lymphatic vasculature** and different lymphatic organs; and
2. Nonspecific and specific immune systems.

Let's discuss each of these.

The Lymphatics

The lymphatic vasculature is the network of vascular channels that:

- Drain all tissues and remove bacteria and certain proteins;
- Process the drained fluid through **lymph nodes**;
- Return the fluid to the blood;
- Transport fat from the **small intestine**; and
- Supply mature lymphocytes (cells related to immunity) to the blood.

It is also a system of tissues and organs that produce, store, and carry white blood cells (specifically lymphocytes) that fight infection and disease. The lymphatic system includes the **bone marrow**, **spleen**, **thymus**, **lymph nodes**, and a network of thin tubes that branch, like blood vessels, into most tissues of the body and carry **lymph fluid** and white blood cells. This lymphatic vasculature picks up excessive fluid that has leaked from the blood capillaries into the extravascular tissue (the tissue outside the blood vessels) and returns this fluid (called lymph) to the blood stream. The lymphatic fluid does not really circulate (going around and around the body) but rather it travels in one direction only—toward the heart. The lymphatic system is made up of various lymphoid tissues and organs that populate the path followed by the lymphatic fluid.

Let's be a little more specific about each of these components of the lymphatic system so that you will have a greater appreciation of this elegant defense system. To really understand how the lymphatic system works, it is important to understand how we get lymph in the first place. Remember from our previous discussion, lymph is a somewhat clear fluid that carries protein molecules, salts, glucose, urea, white blood cells (the germ fighters), and other substances.

As you might imagine, the body contains different concentrations of proteins, salts, and other substances in various parts of the body. Because of these different concentrations both inside and outside an organ or vessel (let's take a capillary as an example), a natural phenomenon known as **osmosis** occurs. Understanding osmosis is fundamental to understanding the movement of water and the effect of **concentration gradients** (differences in the concentration of solutes) in the body. Osmosis is the passage of a solvent (a liquid that dissolves or is capable of dissolving), such as water, from the dilute side to the concentrated side of a membrane, filter, or other semipermeable border (the word *semipermeable* comes from the Latin words *semis* = half ; *per* = through ; *meare* = to pass). Without added pressure, a solution divided in this way will undergo osmosis to equalize the concentration on both sides of the membrane or border (Figure 86).

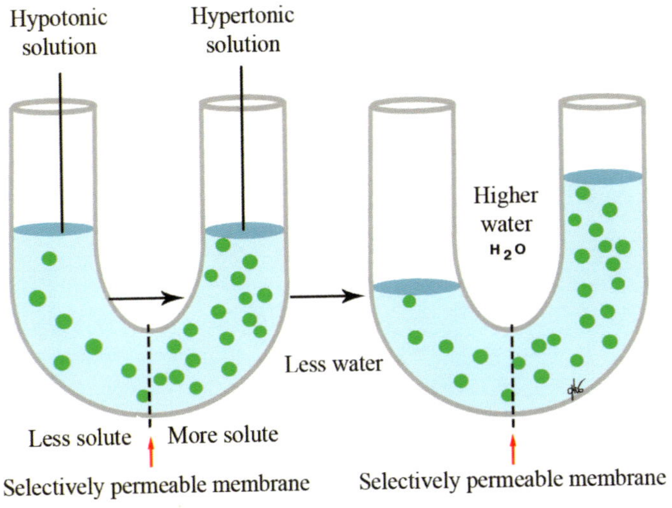

Figure 86. Osmosis across a concentration gradient

Thus, osmosis is the movement of water from an area of lesser concentration to an area of greater concentration so that this concentration difference is eliminated. For example, if you put a cell in pure water (that has no dissolved chemicals in it), the water outside the cell would move to the inside of the cell to decrease the concentration of the solute inside the cell. Because most of the dissolved material in a cell cannot get out, water will keep coming inside until it bursts the cell. This movement of water is a special case of the principle of **diffusion**, which applies to dissolved substances, which also tend to distribute evenly if there are no barriers.

When the body produces lymph, water moves in and out of the capillaries because of differences in the amount of dissolved proteins in the space inside the vessels (called intravascular space because it is located "inside" of the vessels) versus that outside the vessels (extravascular). Water is drawn to any location that has the greatest concentration of these proteins. As mentioned earlier, it is the unequal concentration of solute on the two sides of the capillaries (inside versus outside) that causes the water to be drawn from one area to the other. This water movement produces an osmotic pressure, moving water into the capillary vessels where the higher concentration of protein molecules, salts, glucose, urea, and other substances are. This flow of water is opposed by a **hydrostatic pressure** within the capillaries. Hydrostatic pressure is the pressure due to the weight of a fluid. The term *hydrostatic* comes from the Greek words *hydro* = water ; *statikos* = standing.

If the concentration of proteins and other materials is greater on the outside of the capillaries, the fluid inside the capillaries tends to move out of the vessels (through osmosis), which then moves water to the outside of the vessels and into the extravascular space. Because of osmotic and hydrostatic pressure differences along the body's capillaries, not all the vascular fluid that has been forced out of the blood vessels into the extravascular tissue can be reabsorbed back into the blood stream. These two forces, osmotic and hydrostatic pressures, oppose each other. Osmosis wants to force the fluids into the vessel where there is a place of higher concentration, and the hydrostatic pressure wants to push the fluids from inside the vessels to the extravascular space.

Despite the efficiency of this process, fluid is left behind in the extravascular compartments, and were it not for the efforts of the lymphatic system, the body would get **edematous** (swollen) with increasing fluid collection in the extravascular space. Without the lymphatic's drainage system, fluid that was just released from the capillaries would continue to accumulate in the body's tissues, producing **edema** (a swelling caused by accumulation of fluid). Highly permeable (meaning that fluids can easily enter them), these lymphatic capillaries begin as conduits that permit their contents to flow in only one direction through the use of one-way valves until the fluid is released back into the venous circulation. But where?

As you can see in Figure 87, the right lymphatic duct only receives the lymph flow from the right arm and the right side of the chest, neck, head, and lower left lobe of the lung, while the larger thoracic duct *drains* the lymphatic fluid from *the rest of the body*. In adults, the thoracic duct transports up to 4 L or about 1 gallon of lymph per day. (You may ask why these two lymphatic ducts aren't just called the "right" and "left" lymphatic ducts. Although you will see in some drawings that the terms *right* and *left* lymphatic ducts are used, it is important to note that the right lymphatic duct handles a much smaller portion of work than the thoracic duct. Since the thoracic duct handles the lion's share of the filtering, it perhaps justifies a special name.) Before reaching these ducts, however, the lymph must be filtered, and this filtering occurs in the various lymphoid organs discussed next.

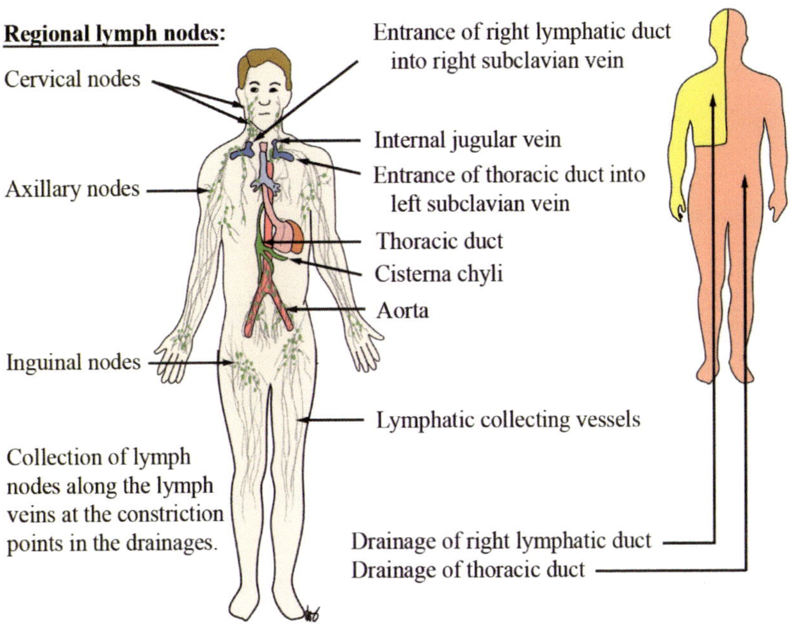

Figure 87. Location and drainage of right lymphatic duct and thoracic duct

Test Your Knowledge

1. What is the job of the lymphatic system?

   ____

   ____

   ____

2. How do we get lymph?

   ____

   ____

Lymphoid Organs

The lymph nodes and other lymph structures (including the spleen, thymus, tonsils, and special areas around the GI tract called **Peyer's patches**; refer back to Figure 85) are responsible for the filtering process where foreign material is identified. Let's look at each one of these structures so that you can understand their respective roles in your body.

Lymph Nodes

Lymph nodes, typically small collections of lymph tissue, serve as the primary filters of lymph. As lymph fluid passes through them, white cells and other **phagocytic** cells (large cells that surround, engulf, and digest invaders) identify foreign matter, specifically bacteria, virus-infected cells, and cellular debris. These potentially harmful intruders are then removed from the ongoing lymph flow by the white cells and other phagocytic cells (phago from the Greek word *phagein* meaning "to eat" ; *cyte* = cells ; *ic* = pertaining to). When this process of "capturing the invaders" is taking place within a node, the node itself may become bigger and tender, and depending on its location in the body, may become palpable (that is, "feel-able" with the fingers).

Other Lymph Structures

- **Spleen**

  The **spleen** (Figure 88) filters blood, creates lymphocytes that are needed for the destruction and recycling of old red-blood cells, and supplies the body with blood in emergencies such as internal bleeding or a bad cut. The spleen is also a blood reservoir. The spleen is oval shaped and is indented on its inner surface to form the **hilum**, or stalk of attachment to the **peritoneum**. The spleen is tucked under the left side of the diaphragm. It normally measures about 1 by 3 by 5 in. (2.5 × 7.5 × 12.5 cm) and weighs less than one-half pound (230 g). The spleen is also the location where white blood cells trap organisms by using phagocytic white cells (those lymphocytes that can ingest invading microorganisms and other foreign material) to remove foreign invaders.

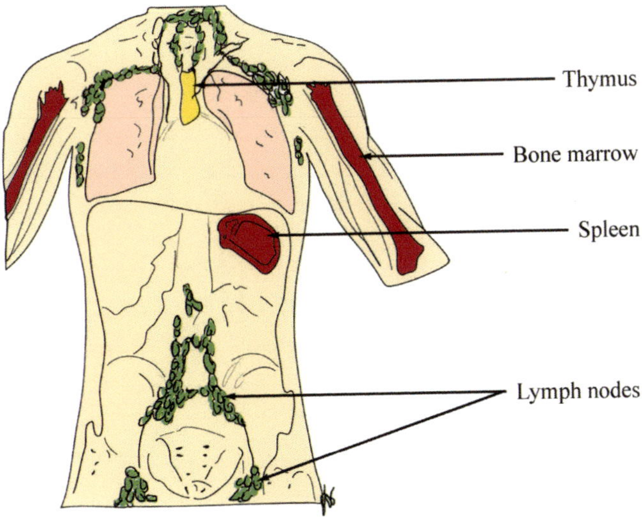

Figure 88. Thymus and spleen

- **Thymus**
  The **thymus** (Figure 88), a lymphoid structure located in the mediastinum (a space located in the upper chest between the two lungs), plays a pivotal role in the specific immune system, which we will discuss in more detail later in this chapter. For now, know that the thymus gland is most active during early life, playing a critical role in the development of a child's immune system before birth and for a time thereafter. Usually by the age of two, the thymus gland has reached its maximum size (weighing about 30 to 40 grams or 1.06 to 1.41 ounces) with its immune capabilities being

fully functional. Because of this, vaccinations before the age of two are less effective, since these young immune systems are not mature enough to maintain a significant immune response. After puberty, the gland begins to shrink and is replaced by connective tissue and fat.

- **Tonsils and Adenoids**
  The **tonsils**, much like the lymph nodes, spend their lives filtering lymph. The tonsils are clumps of tissue, on either side of the throat, found in a pocket at the side of the **palate** (roof of the mouth). The lower edge of each tonsil is near the tongue and in the posterior (way in the back) of the throat. The adenoids are a single clump of tissue in the back of the nose (nasopharynx). They are located (in the adult) on the back wall of the throat (pharynx) about one inch above the **uvula** (the little teardrop-shaped piece of tissue that hangs down in the middle of the **soft palate**).

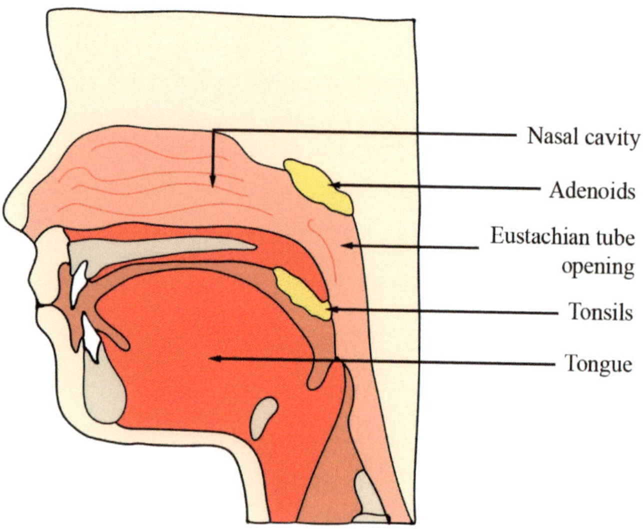

Figure 89. Tonsils and adenoids

The tonsils and the adenoids (Figure 89) are composed of lymphoid tissue involved in antibody production. **Tonsillectomy** (the removal of tonsils) was once a common procedure done in young people who experienced frequent or chronic bacterial infections. Tonsillectomy is not as common as it once was because of the increased efficiency of antibiotics.

- **Peyer's Patches**

  Peyer's patches are a collection of lymphoid tissues that are usually found in the lower portion of the small intestine (**ileum**) and as such, they distinguish the ileum from the **duodenum** and **jejunum** (Figure 90). The location of these Peyer's patches is of utmost importance in supervising the immune response of the intestinal lumen and in facilitating the generation of the immune response within the mucosa.

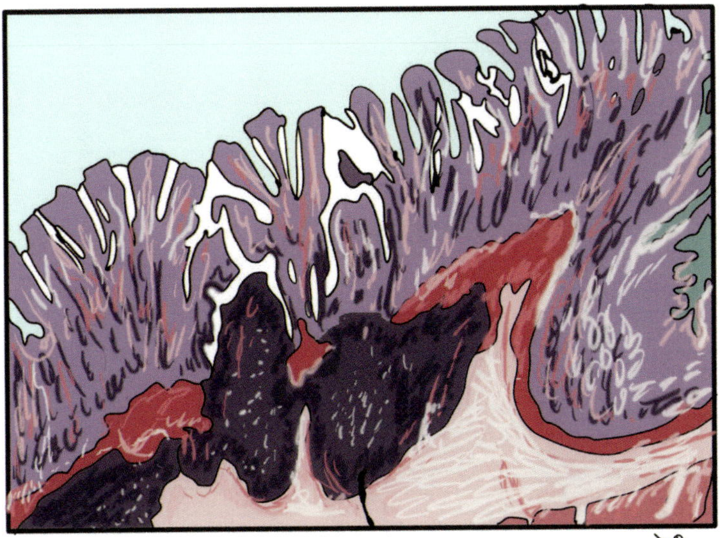

Figure 90. Peyer's patches

Test Your Knowledge

1. What is the job of the lymph nodes?

   ____

   ____

   ____

2. What is the job of the thymus?

____

____

____

3. What is the job of Peyer's patches?

____

____

____

The Body's Immune Response

To effectively protect you, the body must be able to distinguish "self" from "nonself." Put another way, it needs to be able to tell the good guys from the bad guys. To accomplish this it must be able detect pathogens (disease-producing organisms) from normal body components. This remarkable accomplishment is the defining characteristic of the immune system.

The immune system of the human body falls into two categories: the **nonspecific immune system** and the **specific immune system**. Let's look at each of these separately.

The Nonspecific Immune System

The nonspecific immune system is the first line of defense. It prevents most things from entering the body. The words most associated with the impact that the nonspecific immune system has on the body are "generalized" and "fast." The skin is one example of the nonspecific immune system. Because the skin covers the entire person, it is an effective barrier to prevent entry of pathogens into the body. Both intact skin and mucous membranes of the mouth, for example, are extraordinarily good at turning back a pathogenic invasion, but when these defenses are breached, as in the case of a cut or abrasion, other nonspecific immune fighters must be mustered.

Clinical Correlate

The importance of the skin (which is often underappreciated as being part of our nonspecific immune system) is clear when a hospital must care for a burn victim who has lost a significant portion of skin. The battle for the medical team from the onset is how to keep the patient from getting infected. Why? Because pathogens have unhindered access to the inside of the patient's body due to the skin tissue being nonexistent or severely damaged.

Blood-Borne Immune Proteins

Some proteins play essential roles in the nonspecific immune system. These are primarily **cytokines**, which can be further subdivided into both **interleukins** and **interferons**.

Cytokines are like short-range hormone proteins that are secreted (or leaked) by infected cells to warn its neighbors of potential danger. Cytokines (Greek *cyto-* = cell ; *-kinos* = movement) are any of a number of substances that are secreted by specific cells of the immune system and that carry signals locally between cells, and thus have an effect on other cells. They are a category of signaling molecules that are used extensively in cellular communication. They are **proteins**, **peptides**, or **glycoproteins**. Although there are many different types of cytokines, two that are particularly important are interferons and interleukins. We will discuss each of these.

- **Interferons** are a kind of cytokine protein released by virus-infected cells. They stimulate the immune response and help regulate the manufacture of antibodies. They provide no protection to the cell that released them, but they induce neighboring cells to produce proteins that hinder further spread of the infection. They are a type of nonspecific defense assistants.

- **Interleukins** are a second group of cytokines that also provide nonspecific defensive assistance. This group of chemicals is released predominately by white cells, specifically macrophages (*macro* = large ; *phage* = swallow or eat) and lymphocytes (*lymph/o* = lymph ; *cyte* = cell). Of the various duties of interleukins, one is to reset the body's "thermostat," thus inducing a fever that, in moderation, may actually destroy some bacteria and inhibit the growth of others. This then brings us to a discussion of **complement**. As the name suggests, complement is a part of more than 20 blood-borne proteins that when activated "complement" the actions of other immune responses by causing a series of reactions that occur as a result of a single triggering reaction. They are another part of the nonspecific immune system. They will frequently release **perforins** that punch holes in the membranes (perforate) of target cells, causing the infected cell's cytoplasm to leak out, resulting in cell death and finally removal of the dead cell by phagocytes.

Let's pause to consider some of the cellular components of this nonspecific system. The predominant players are neutrophils (the most common kind of white cell) and macrophages, both of which are aggressive phagocytes that engulf bacteria, viruses, abnormal cells, and debris. In addition, there are cells called **natural killer cells** that are lymphocytes that perform immune surveillance, meaning they clear the body of spontaneously produced tumor cells. The actions of these various defenses can produce inflammation, sometimes referred to as the **inflammatory response**. Think of it this way: As your body tries to defend you against disease, and all of these immune responses take place, more cells are produced to get rid of the disease. As a result, the body responds to those calls for help. The cardinal features of this response are well known to most of us. They are heat, redness, swelling, and pain.

The local heat of a fever is attributed to the increased blood flow to the area produced by chemicals released by certain white cells already in the vicinity. This also causes the redness so typical of local inflammation. The swelling or edema that one may see during an infection or immune response is produced by the increased capillary permeability (the blood vessels in the area become leaky) caused by these same chemicals. All these factors stimulate pain receptors locally and may cause a person to feel pain in the area.

To summarize, the nonspecific immune system is effective, generalized, and fast in response. It covers the bases while the slower-to-respond specific immune system is getting activated. However, it has no "memory" of previous battles. That remarkable characteristic falls to the specific immune system, discussed next.

The Specific Immune System

The specific immune system is composed of an army of lymphocytes (white blood cells), numbering in the trillions, that are the primary soldiers in this defensive system, but they take time to get organized. These lymphocytes fall into two general categories: **T-lymphocytes**, labeled such because, while born in the bone marrow, they complete their maturation in the **T**hymus, and **B-lymphocytes**, entirely born and bred, so to speak, in the **B**one marrow.

T-lymphocytes are responsible for what is referred to as **cell-mediated immunity**. This is analogous to hand-to-hand combat where the body's defensive cells attack the invaders in close contact. The external or foreign pathogens (*path/o* = disease ; *gen* = producing or forming) are met at close quarters (on the front line) and are usually dispensed with. Unlike the white cells of the nonspecific defense system, these cells respond to and attack only *specific antigens* (pathogens that carry an identifiable protein on their surface). As these invaders are "digested," portions of their protein structure are broken up and displayed on the defender's cell surface, and a host of T-cells are created to respond solely to that particular invader. Consider these broken proteins like badges of honor for the T-cells. All of this takes time, however, and although the resulting mass of freshly made, highly specific T-cells will likely be of benefit when that same pathogen is seen again, it does not affect the first exposure. That is, the body develops an immune memory, and with the second exposure, a massive preplanned attack ensues. Suppose we liken the human body to a large mansion containing many rooms and closets. After a new invader (one never encountered before) has been identified, the body orders T-cells to be made specifically for use against that particular pathogen. These new T-cells are hidden (by the thousands) in various closets through out the mansion. If the invader they are designed to attack shows up again, they will pour out of the closets and easily overwhelm the intruder.

Several varieties of T-cells have been identified. For our purposes, one that is particularly important is the killer or **cytotoxic** T-cells (*cyt/o* = cell ; *tox* = poison; *ic* = pertaining to). Once their invader has been targeted, they release a host of highly caustic cytokines and other chemicals that destroy the foreign cells or bacteria. Not all the T-cells are actively attacking, however; some are becoming memory T-cells, held in reserve to reproduce and make more of the same highly specific T-cells should future encounters with the same antigen occur. It is this induced immune memory that sets the specific immune system apart from the nonspecific one.

This brings us to **humoral** or **antibody-mediated immunity**. The term *humoral* refers to elements in the blood or other body fluids. As you will recall from our discussion a little earlier, B-cells are born and bred in the bone marrow. As you also know, the bone marrow is also where blood is made. Therefore, lymphocytes (white blood cells) made in the bone marrow are called B-cells. Like their T-cell counterparts, they are highly specific in that they only attack a specific antigen-containing invader, but they don't wage hand-to-hand combat. Instead, they release antibodies *into the blood*, which locate and attach themselves to the foreign invaders, allowing local phagocytes and complement to do their job of destroying such trespassers. Like T-cells, B-cells also produce memory cells, ready to reproduce with only a moment's notice should a future encounter with the same antigen occur.

It is these T and B memory cells that form the basis for vaccinations. The body is exposed to a dead or greatly weakened form of the antigen invader, to which it responds by making long-lasting memory cells to deal with any future exposures to the real thing. An antigen is defined as a substance that is not normally found in the body, but if there, will produce an immune response.

When antigens are in the body (in this case through a vaccine), the person has an active immunity because the antibodies made come from his or her own body. Passive immunity occurs when you are exposed to an antigen, and to keep you from contracting the disease you are given antibodies from some other source to attack any pathogens you might encounter from that recent exposure. However, the antibodies are only temporary and provide you only short-lived protection since your body has not "seen" the pathogen yet and thus has not made any memory cells. A good example of this would be when a person is exposed to **hepatitis** and is given a shot of **gamma globulin** (premade antibodies to hepatitis). Another example is the antibodies an infant gets through its mother's breast milk. In both cases, the person has not had to "make" the antibody but has received it from another source (the gamma globulin or the mother's milk).

Test Your Knowledge

1. What is the purpose of the nonspecific immune system?

   ____

   ____

   ____

2. What is the purpose of the specific immune system?

   ____

   ____

   ____

Common Conditions and Diseases of the Lymphatic and Immune System

Lymphedema is characterized by swelling (edema) and the accumulation of lymph in affected areas. It often occurs with female patients who have had a significant **lymphadenectomy** (removal of most of the lymph nodes), perhaps following a surgery for early ovarian cancer, resulting in significant swelling in the legs. This edema is a reflection of the lack of lymphatics in the pelvis and the subsequent accumulation of lymph there and in the lower extremities. This condition can be quite uncomfortable.

Neutropenia is, literally, a reduction in the number of neutrophils. Recall that these are granulocytic white cells that are critically important in fighting infections. Neutropenia can be caused by certain medications, marrow failure, and immunologic factors, among other things.

Lymphatic System Glossary

acquired immune deficiency syndrome (also known as AIDS) viral disease associated with diminished immunocompetence; fatal if left untreated

AIDS (also known as acquired immune deficiency syndrome)

anaphylactic an immediate hypersensitivity; allergy that can be life-threatening associated with significant hypotension and bronchial constriction

antibodies blood-borne proteins that are produced specifically against a particular antigen

antigens foreign substances capable of producing disease or tissue damage

artificially acquired active immunity comes when a dead or attenuated antigen is introduced to the body and results in the production of antibodies and immune memory; an example of this is a vaccine

artificially acquired passive immunity comes when a person has been exposed to a disease such as hepatitis and receives a gamma globulin shot which are specific antibodies against that disease; It only provides protection for a short while thus it is passive and it is artificial

B cells type of lymphocyte that produces "humoral" immunity by the production of antibodies

cellular immune response production of T cells against the specific antigen in which the T cells themselves attack the antigen rather than antibodies attacking the antigen

edema excessive fluid collection in the body; in the case of the lymphatic system, edema is the swelling of the lymph nodes

fever elevated body temperature; offers powerful protection against germs; one of the cardinal signs of inflammation; there is redness, fever, pain, and swelling

first line of defense skin and mucous that provide a barrier to foreign pathogens or antigens from entering the body

HIV (also known as human immunodeficiency virus)

humoral immune response body fluids carry antibodies to destroy specific antigens or antigen-bearing particles

human immunodeficiency virus (also known as HIV) causes AIDS

immunoglobulin blood proteins (antibodies) that attack specific antigens for which they are made; they attack specific antigens

inflammation tissue response to injury or infection producing local redness, warmth, pain and swelling

innate (nonspecific) defense provides a rapid, non-specific attack against pathogens or anything it does not recognize); include species resistance, mechanical barriers, chemical barriers, fever, inflammation, phagocytosis

interferons hormone like proteins released by virus infected cells that stimulate the immune system but provide no protection to the cells that released them but induce the neighboring cells to produce the necessary proteins to hinder further spread of the infection

leukemia malignant blood disorder where there is an over abundance of immature WBCs; typically hampers the body's ability fight infection because the WBS's are so immature

lymph fluid that cannot be absorbed back into the capillaries and thus prevents swelling and edema from occurring by transporting the lymph back to the bloodstream and along the way is filtered many times

lymph nodes mass of lymphoid tissue which predominately filters lymph that passes through it

lymphadenopathy swollen lymph nodes

lymphatic vessels thin-walled vessels that direct lymph in only one direction as a result of valves returning the lymph fluid to systemic circulation

lymphocytes type of white blood cell that provides immunity

macrophages large phagocytic cell

mechanical barriers formed by skin and mucous membranes that line the passage ways to the respiratory, digestive, urinary, and reproductive system; also considered to be the nonspecific first line of defense

metastasis movement of cancer cells from one part of the body to another

naturally acquired disease — occurs when a person is exposed to a pathogen and develops a disease (e.g., a cold)

naturally acquired passive immunity — temporary immunity acquired by a fetus or an infant where antibodies are acquired from its mother; the form of immunity acquired from another source

pathogen — potentially a disease producing entity

pus — fluid that contains white cells, debris, etc. from a recent infection or damaged tissue

right lymphatic duct — receives lymph from the right side of the chest, right side of the head and neck and right arm

spleen — largest lymphatic organ; it filters blood, creates lymphocytes, serves as a blood reservoir and is located in the retroperitoneum in the upper left portion of the abdomen

splenomegaly — enlargement of the spleen

T cells — mature lymphocytes that provide cell mediated immunity (where the cells attack directly as in hand to hand combat)

thoracic duct — a duct that drains everything that the right lymphatic duct does not get including both the lower extremities, left side of the chest and abdomen, the left arm, and the left side of the head and neck

thymus — lymphoid structure located in the mediastinum (in the center of the chest between the two lungs) that plays a pivotal role in the specific immune system were some lymphocytes are matured

tonsils — mass of lymphatic tissue located on the back of the pharynx; primary responsibility is to detect infections and filter lymph; partially encapsulated lymph nodules

vaccine — artificial means of producing an immune response without having to have the disease first; it usually consists of a dead or attenuated antigens

Chapter 6
The Digestive System

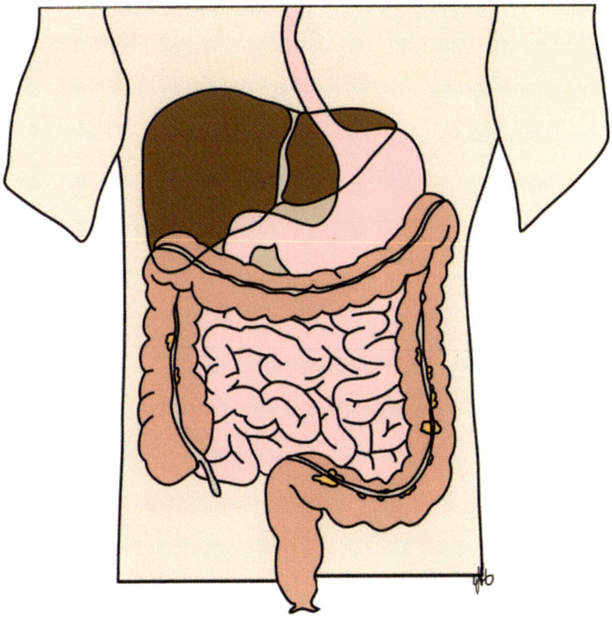

Figure 91. The digestive system

The food we ingest (eat) must be broken down so that its nutrients can be absorbed. Then, any unprocessed portions must be stored temporarily until we can eliminate them at our convenience. The digestive system accomplishes these tasks. We will review these major processes briefly and then look at an overview of the digestive anatomy (Figure 91), followed by a more detailed description of each step in the digestive process.

Food Processing

Digestion begins almost immediately, as food enters the mouth. The tongue—along with the **mastication** (or chewing) muscles and the **saliva**—are the first step in the digestive process, breaking whole food into smaller chunks.

This mechanical breakdown prepares the food just eaten for more sophisticated processing that involves chemical digestion. Let's say you just enjoyed a steak dinner with a loaded baked potato and a nice glass of wine. The **carbohydrates**, **fats**, and **proteins** in your meal can then be "attacked" by highly specialized digestive **enzymes**, permitting the valuable nutrients to be eventually absorbed. **Absorption** refers to the transport of nutrients across the wall of the digestive tract and into the bloodstream, where the body's cells can use them for metabolic purposes. Finally, **elimination** describes the process whereby the body, once it has extracted most of the nutrients from the ingested food, briefly stores the remaining indigestible contents (e.g., cellulose from plants) until they can be evacuated from the body.

Digestive Anatomy

Many people think that **the kidney** is to liquids as the **digestive tract** is to solid food; that is, the kidney digests the liquid we drink like the digestive tract digests our food. This is not correct! Once foods, both liquids and solids, are absorbed in the digestive tract, they enter the bloodstream and are processed. Any leftover or unusable substances are either eliminated by the digestive tract or the kidneys.

You might compare the digestive tract to a snakelike tube whose width varies along its considerable length. Extending from mouth to **anus**, the digestive tract measures some 22 to 24 feet. Let's take a moment now to review the sequence of the digestive anatomy (Figure 92).

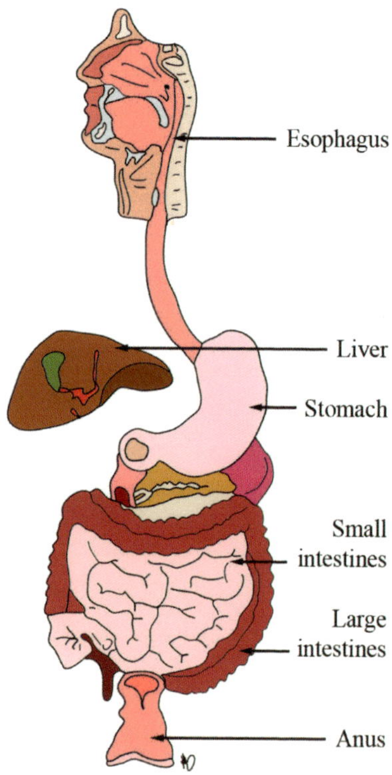

Figure 92. Anatomy of the digestive system

Once food enters the mouth, it travels through the pharynx (throat), the esophagus, the stomach, the small intestine, and the large intestine. It is then expelled through the anus.

The digestive tract is lined with a layer of cells called the **mucosa**. This is the layer that comes into actual contact with the swallowed food. The composition of the mucosa changes along the length of the digestive tract. It consists of a friction-resistant structure called **squamous epithelium** in the mouth, the esophagus, and the anus, which prevent tearing of those areas by food and waste products. (Squamous epithelium looks like fried eggs under the microscope.) There is also another kind of epithelium in the digestive tract. This is a simpler, one-layer **columnar epithelium** that is tall in shape and is responsible for absorbing the nutrients (Figure 93). Beneath the mu-

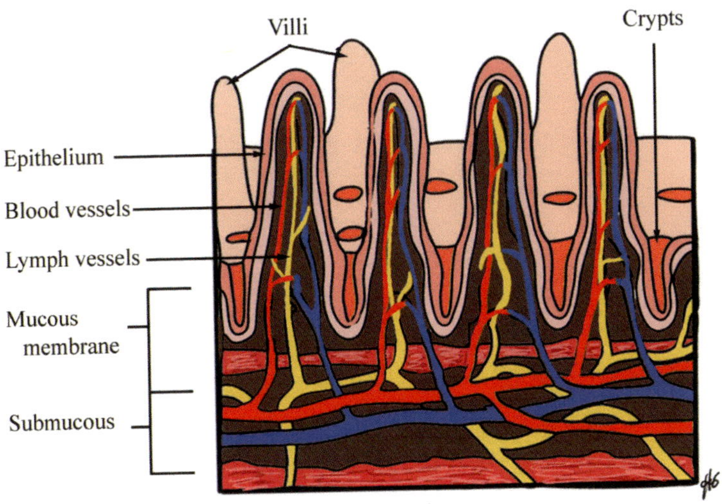

Figure 93. Gastrointestinal cross section

cosa is the **submucosa**, a layer of connective tissue containing blood vessels and nerves. These two layers (the mucosa and submucosa) are surrounded by a smooth muscle layer that moves the contents along the digestive tract. This movement is called **peristalsis** (*peri* = around ; *stalsis* = contraction in the **alimentary canal**.) Peristalsis is an automatic smooth-muscle process that moves food through the digestive system (Figure 94).

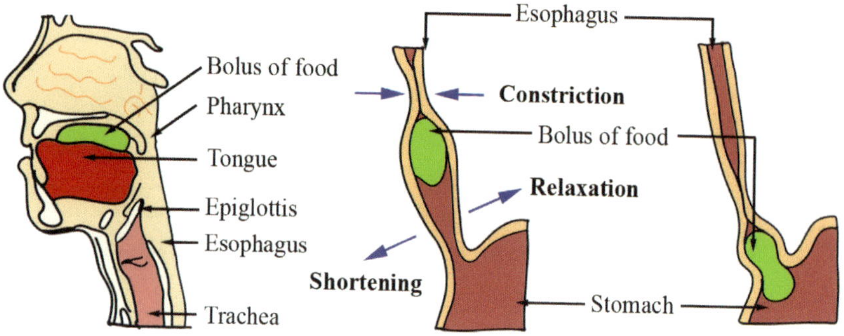

Figure 94. Peristalsis

The outermost layer of the digestive tract is sometimes called the **adventitia** (Figure 95) or **serosa** but is more commonly known as the **peritoneum** below the diaphragm. The term *adventitia* is not an unusual one as

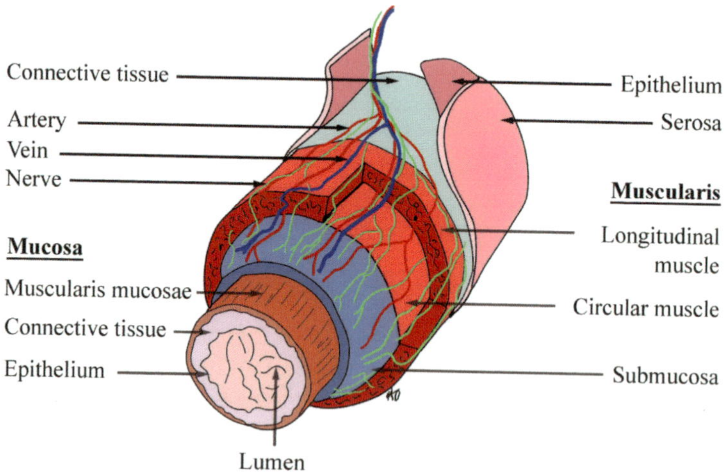

Figure 95. Cross section of bowel

adventitia is the outermost connective tissue covering of any organ, vessel, or other structure. This adventitia layer is the same surface coating both above and below the diaphragm; only the name changes depending on the location. This layer provides a moist, friction-free surface that allows the small and large bowels to slide across one another without causing discomfort. When the peritoneum becomes inflamed, the result is significant pain and a condition known as **peritonitis** (from the Latin and Greek words *per* = around ; *teinein* = to stretch ; *itis* = inflammation of). Simply put, peritonitis is an inflammation of the **serous membrane** lining the abdominopelvic walls.

The **small** and **large bowels**, also known as the **small** and **large intestines**, are supported by blood vessels, lymph, and nervous tissue provided through the **mesentery**. The mesentery is a filmy fold of the peritoneum that anchors the intestine and usually prevents it from "kinking." You've probably experienced the effects of kinking if you've ever used a hose. If you were to literally fold or bend a running hose you would notice that the water would cease flowing out of the open end. Similarly, your bowels (intestines) would bend or kink (which could reduce or even cut off the blood supply to the intestines or produce a bowel obstruction) if it were not for the aid of the mesentery.

There are two fatty curtains that lie over the bowel. These are called the **greater omentum** and the **lesser omentum**. A healthy omentum looks like a fatty drape (Figure 96). The terms *greater* and *lesser* omentum were chosen because the greater omentum is suspended from the "greater" curvature of the stomach and attached to the anterior surface of the **transverse colon**, whereas the lesser omentum joins the "lesser" curvature of the stomach and the first part of the **duodenum** to the liver. (As you can see in Figure 96, the greater curvature of the stomach is the side of the stomach that has the largest curve and is four or five times as long as the lesser curvature.)

There is no clear-cut answer as to the purpose or function of the omentums.

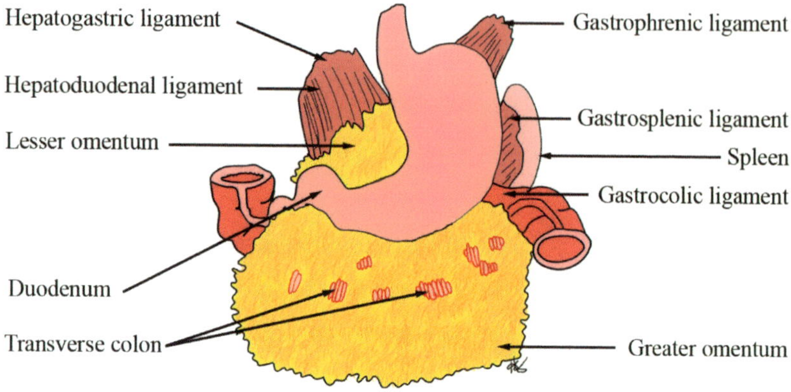

Figure 96. Omentum

Clinical Correlate

The omentum is important in ovarian cancer. Often, cancer cells that have broken away from the ovary like to implant and grow in the omentum. This condition is known as omental metastasis.

Test Your Knowledge

1. Approximately how long, from mouth to anus, is the digestive tract?

   ____

2. Name the structures that food travels through from start to finish.

   ____

   ____

   ____

3. What is the purpose of either the greater or lesser omentum?

   ____

Esophagus

The **esophagus** permits swallowed food to travel from the mouth, where it has been torn and shredded, to the stomach. At the meeting of these two structures, a ring of smooth muscle surrounds the **esophageal sphincter** and usually prevents the highly acidic stomach juices from **refluxing**, or shooting back up into the esophagus. Unlike the stomach, which is equipped with a thick coating of **mucus** to protect itself from its own acids, the esophagus can be damaged by repeated exposure to this burning fluid. In some people, reflux leads to a condition called **GERD**, which stands for **gastroesophageal reflux disease**.

Clinical Correlate

Some people are more prone to relaxation at the gastroesophageal junction and are at increased risk of the acidic contents getting up into the esophagus. There are certain foods that also create a higher risk of reflux (e.g., chocolate) by virtue of their relaxing effect on the esophageal sphincter. People with GERD (gastroesophageal reflux disease) often benefit from sleeping with their upper bodies propped up on several pillows, making it more difficult for the gastric juices to gain access to the lower esophagus. Certain medications (e.g., Pepcid) are acid inhibitors that reduce gastric acidity and help prevent reflux.

Stomach

After food has entered the stomach, mechanical digestion continues, and chemical breakdown kicks into high gear. Well supplied with smooth muscle, the stomach churns the food until it turns into a thick, cream-like substance called **chyme** (pronounced "kime"). The lining of the stomach is studded with tiny pits (Figure 97) that serve as outlets for millions of **gastric glands**. There are specialized cells in these pits that produce a variety of chemicals that are needed for digestion. These cells include **parietal cells** and **chief cells**. Parietal cells secrete **hydrochloric acid (HCl)** as well as **intrinsic factor**. (Intrinsic factor is a relatively small protein secreted by the gastric mucous membrane and required for adequate absorption of vitamin B12, which is necessary for the production of red blood cells.) The HCl protects against bacteria in the food, but it also makes chemical digestion possible by dissolving connective tissues in certain meats.

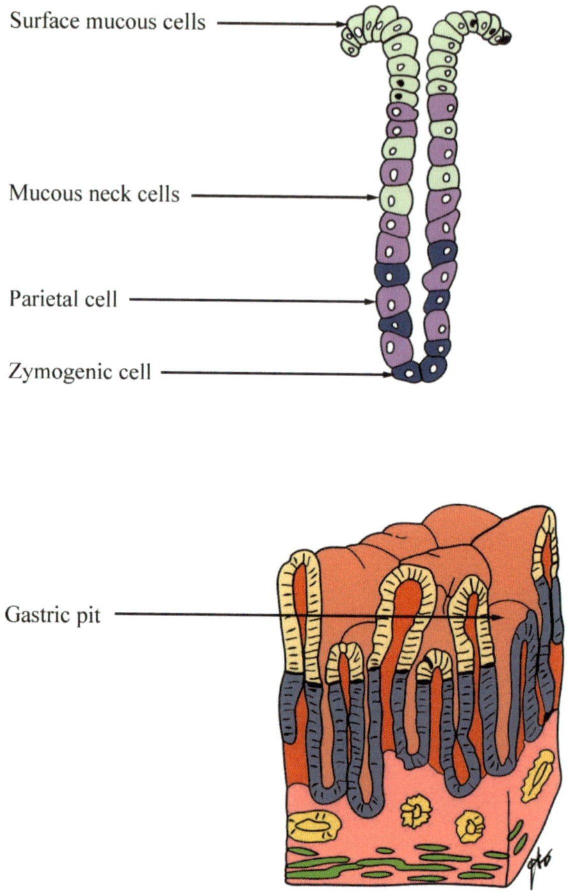

Figure 97. Gastric pits - a cross section

Chief cells in those same glandular pits produce **pepsinogen**, which is activated to **pepsin** when it is exposed to the high acidity of stomach juices. Pepsin permits the breakdown of ingested proteins. Relatively little absorption of nutrients occurs in the stomach, however, because of the presence of the thick mucous coating already mentioned. In other words, the stomach is a churner. Its purpose is not really to absorb anything but rather to digest/break down the food. The lion's share of absorption falls to the small intestine.

Test Your Knowledge

1. What is the purpose of the esophagus?

   ____

   ____

2. What is the purpose of the stomach?

   ____

   ____

3. What do parietal cells do?

   ____

4. What do chief cells do?

   ____

Small Intestine

Chyme (the partially digested food) exits the stomach through the **pyloric sphincter** (a smooth muscle-controlled "gate") (Figure 98) and gains entry to the next part of the digestive tract—the small intestine. It is here where most of the body's digestion and absorption take place.

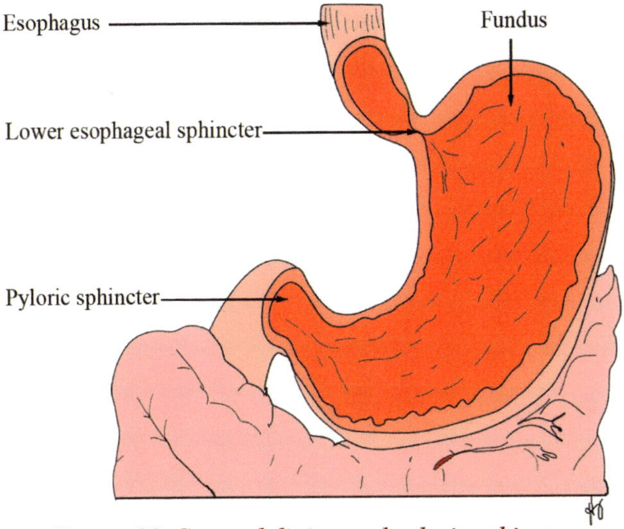

Figure 98. Stomach lining and pyloric sphincter

The small bowel (intestine) is divided into three sections, each one longer than the one before it. The **duodenum** (Figure 99), which makes up the first 9 to 10 inches, receives the highly acidic chyme from the stomach, and consequently is at risk for **duodenal ulcers**. Unlike the rest of the small intestine, the duodenum is **retroperitoneal**, meaning that it lies beneath the peritoneum (it is held up against the posterior wall of the abdominal cavity).

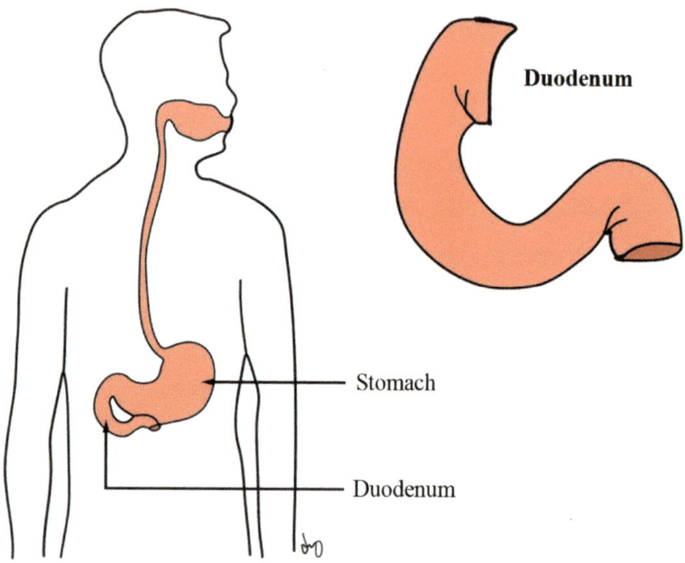

Figure 99. Duodenum

The battle to protect the lining of the small intestine from the stomach's acidic contents first comes from the small bowel itself. Millions of intestinal glands secrete highly alkaline mucus, which helps neutralize the acid while keeping the chyme in a liquid form to further aid in its digestibility. Two key accessory digestive organs, the pancreas and the liver, aid in the digestive process.

Pancreas

The pancreas (Figure 100), which lies just inferior to and posterior to the stomach, has two very important functions. As an **endocrine gland**, it releases **insulin** and **glucagons** into the bloodstream to regulate glucose (sugar) levels. As an **exocrine gland**, it secretes pancreatic juices into the duodenum that contain a variety of digestive enzymes. These enzymes are transported to the small intestine by way of the **pancreatic duct**, which joins the common bile duct and leads to the inside of the duodenum. The pancreas also releases compounds that are basic and help neutralize the acidic chime that arises from the stomach.

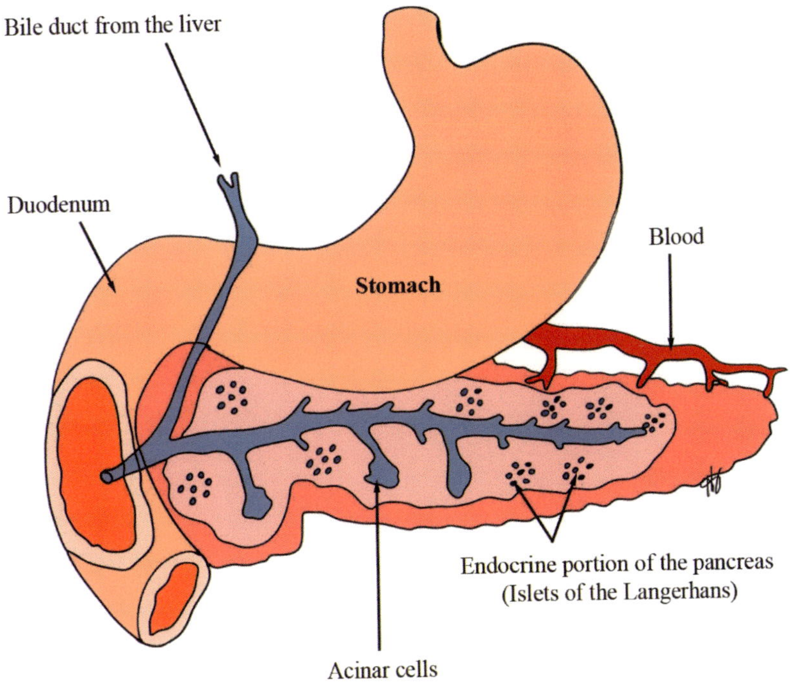

Figure 100. The pancreas

Liver

Among its many tasks, the **liver** deactivates drugs and toxins, stores glucose in the form of glycogen, stores iron and vitamins, and produces many important blood proteins. The liver receives blood from two sources. It takes oxygen-rich blood from the **hepatic artery** (*hepato-* or *hepatic* from the Greek word for liver, *hēpar*), but it also receives blood from the **portal vein** (Figure 101). This vein delivers nutrients and other products from the digestive tract. You can remember that this is a portal vein by thinking of a port where the ships come in to deliver goods (and maybe pick some up) from other countries. The portal vein receives the blood from the digestive tract and delivers the nutrient-rich blood to the liver. The liver is the first organ to receive nutrients brought in by the portal vein as well as a variety of potential toxins from the digestive tract. The liver is considered the "great trash can" of the body. It is the liver that deactivates many of the medications we take to cure our ills in what is referred to as a "first pass effect."

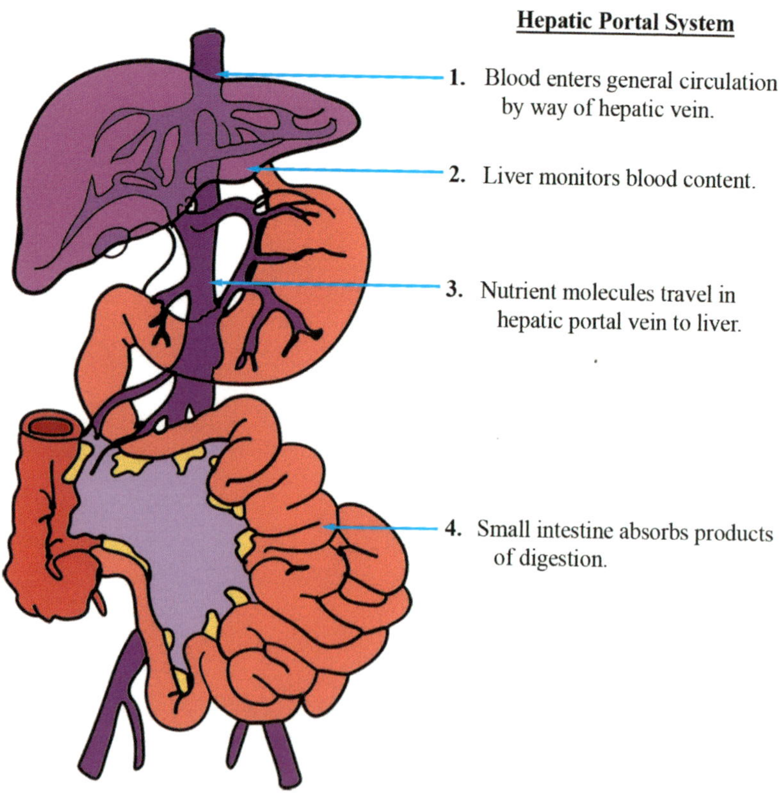

Figure 101. Hepatic circulation

Clinical Correlate

A "first pass effect" refers to the liver's first access to clear the body of nutrients and toxins before they get to the other parts of the body. Remember: All the digestive tract does is break down and absorb nutrients. It is not necessarily selective in what it absorbs. The liver, however, helps rid the body of harmful and potentially harmful substances. In severe ***alcoholism****, it is the liver that can be dangerously affected, sometimes causing cirrhosis (shrinking of the liver). The liver shrinks because of the destructive affect the alcohol has on the liver tissue, making it more difficult for the nutrient-rich blood to get through. When this happens, the portal veins that bring this nutrient-rich blood to the liver can develop* ***varicosities****, where the veins become abnormally swollen or knotted due to increased pressure in the portal system, making these varicosities more likely to bleed profusely if torn.*

The primary digestive product of the liver is **bile**. Bile helps break down fats into fatty acids, which can then be absorbed into the body by the digestive tract. Although it is manufactured in the liver, bile is stored in the **gallbladder**. There, bile is concentrated and released when fat-containing chyme is present. The intestinal hormone **cholecystokinin** or **CCK** is secreted by cells in the mucosa of the small bowel in response to these

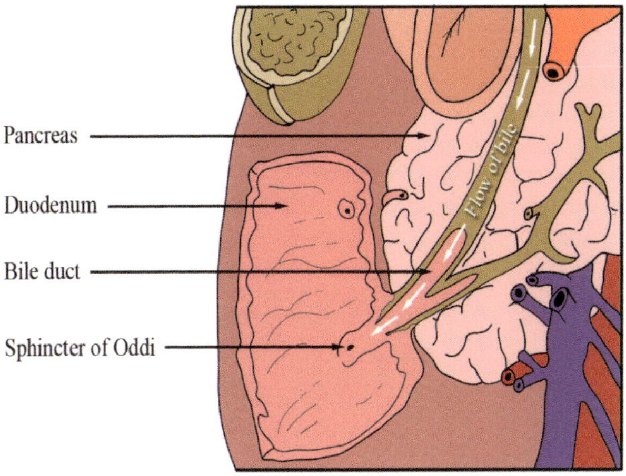

Figure 102. The anatomy of bile flow

fats. CCK causes the gallbladder to contract, releasing bile into the lumen (opening) of the small bowel/intestine (Figure 102). Bile then emulsifies the fat (that is, it breaks down the fat droplets into smaller sizes), permitting easier digestion by increasing the exposed surface area.

Digestion

The secretion of digestive enzymes and other important juices is prompted by the presence of acidic chyme, as well as simple stretching of the small bowel. The body's three major energy sources are carbohydrates, fats, and proteins, and their digestion and absorption is accomplished by specific enzymes at specific locations in the **gastrointestinal tract**. The digestion of carbohydrates (sugars) begins in the mouth, through the secretion of a substance called **salivary amylase**.

Although most fats must wait until they arrive in the duodenum, where their presence triggers the release of bile from the gallbladder and the emulsification process begins, some digestive action on dietary fats occurs in the mouth through the presence of substances called **lingual lipases**.

Protein digestion, which results in the release of amino acids, starts in the stomach with the release of pepsin and continues in the duodenum (followed by the other two parts of the small intestine, the **jejunum** and the **ileum**) where other enzymes, like **trypsin**, continue to yield free **amino acids**, which are the building blocks of proteins in the body. The efficient absorption of these nutrients requires a large surface area, which is provided by the fine hair-like structures called **villi** (from the Latin word meaning "tuft of hair") that line the walls of the center of the small intestine (Figure 103). As chyme makes its way to the end of the small bowel, it is still a semiliquid, composed of water and nearly indigestible food remains. It is at this point that the large bowel enters the picture.

The end of the small intestine (called the ileum) marks the transition from the small intestine to the large intestine (also called the **colon**). The **appendix** is located at the **cecum**, near the spot where the small bowel ends and the **ascending colon** begins. Its purpose is unknown (although a role in the lymphatics system is likely), but when the appendix becomes inflamed, the result can be **appendicitis**.

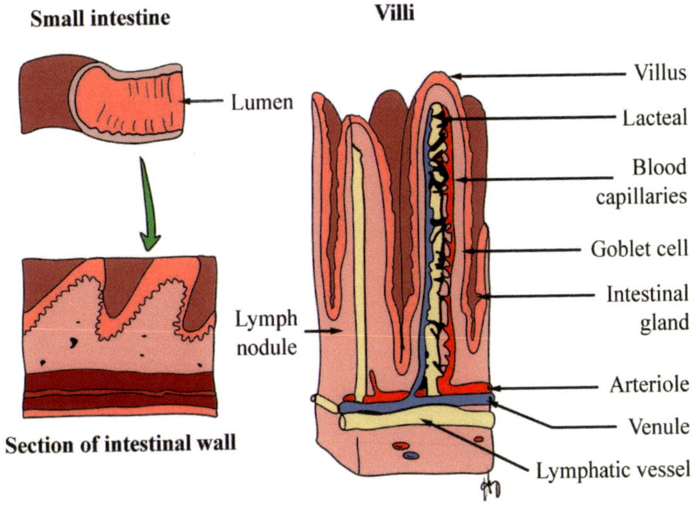

Figure 103. Villi and the anatomy of the small intestine

Test Your Knowledge

1. What is chyme?

   ____

   ____

2. In what structures does the primary absorption of nutrients take place?

   ____

   ____

3. What is the primary responsibility of the liver?

   ____

   ____

4. From which two structures does the liver receive its blood supply?

____

____

5. What is appendicitis?

____

____

Large Bowel

Frequently referred to as the, the large intestine or bowel is about 4 feet long. While the large intestine is not as long as the small intestine, it is much larger in diameter than the small intestine. The large intestine is divided into several distinct segments (Figure 104). These include the **ascending colon**, the **transverse colon**, the **descending colon**, the **sigmoid colon**, and the **rectum**. The digestive tract ends at the anus. The function of the large intestine is simple: absorb water, absorb vitamins (created by bacteria inside the intestine), compact the feces, and store them until they can be discharged via the anus. NOTE: Bacteria, when confined to the in-

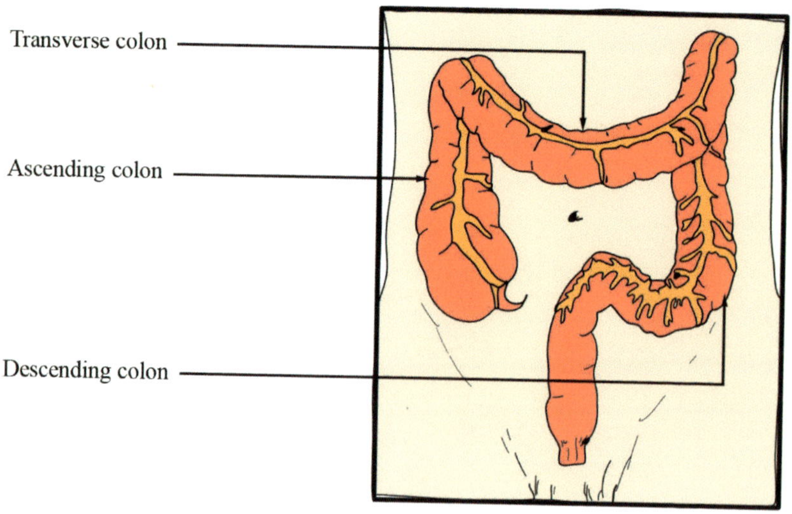

Figure 104. Large intestine or colon

side of the colon, are helpful because they help create vitamins. You may have heard many commercials for supplements like Activia, which are supposed to provide "good" bacteria to the intestine. All bacteria, whether "good" or "bad" can be harmful if they get out of the lumen of the bowel and into the abdominal cavity.

Test Your Knowledge

1. Name the segments of the colon or large intestine.

   ____

   ____

   ____

   ____

2. What is the purpose of the large intestine?

   ____

   ____

   ____

3. Which intestine is larger in diameter: the large intestine or the small intestine?

   ____

   ____

Common Conditions and Diseases of the Gastrointestinal Tract

Crohn's disease is a form of **inflammatory bowel disease**. It causes inflammation of the lining of the digestive tract. Typical signs and symptoms include abdominal cramps, fever, decreased appetite, and fatigue. Treatment is usually centered on changes in diet, steroids, and occasionally surgery. Symptoms often wax and wane and are frequently lifelong.

Appendicitis refers to an inflammation of the appendix. A patient may first complain about pain around the **umbilicus** (the belly button). This is often associated with nausea, diminished appetite, and fever. The treatment is commonly surgical removal of the appendix.

Small bowel obstruction may be a mechanical or functional obstruction and slows or completely blocks the passage of digestive products. Causes include **adhesions** (scar tissue) that form after surgeries or infections, cancers, and Crohn's disease.

Colon cancer starts in the rectum or large bowel. It frequently is without symptoms until advanced in its spread. How it is treated depends on the stage of the cancer and could involve **chemotherapy**, radiation, or surgery.

Digestive System Glossary

absorption	transfer of nutrients into bloodstream
amino acid	building blocks of proteins
BM	bowel movement
carbohydrates	most important source of energy for your body changed by the digestive system into glucose (blood sugar) used for energy for your cells, tissues and organs; best sources of carbohydrates—whole grains (the less processed, the better), vegetables, fruits and beans—since they promote good health by delivering vitamins, minerals, fiber, and a host of important phytonutrients
chemical digestion	process that breaks down large molecules that can be absorbed by the body's cells; takes place in the mouth, stomach & small intestine
chief cell	cell which releases a precursor enzyme to another cell; found in gastric pits and produces pepsinogen (activated to pepsin in the presence of high acidity) which permits the breakdown of protiens
chyme	material that includes food and gastric juice found in both the stomach and small intestine
defecation	process of eliminating feces
duodenum	first part of the small intestine that receives chyme from the stomach and is the first part of the digestive system that absorbs nutrients
enzyme	molecules that speed up the rate of chemical reactions in the body but don't necessarily participate in their action
feces	solid waste material
gastric juice	fluid which contains the enzymes pepsin, hydrochloric acid, and thick, slippery mucus to help break down whatever you have ingested; the mucus portion helps protect the lining of the stomach from the acidic contents of the chyme
gastric pits	found among columnar cells; holes that go into the lumen of the stomach; pits that secrete a variety of digestive juices to break down chyme

hepatitis	inflammation of the liver caused by a variety of conditions
ileum	last portion of the small intestine important in the absorption of vitamin B 12
jejunum	middle portion of the small intestine
large intestine	horseshoe shaped organ that fits over the coils of the small intestine responsible for storing feces until they can be eliminated, absorbs water, and a variety of vitamins
lipids	(also known as fats) together with carbohydrates and proteins, lipids are the main constituents of plant and animal cells
mastication	chewing
mesentery	fan-shaped membrane that attaches small intestine to it's blood and nerve supply
pancreas	produces enzymes that break down digestible foods; both an exocrine and endocrine organ; over 90% of its bulk is for exocrine juices that are released into the small bowel and a small portion is an endocrine organ which releases insulin and glucagon thus regulating glucose levels in the blood
pancreatic lipase	digests lipids along with the help from bile; breaks down fats in the diet into fatty acids and glycerol
parietal cells	secrete hydrochloric acid which produces an acidic environment that helps break down proteins and intrinsic factor (important in the absorption of vitamin B12)
pepsin	released by chief cells in response to high acidity in the stomach for the breakdown of proteins; an enzyme that works on protein and changes it to simpler proteins
pepsinogen	inactive form of pepsin; activated as soon as it is in contact with Hcl (high acidity)
peptic ulcer	erosion of the mucosa of the stomach or duodenum produced by a variety of conditions
peristalis	wave-like muscular contractions that move chyme (partially digested food) through the digestive system
peritoneum	serous membrane that lines the abdominopelvic cavity
peritonitis	inflammation of peritoneum frequently caused by infection

pylorus	end of stomach before it joins with the small intestine; controls the release of chyme from the stomach into the small intestine (duodenum)
rectum	temporary storage area for indigestible food residue
saliva	liquid released from several sites in the mouth that begins the process of digestion
small intestine	organ of the digestive system in which most digestion takes place
stomach	organ that churns ingested food into a liquid like substance known as chyme and stores it for release into the small bowel

Chapter 7
The Urinary System

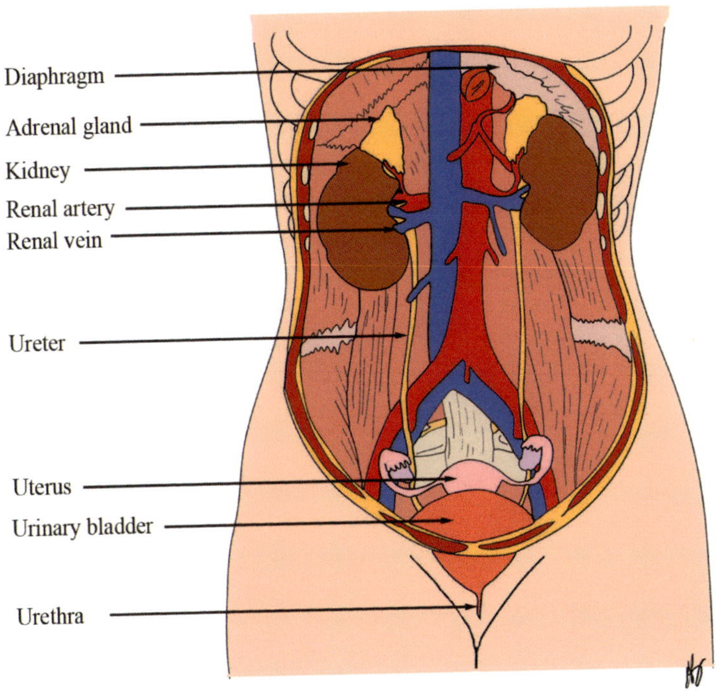

Figure 105 - The urinary system

When we consider the human body's urinary system (Figure 105), most of us think only about the production and storage of **urine**. Interestingly, the kidneys and a variety of hormones are responsible for a good deal more than that.

Fluid and Electrolyte Control

The fluid and **electrolyte** content of the body's **intracellular** (*intra* = inside ; *cellular* = cell) and **extracellular** (*extra* = outside ; *cellular* = cell) compartments must be carefully controlled, and this control falls to the urinary system to accomplish. An electrolyte is a chemical substance that, when dissolved in water, turns into electrically charged atoms called **ions**. Therefore, electrolytes are capable of conducting electric current.

For example, let's say you and a friend go to the movies. After buying your tickets, your friend decides to order two sodas. Not knowing that you are trying to diet, your friend buys one for you and one for himself. Once inside the theatre he offers the soda to you. You decline, stating your plans to be a size 10 by the time the holidays roll around. Because the movie ends up being quite long (and because your friend is as skinny as a rail and can afford to guzzle these drinks), he consumes both of them by the end of the show. Then let's say that afterward, both of you have your blood drawn. You might suspect that your skinny friend would have a higher glucose level in his blood than you do. After all, he drank the sodas and you did not. Believe it or not, however, you'd find only a slight difference, if any, between your body's fluid balance and that of your friend. You may wonder how this would be possible, and you might be surprised to know that the answer lies in your body's ability to balance the fluids through the work of the kidneys, brain, heart, and the **adrenal glands**, which are small glands located just above each kidney.

This balancing act is called **homeostasis**, which comes from the Greek *homoios* (same, like, resembling) and *stasis* (to stand, posture). It simply means the ability or tendency of a cell to maintain internal equilibrium by adjusting its physiological processes. Put another way, homeostasis is the tendency of the body to seek and maintain a condition of balance or equilibrium within its internal environment, even when faced with external changes. Homeostasis in a general sense refers to stability, balance, or equilibrium. It is the body's attempt to maintain a constant internal environment. Maintaining a stable internal environment requires constant monitoring and adjustments as conditions change. This adjusting of physiological systems within the body is called **homeostatic regulation**. If you're having trouble understanding this concept of homeostasis, think stability, balance, or equilibrium. Although there are precise mechanisms for understanding homeostasis that will be discussed a little later, for now just know that the urinary system maintains homeostasis in the following ways:

- Adjusting the water and electrolyte content of the urine on an as-needed basis
- Eliminating waste products through urine
- Managing the concentration of hydrogen ions responsible for the acid–base balance of the body

- Secreting **renin**, a hormone involved in blood pressure regulation
- Releasing **erythropoietin** (*erythr/o* = red ; *poietin* = substance that forms), a hormone secreted by the kidneys that acts on stem cells of the bone marrow to stimulate red blood cell production or **erythropoiesis**
- **Elaborating** (which means making and releasing) a hormone that can influence the rate of calcium absorption from the **gastrointestinal** or GI tract. *Gastrointestinal* is a term that means "pertaining to the stomach and intestines"

We will touch on each of these **renal** functions as we review the anatomy of the urinary system.

Test Your Knowledge

1. Which hormone, secreted by the kidney, acts on the stem cells of the bone to stimulate red blood cell production?

   ____

   ____

2. Renin, secreted by the kidneys, is important in regulating what?

   ____

3. T or F: Homeostasis is the body's attempt to maintain a constant internal environment.

   ____

The Kidneys, Ureters, Bladder, and Urethra

The kidneys, ureters, bladder, and urethra are vital organs covered by smooth, moist **peritoneum**. As already mentioned, the peritoneum is a membrane that lines the abdominal cavity and covers most of the organs inside of it. The word *peritoneum* comes from the Greek *peri-* = around ; *tonos* = to stretch. Thus, the peritoneum "stretches around" the inside of the abdominal area. Because they are protected by the lower ribs, the **kidneys** remain fairly

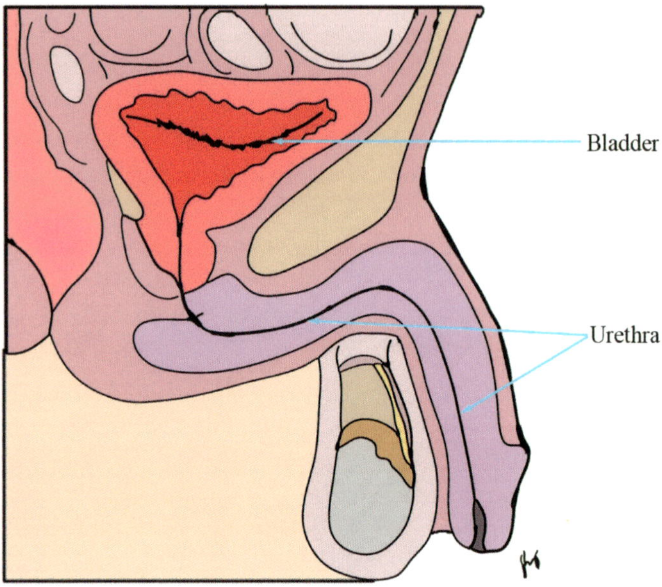

Figure 106. The bladder and urethra: a lateral view

safe from external injury. The **ureters** (tubes composed of muscle fibers), transport urine from the kidneys to the bladder. The **bladder** is a muscular bag that stores urine until the person voids (urinates). The urine leaves the bladder through a tube called the **urethra** (Figure 106).

Kidneys

The kidneys have several very important jobs. They

- Maintain the balance of fluids in the body;
- Filter out the waste products of metabolism. The minerals, water, and glucose needed by the body are then returned to the blood by a process called **reabsorption**. The remaining fluid and wastes pass into collecting ducts, flowing to the ureter and bladder as urine; and
- Secrete renin. Renin is a substance important for the control of blood pressure.

The kidneys receive their blood supply directly from the aorta by way of the **renal arteries**. Each kidney has one renal artery. The kidneys are drained by the **renal vein**. Each kidney consists of two layers: the **outer cortex** and the **inner medulla**. The cortex contains the **glomeruli** and **convoluted tubules**, and the medulla, a smooth, somewhat striated inner section, contains many of the **loops of Henle** and the **collecting tubules** (Figure 107). We will discuss these structures shortly. In Figure 108 you can see the microscopic urine-producing units of the kidney in the cortex. These units are referred to as **nephrons**. More than one million nephrons are found in the cortex of each kidney.

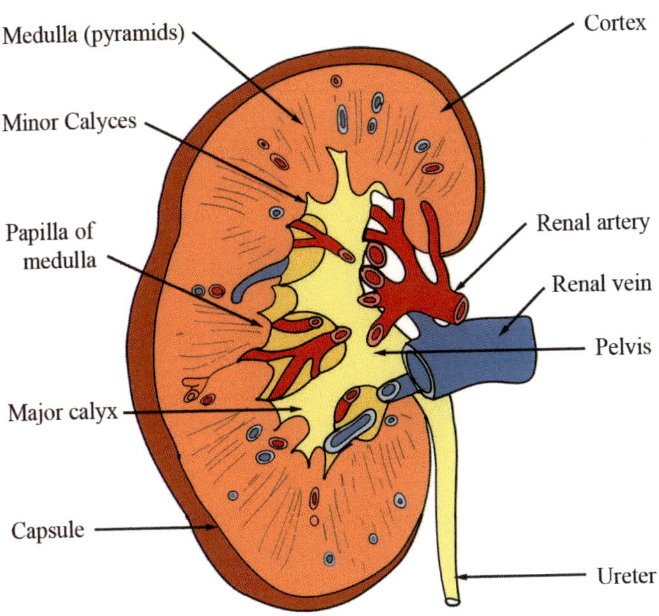

Figure 107. Cross section of kidney

Each nephron is equipped with two structures. The first is the **renal corpuscle**, a round structure that is composed of capillary blood vessels actively involved in the filtration of the blood to form urine. The renal corpuscle is also called the **glomerulus**. The glomerulus or renal corpuscle makes up part of the nephron, which is considered to be the functional unit of the kidney. The second structure found in the nephron is the **renal tubule**.

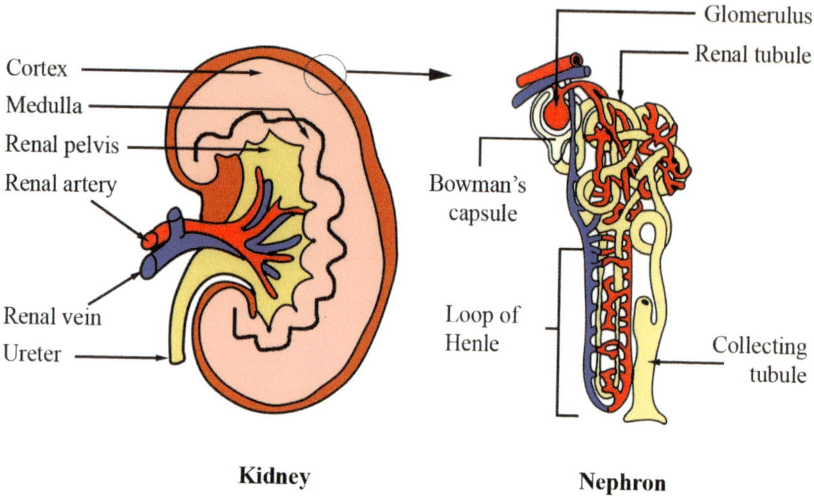

Figure 108. Nephron

As blood enters the glomerulus (located in the cortex), the plasma (blood fluid) is filtered. This produces a fluid called **plasma filtrate**, which enters the renal tubule (Figures 109 and 110). The plasma filtrate consists of water containing electrolytes, glucose, and other substances, but normally no proteins or red cells. The volume of filtrate produced is dependent on the blood pressure inside the **glomerular blood vessels**. The higher the pressure, the greater the volume of filtrate produced.

Clinical Correlate

The filtration of the liquid from the blood is not selective, meaning glucose and important ions are filtered out along with the liquid. The body wants to reserve most of the liquid and all of the important ions. The nephron is very effective in doing this. In people with ***diabetes****, whose glucose levels are much higher than those who do not have the disease, the kidneys' absorption abilities (for glucose) are overwhelmed and nonabsorbed glucose begins to appear in the urine. From a practical standpoint, you may do a routine* ***urinalysis*** *on a patient and discover that there is a lot of glucose in the urine. This could be indicative of diabetes. Additionally, you may notice that a diabetic patient tends to urinate more frequently than a nondiabetic patient. This is because the amount of glucose in the* *nephrons literally "sucks out" water from the surrounding tissue outside the nephrons, producing more urine. This process is called* ***osmosis****, which we have already discussed.*

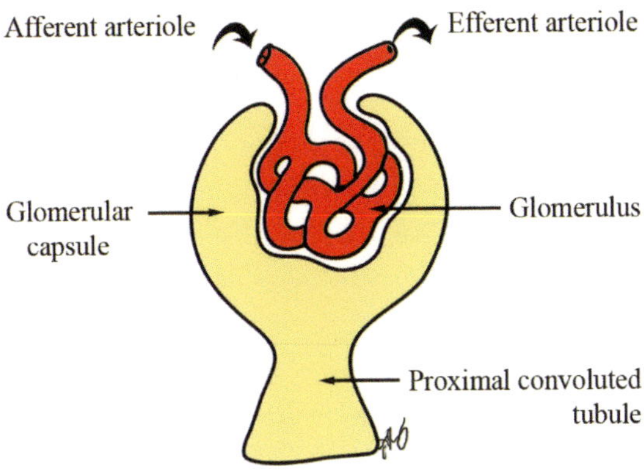

Figure 109. - The glomerulus

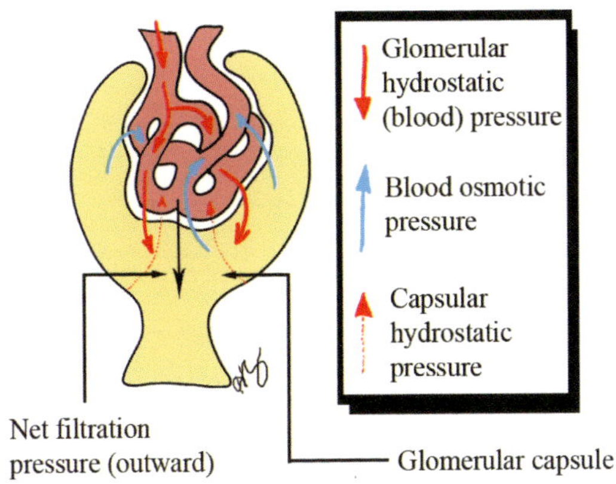

Figure 110. - Filtration in the nephron

Since this fluid contains important substances that the body does not want to lose, the renal tubule's job is to reclaim those substances along its length. (The reabsorption of water, electrolytes, and glucose is just one of the many wonders of the urinary tract specifically and the body in general, and the secretion and elimination of unwanted substances is another.) The filtrate, after being produced in the glomerulus, enters the nearby convoluted tubule first (Figure 111). Here the majority of the filtered water, sodium, chloride, and glucose are reabsorbed.

To get a better picture of how the tubules reclaim important components for the body, imagine a woman crossing a small stream on a footbridge. She accidentally spills the contents of her purse into the fast-moving stream. Two fishermen downstream see what happened and begin collecting the various items as they float toward them. Unable to retrieve all of them, they concentrate only on the important things like car keys, money, and jewelry, and they return these items to the woman. This is a good example of how the kidneys work. The most important items (e.g., glucose, sodium) are reabsorbed as quickly as possible in the proximal (close by) convoluted tubule.

The remaining filtrate then enters the loop of Henle (Figure 111). As the name suggests, this portion of the nephron tubule dips down into the cortex creating a descending arm that connects with the medulla and an ascending arm that travels back to the cortex. As fluids move down the loop of Henle into the medulla, water is filtered out, moving into the interstitial fluid of the medulla. When the fluid moves up the ascending arm, salts are pulled out, and the cell walls are impermeable to water, so no additional water is lost. The filtrate, which is becoming increasingly more urine-like during these steps, next enters the distal (farther away) convoluted tubule (Figure 111). There, final adjustments are made before the filtrate enters the collecting system and leaves the kidney as urine. This fine-tuning includes not only absorption but also secretion of critical ions like hydrogen and potassium. The urine is directed toward the renal pelvis and on to the bladder via the ureters.

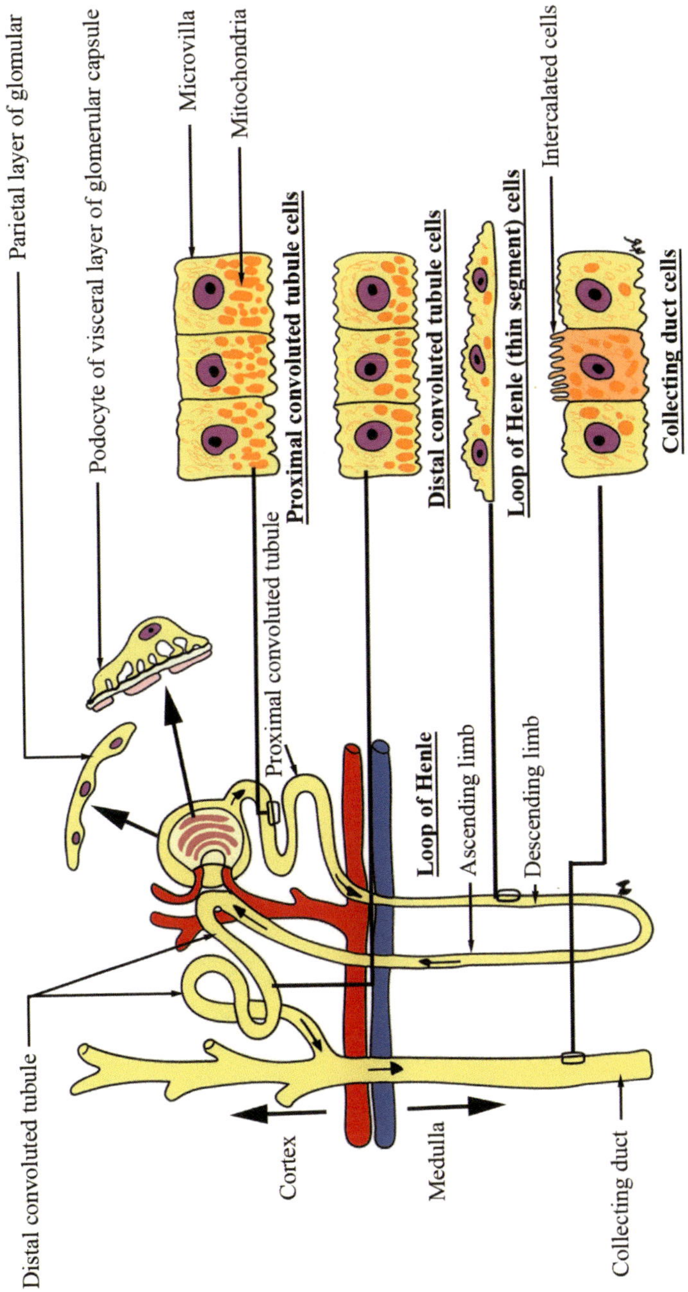

Figure 111 - Close-up of nephron

Clinical Correlate
*The ureters are in harm's way and difficult to see because they are underneath the peritoneum (i.e., they are **retroperitoneal**) and thus are prone to injury during surgery.*

One additional structure must be reviewed before we leave our discussion of the kidney's nephrons. This specialized structure has a long name: the **juxtaglomerular apparatus**. To better understand this structure, please follow along with our discussion here by looking at Figure 112. Notice that the tube of the distal convoluted tubule coils around and superficially "joins" the artery that carries blood into the renal corpuscle (also called the glomerulus or **afferent arteriole**). There, specialized cells release renin. If the blood pressure is too low, this hormone produces **vasoconstrictive** effects by yielding **angiotensin II** (*angio* = from Greek *angeio-* meaning vessel, blood vessel ; *tensin* = constrict), and it promotes a rise in blood pressure. Too much renin can result in **chronic hypertension** in some people.

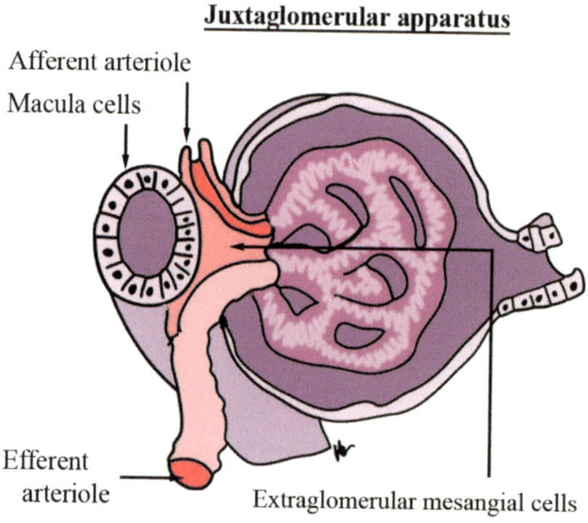

Figure 112. Juxtaglomerular apparatus

A final, frequently overlooked task of the kidneys is to stimulate red blood cell production in the **bone marrow**. They do this by releasing erythropoietin in response to low oxygen content in the **renal arterial influx** to the kidneys (the blood coming into the kidney). The practical application of this process could be illustrated in the following way. Suppose a person who lives at sea level goes to a region such as Colorado where the oxygen content of the air is less due to the higher altitude. The kidney senses the drop in oxygen tension in the renal arteries and turns on erythropoietin and release rennin, which will increase the blood pressure to improve the body's oxygen content. This increases blood volume and blood pressure to counteract the lower oxygen tension of this new environment. This is also why people who are new to a high altitude area tend to huff and puff. It is an effort by their bodies to try to get more oxygen into their blood.

Test Your Knowledge

1. T or F: Ureters transport urine from the kidneys to the loop of Henle?

   ____

2. T or F: Each nephron is equipped with two structures?

   ____

3. T or F: The majority of the filtered water, sodium, chloride, and glucose are reabsorbed in the proximal tubule?

   ____

4. T or F: Osmosis is the process through which homeostasis is achieved?

   ____

Ureters

The two ureters are tubes that contain smooth muscle that travel in the **retroperitoneal space** and transport urine from the kidneys to the bladder (Figure 113). From 10 to 12 inches in length, they actively propel urine along by **peristalsis**. Peristalsis is an involuntary, coordinated contraction of smooth muscle that, in this case, pushes urine ahead. Great care must be taken to avoid injuring these delicate structures during pelvic surgeries such as **hysterectomy**.

Bladder

The bladder, which serves as a temporary storage site for urine, is a **muscular distensible sac** (able to stretch and expand) also located in the retroperitoneal space. The ureters join the bladder at a site known as the **trigone** (Figure 114). The bladder's three layers of smooth muscle (Figure

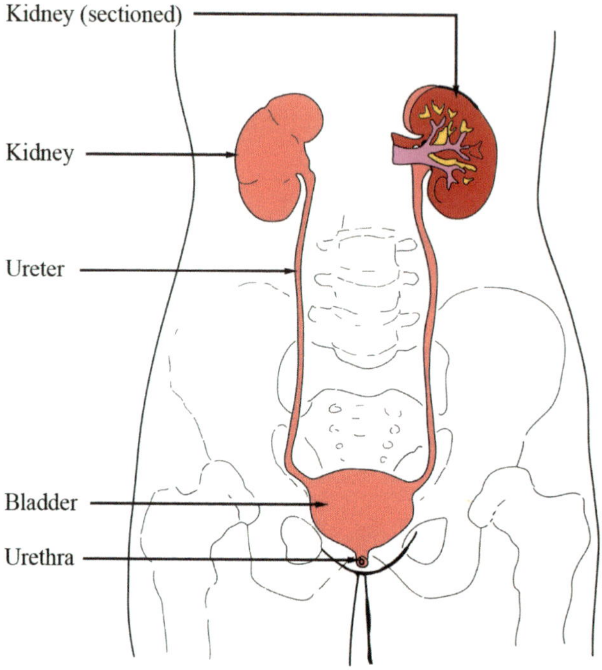

Figure 113. Ureters

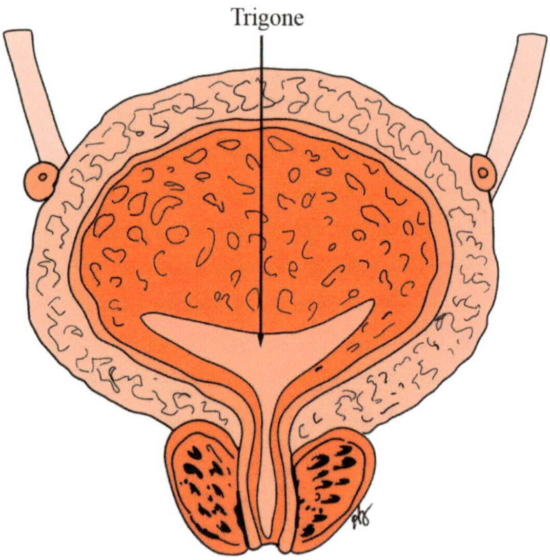

Figure 114. Trigone of the bladder

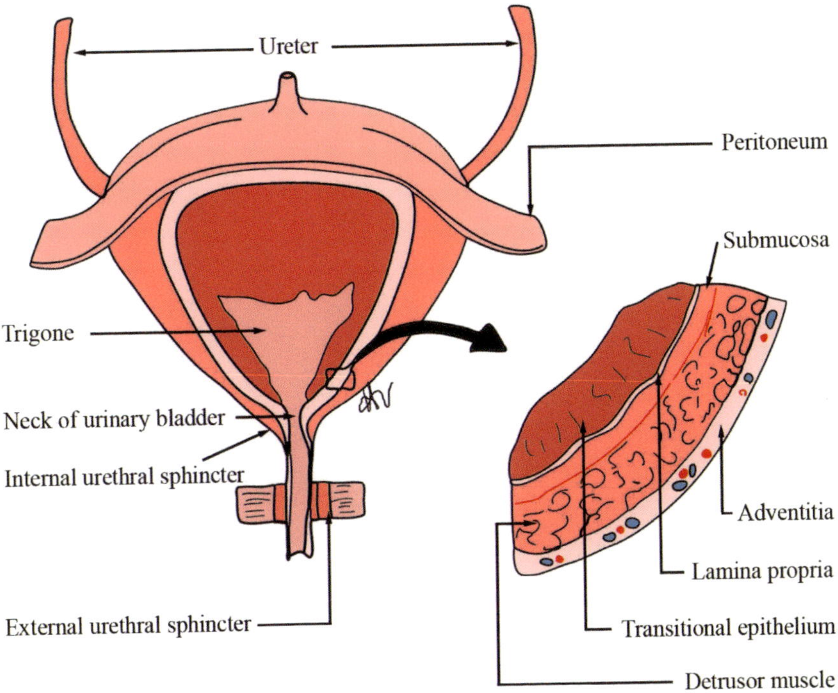

Figure 115. Close-up of bladder anatomy

115) are collectively referred to as the **detrusor**, and the inner lining of the bladder is covered by **transitional epithelium**. Transitional epithelia is a type of tissue that consists of multiple layers of epithelial cells.

Trigone

These cells can contract and expand as needed. They appear to be **cuboidal** when the organ or the tube is not stretched, and when stretched they look flat and irregular, hence the name "transitional." Two functions of the transitional epithelial cells are:

- To accommodate fluctuation in volume of the liquid in an organ or tube (i.e., urinary bladder); and
- To protect against the caustic effects of urine.

Clinical Correlate

Detrusor instability *(also known as* ***D.I.****) is a condition that occurs when the detrusor muscles contract involuntarily, pushing the contents of the bladder out of the body in large quantities. The patient has no control over the exit of the urine from the body. This form of* ***incontinence*** *can, and often does, occur unpredictably and can be an embarrassment to the patient.*

Urethra

The urethra is the thin-walled tube through which urine passes to the outside of the body. It has two "gates" to prevent urine leakage. The innermost gate, the **internal sphincter**, is constructed of smooth muscle and is not under voluntary control. It is almost always closed unless the **external sphincter** opens by choice for the person to use the bathroom. The external sphincter, however, is made of skeletal muscle and is under voluntary control, permitting urination.

Test Your Knowledge

1. What are the ureters?

   ____

   ____

2. What is the trigone?

   ____

   ____

3. Is the bladder located retroperitoneally?

   ____

4. What is the purpose of the transitional epithelium in the bladder?

   ____

   ____

5. How does urine travel to the outside of the body?

   ____

   ____

Fluid and Electrolyte Balance

The body is composed primarily of water—about 60%, in fact. The body fluids contain this water and the variety of materials dissolved in it. Body fluids can be divided into two compartments: **intracellular** (those inside of the cells) and **extracellular** (those outside of the cells). Intracellular fluids account for about two-thirds of total body fluids (Figure 116) and extracellular fluids make up the remaining one-third. Fluids constantly shift between the intracellular and extracellular compartments as a result of changes in blood pressure and osmosis.

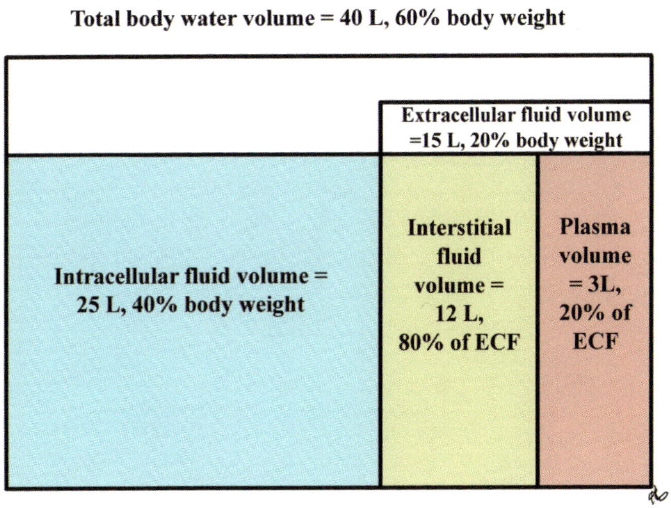

Figure 116. Distribution of body fluids

Recall that osmosis is the movement of water from areas of low solute concentration to areas of high concentration and helps maintain homeostasis.

Blood pressure is a force that is always trying to push water from inside the blood vessels to the interstitial spaces (the spaces outside of these vessels). Osmosis, a force that generally attempts to "suck" the water back into the blood vessels, works against blood pressure in this way. In healthy people, the amount of water or fluids taken in is about the same as the amount of water lost when they urinate, perspire, and exhale air from the lungs. And while body fluids move back and forth between the intracellular and extracellular compartments, the total amount of body fluid changes very little.

When excessive body fluid losses occur, for example, in the case of severe **diarrhea**, the result is **dehydration**. The body's fluid balance is orchestrated by the **hypothalamus**, an organ at the base of the brain. The hypothalamus has several important jobs. One of these is to monitor the **osmotic pressure** in the blood (Figure 117). When the osmotic pressure gets too high, the hypothalamus directs the pituitary to release **ADH** (short for **antidiuretic hormone**). A **diuretic** is anything that promotes the formation of urine by the kidney. (The word *diuretic* comes from a combination of the Greek *dia-* = thoroughly ; *ourein* = to urinate, to urinate thoroughly. An antidiuretic is something that does the opposite of a diuretic). The ADH is then released by the gland near the hypothalamus (Figure 118) called the **pituitary gland** and activates the thirst centers. ADH also works against further fluid losses by speeding up the reabsorption of water in the distal convoluted tubule and other parts of the kidneys' collecting system we described earlier. This helps to re-establish the normal fluid content of the body.

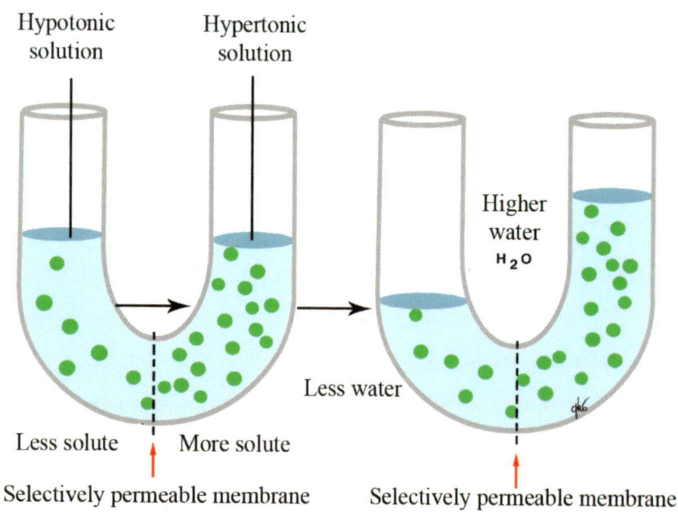

Figure 117. Example of osmotic and hydrostatic pressure

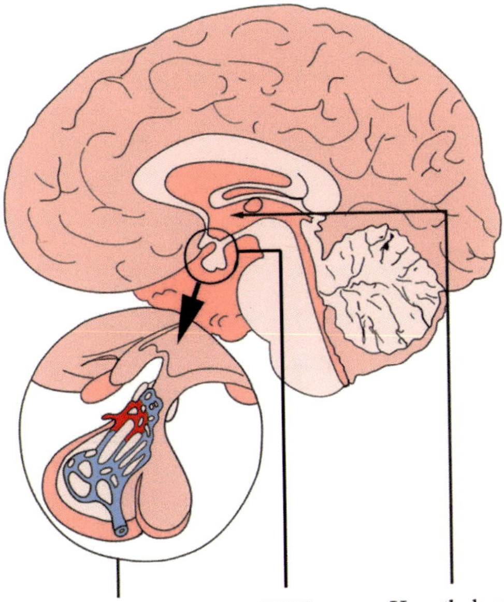

Figure 118. Hypothalamus and pituitary gland

Other hormones are also released by other organs (e.g., the heart, receptors in the carotid artery, etc.) in response to changes in blood volume or blood pressure. These include **ANP** (short for **atrial natriuretic peptide**), a hormone released by the heart when sensors called **stretch receptors** detect excessive blood volume. (Stretch receptors are called such because they sense a stretch when there is an increase in the blood volume that presses against them.) The ANP hormone increases the quantity of filtrate produced in the glomerulus of the kidneys, resulting in a greater volume of urine and lowering of the blood pressure. **Aldosterone**, a hormone secreted by the adrenal gland in response to drops in blood pressure, acts on the renal tubules to increase the reabsorption of sodium by the kidneys. Because water tends to follow sodium, this results in an increase in blood volume and thus a rise in blood pressure.

Clinical Correlate
When a person is shot, the blood pressure drops due to blood loss. In response, aldosterone is released in an attempt to increase the body's blood pressure to a normal level.

Maintaining the fluid content is only part of the challenge for the kidneys.

The body's electrolytes (important salts, acids, and bases that conduct electricity) must be kept within narrow limits if the body is to continue functioning efficiently—or at all, for that matter. The volume of electrolytes taken in, plus those that are created inside the body, must match the volume lost through urination and sweat. This is called **electrolyte balance**, and it's achieved by both the kidneys and the many functioning cells in the body that must maintain their electrolytes inside the cells at very different levels from those maintained on the outside.

The kidney also affects the rate of calcium and phosphate absorption from the small intestine. It does this (with the help of the liver) by elaborating (making and distributing) the hormone **calcitriol**.

Finally, the body's **acid–base status** (also called **acid–base balance** or **acid–base equilibrium**) must also be closely monitored and adjusted by the kidney. This means that the hydrogen ion concentration (which is a measure of the body's pH acidity) must be kept within a tight range if the heart, **enzyme systems**, muscles, and nervous system are to operate normally. (There are two major enzyme systems in the human body. One is digestive and the other is metabolic. The **digestive enzymes** help break down all of the food we eat so it can be absorbed by the body. The **metabolic enzymes** help to run all of the systems of the body from respiratory to nervous.) **Acidosis** refers to the presence of a greater-than-usual number of hydrogen ions. **Alkalosis**, on the other hand, refers to the presence of a lower-than-usual number of these ions. A **buffer** is a substance that acts to minimize the changes in pH (a measure of the degree to which a solution is acidic or alkaline). The body has several buffer systems to accomplish this goal.

This completes our review of the most important features of the body's renal system.

Test Your Knowledge

1. What is a diuretic?

 ____

 ____

2. What part of your body controls fluid balance?

 ____

 ____

3. What hormone secreted by the adrenal glands acts on the renal tubules to increase reabsorption of sodium by the kidneys?

 ____

4. How much of the body is composed of water?

 ____

5. Acidosis refers to:

 ____

 ____

6. Alkalosis refers to:

 ____

 ____

Common Conditions and Diseases of the Urinary System

Acute renal failure is the sudden loss of the kidneys' ability to remove waste products and concentrate the urine without losing important electrolytes. This can result from severe dehydration, **septic shock**, and a variety of other clinically dangerous conditions. Treatment depends on the cause, but **dialysis** is sometimes necessary.

Pyelonephritis, unlike a bladder infection, is an infection of the kidneys and ureters. It is usually characterized by spiking fevers and back or flank pain or tenderness. Treatment is directed toward **broad-spectrum antibiotics** until a urine culture identifies the infective organism.

Renal artery stenosis occurs when the artery becomes so narrow that blood flow to the affected kidney is reduced. This can produce a severe **hypertension** that is difficult to manage medically. The cause of the narrowing is usually **atherosclerosis**.

Urinary System Glossary

electrolyte	chemical that carries an electrical charge in a solution
erythropoietin	(also known as EPO) hormone secreted by the kidney to stimulate the production of red blood cells
filtration	passive process whereby some substance, but not all, pass through a filter or other material
golmerulus	tiny ball or capillaries in cortex of kidney
hilum	depression or pit in that part of an organ where blood vessels and nerves enter and leave
kidney	one of two bean-shaped organs located behind the abdominal cavity on either side of the backbone in the lumbar region
meatus	opening canal
medulla	inner region
micturition	urination; act of voiding
nephron	combination of golmerulus and renal tubule where filtration, reabsorption, and secretion take place in the kidney
nitrogenous waste	substance containing nitrogen and excreted in urine
potassium	(also known as K+) salt (electrolyte) secreted from the bloodstream into the renal tubules to leave the body in urine
reabsorption	in this process the renal tubules return materials necessary to the body back into the bloodstream
renal artery	carries blood to the kidney
renal pelvis	central collecting region in the kidney
renal tubule	microscopic tube in the kidney where urine is formed after filtration
renal vein	carries blood away from the kidney
renin	enzymatic hormone synthesized, stored, and secreted by the kidney
sodium	(also known as Na+) salt regulated in the blood and urine by the kidneys
trigone	triangular area in the bladder where the ureters enter and the urethra exits

urea	major nitrogenous waste product excreted in urine
ureter	tube leading from each kidney to the bladder
urethra	tube leading from the bladder to the outside of the body
uric acid	nitrogenous waste excreted in the urine
urinary bladder	sac that holds urine
urination	process of expelling urine; also called micturition
voiding	emptying of urine from the urinary bladder

Chapter 8
The Reproductive System

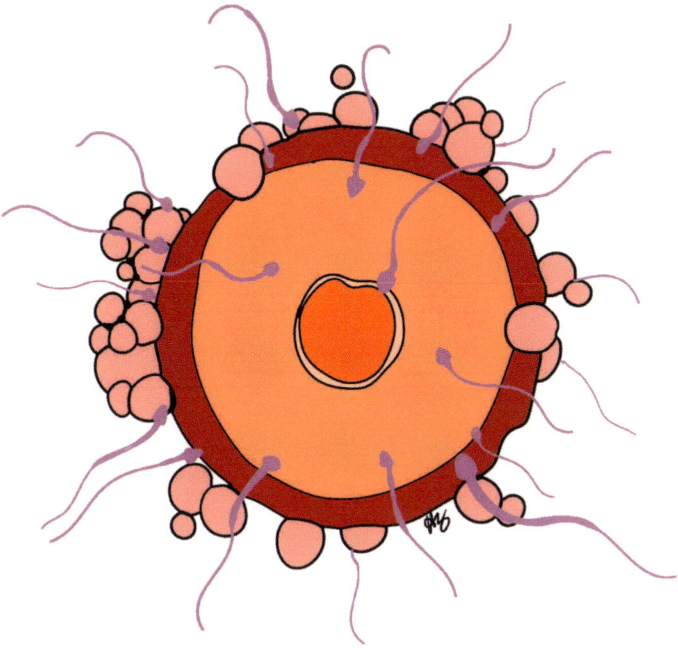

Figure 119. The male sperm and female egg

In this chapter, we will discuss the male and female reproductive process (Figure 119).

The Male Reproductive System

Great advances in our understanding of the male reproductive system have come only over the past few decades, as attention has been directed toward a better explanation of male infertility. From that research, we have gained a more complete picture of male reproductive physiology and the male's contribution to infertility as a whole.

Male Reproductive Anatomy

The primary sex organs of the male, the **testes** (also called **gonads**), produce **sperm** cells, or **gametes**. (Interestingly, the word *gamete* comes from the Greek words *gamete* = wife and *gametes* = husband). We will address

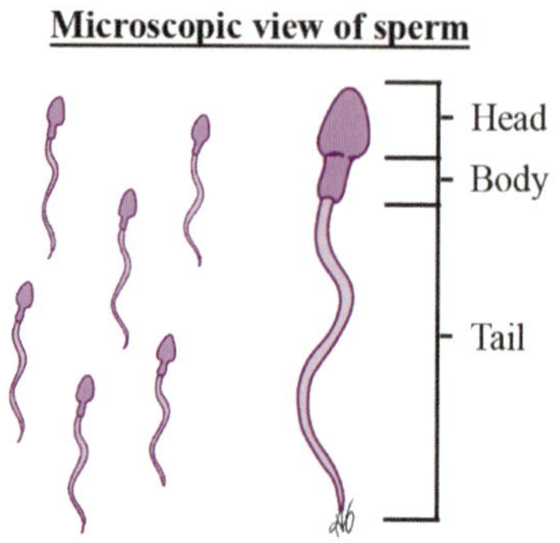

Figure 120. Sperm cell (spermatozoa)

how various anatomic structures contribute to the production, and eventual maturation of, sperm cells, or **spermatozoa** (Figure 120).

A normal male has two testes, also called **testicles**. These sex glands are housed in the **scrotum**, a two-chambered sac suspended outside of the body, behind the base of the penis and in between the legs. The testes serve two purposes:

1. They produce and store sperm cells; and
2. They are the body's primary source of male hormones such as **testosterone**.

Ideally, the developing sperm within the testes are kept slightly cooler than the rest of the body. It helps keep them alive. Higher temperatures can decrease sperm **motility** and/or kill the sperm. This is also why the testes hang down and away from the main part of the body. It is the job of the **cremaster muscle** to contract (pull the testes up closer to the body) to warm them when the outside temperature is too cold and to relax when the outside temperature is too hot.

Clinical Correlate

A common contributor to male infertility is the presence of a ***varicocele****. This is a condition in which a large entangled web of veins keeps the temperature of the nearby testes higher than normal. This can affect the developing sperm by influencing motility and other characteristics not yet fully appreciated. Surgery to correct these varicoceles frequently results in successful pregnancies.*

Contained within the testes are the **seminiferous tubules**. These are extremely long and narrow tubes that give rise to the precursors of sperm cells, called **spermatogonia** (Figure 121). In these tubes, large cells called **sustentacular cells** nurture the immature spermatogonia as they continue their journey down the male reproductive tract.

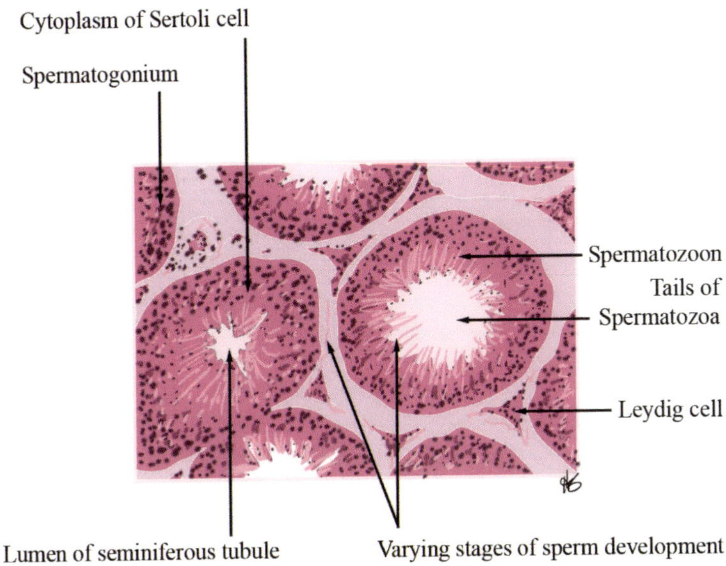

Figure 121. Spermatogonium

The term *spermatogenesis* springs from the Greek prefix *spermato-* for sperm, seed or germ ; *genesis* = the creation of something. Thus, **spermatogenesis** means—literally—the creation of sperm cells. Each spermatogonium that starts the process of spermatogenesis in the seminiferous tubules (Figure 122) eventually develops into four functioning sperm cells. This stands out in stark contrast to the female, who undergoes **oogenesis**, a process that produces only a single egg cell from a maturing **follicle**.

Spermatogenesis, or the making of many sperm, begins with **mitosis**. The important point to remember here is that mitosis is simply the duplication of a cell and all of its parts. In other words, mitosis is responsible for cre-

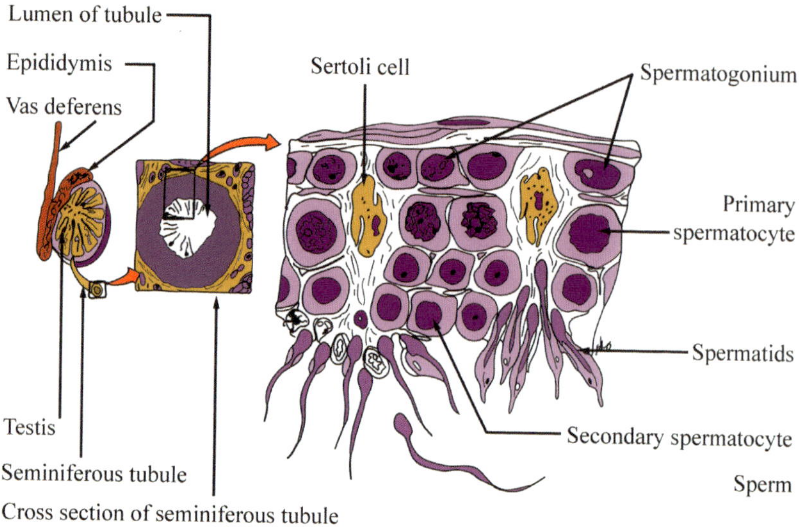

Figure 122. Spermatogenesis

ating new cells that will replace dead or wounded cells. There is no need for **genetic** differences between these cells. In mitosis, **DNA** is duplicated and two new cells are made, each with identical pieces and the exact same genetic code. Two identical copies come from the one original cell sort of like two photocopies from the original document.

Notice that we keep using the word identical here. This is an important concept because the key to mitosis is that identical cells are made. These identical cells are called **daughter cells**. Each of these daughter cells contains 23 pairs of **chromosomes** for a grand total of 46 chromosomes. Forty-six chromosomes are known as the **diploid number** (*diploos* from the Greek word meaning "twofold").

Although mitosis occurs in almost all cells, an additional process, called **meiosis** (which does not occur in all cells) must also take place in order for a human being to be formed. The word *meiosis* comes from the Greek *meioun*, meaning "to make smaller." The end result of meiosis is a reduction in the chromosome number from 46 (remember the ones that came from mitosis?) down to 23 chromosomes. The process of meiosis takes place only in the creation of sperm (spermatozoa) and eggs (**oocytes**), both of which are called gametes. Since both the sperm and the egg (gametes) are responsible for contributing to the specific traits an individual has (like having your dad's nose or your mother's eyes), the chromosomes must be "mixed up." The only way to achieve this mixing of the chromosomes is through the process of meiosis where some of the 46 chromosomes necessary to make a human being come from the mother and some from the father. It is in meiosis that some of the traits of the father cross over with those of the mother. If cross-over does not occur in meiosis, the new gametes will be identical to the original parent cell in every way. In other words, it is through the process of meiosis that people have a variety of traits and are therefore uniquely individual. Yes, we may resemble our parents, but we don't look exactly like them in every way. Thanks to meiosis, we have variations that make us truly one of a kind.

Clinical Correlate

Trisomy 21, also known as ***Mongoloidism*** *or* ***Down syndrome****, is an example of a failure in the genetic division that occurs between gametes. An extra 21st chromosome frequently results in persons with mild to moderate mental and physical impairments. Those affected often have special educational and social needs.*

It is through the process of meiosis that a sperm or egg ends up containing 23 chromosomes (not 23 pairs of chromosomes) so that when combined (during **fertilization**) they form the necessary 46 chromosomes (23 chromosomes from the mom and 23 chromosomes from the dad) for the creation of a human being. These 23 chromosomes in each gamete are known as the **haploid number**. Haploid comes from the Greek word *haplos* = single or simple, and hence this number is not a pair.

Test Your Knowledge

1. How many testes does the male have?

    ____

2. Which muscle helps elevate or drop the scrotum?

    ____

3. What is spermatogenesis?

____

____

____

4. What differentiates mitosis from meiosis?

____

____

____

Spermatogenesis

Returning to spermatogenesis, after a man has reached sexual maturity it takes about nine weeks for a sperm to physically mature. Sperm develop in the testicles and evolve into tadpole-like forms. They have a head and a tail and like tadpoles, they will swim eventually. Millions of sperm are produced in the two testicles (testes) of a male, specifically within the system of tubes called the seminiferous tubules (from the Latin *semen* = seed ; *ferre* = to bear). The testes are located in the scrotum. This bag of skin helps to regulate the temperature of the testicles, which need to be kept cooler than body temperature to produce normal sperm (Figure 123).

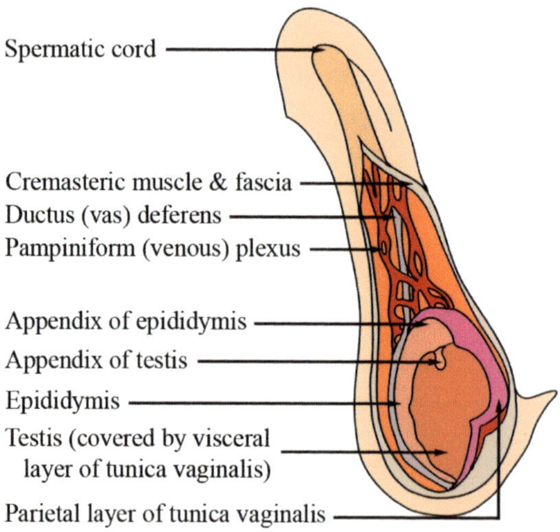

Figure 123. Testes and associated structures

The testes also produce hormones, the most important of which is testosterone, which is needed for the production of sperm. The sperm use fluid waves since they are not yet able to travel from the seminiferous tubules into the **epididymis** (*epi* = above ; *didymos* = testis), where they complete their development. (The epididymis is a set of coiled tubes where sperm are stored and mature. It is located on top of the testicles.) Passage of the sperm cells through the epididymus takes about two weeks. During that time, sperm continue their physical maturation and are stored there. Leaving the epididymus, the sperm cells next enter the **vas deferens** (Figure 124). This is a muscular tube that passes upward alongside the testicles and transports the sperm from the epididymis into the pelvic cavity and funnels it through the **prostate gland** (Figure 125). The vas deferens (*vas* = vessel ; *deferens* = duct), also known as the **sperm duct**, is approximately 2 feet long. From the vas deferens the sperm continue down the **spermatic cord** and **ejaculatory duct**.

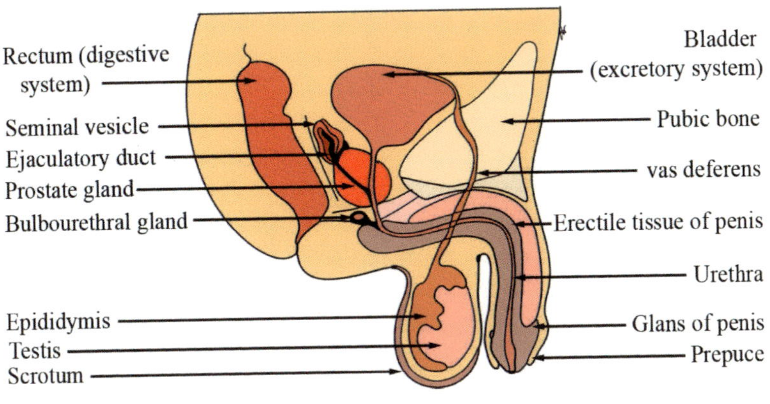

Figure 124. Vas deferens and other associated structures

Both the **seminal vesicles** (located behind the bladder and above the prostate gland) and prostate gland produce a whitish fluid called **seminal fluid**, which mixes with sperm to form **semen** when a man is sexually stimulated. About 60% of this fluid comes from the seminal vesicles, 30% from the prostate gland, and the remaining 10% from the **sustentacular cells**, epididymis, and **bulbourethral glands**. The semen has several functions

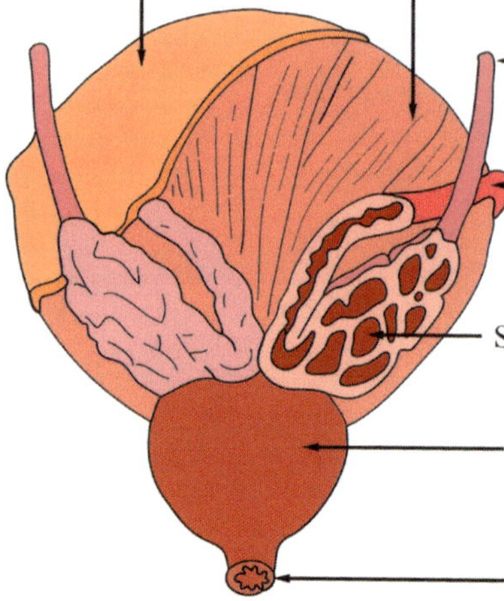

Figure 125. Prostate gland and neighboring structures

including the nourishment of the sperm and neutralizing affects on the acidity of the urethra and **vagina**.

In a normal semen analysis, just one milliliter of semen contains 20 million or more sperm. During intercourse, sperm flow out of the epididymis, through the vas deferens and urethra, and are placed into the vagina where their final maturation occurs. Final maturation involves the sperm cells gaining **motility**, or the ability to move, and **capacitation**, the ability to fertilize an egg once they reach the female genital tract. The sperm must then travel through the **cervix** and **uterus** to reach the **fallopian tubes** and fertilize the egg. Only a fraction of sperm deposited into the vagina will reach the egg in one of the tubes.

Clinical Correlate

*Permanent **sterilization** of the male provides excellent long-term **contraception** to couples no longer desiring pregnancy. The **vasectomy**, a surgical procedure, frequently done on an outpatient basis, involves cutting and tying off the left and right spermatic cords. It has relatively few complications and has become a popular means of male sterilization.*

Some people are afraid that because sperm travel through the urethra (which is the same tube that urine travels through) the **ejaculate** will contain urine. This is not true. "Shut-off" valves that are part of the bladder close off during ejaculation and prevent the expulsion of urine into the ejaculate. Additionally, as the sperm makes its way out of the **penis**, the fluids that are added as part of the overall semen contain certain elements that assist the sperm by neutralizing the acidity of the urethra in the male as well as the female (once deposited into the vagina). Schematically, the passage of the sperm from the beginning of its creation to its ejaculation is the following:

Seminiferous Tubules
↓
Epididymus
↓
Vas deferens
↓
Prostatic Urethra
↓
Out

- Seminiferous Tubules → Epididymus: Both located in the testes
- Epididymus → Vas deferens: Seminal vesicles (about 60% of the fluid is added here)
- Vas deferens → Prostatic Urethra → Out: Prostate adds about 20% to 30% of the fluid here; Bulbourethral glands add about 5% to 10% of the fluids here

Purpose of the Penis

Overall, the penis serves two purposes: urologic (for the passage of urine) and reproductive (for the passage of sperm). The penis contains three masses of spongy erectile tissue with spaces capable of filling and expanding with the pressure of blood (Figure 126). In order for a man to get an **erection**, the penis must fill with blood. This is caused by hormones, blood vessels, nerves, and muscles all working together. In the presence of sexual stimulation (e.g., touching, dreaming, pictures, hearing) an arousal may be triggered. These signals cause the muscles within the penis to relax, allowing blood to flow into the spongy tissue within the penis. When the blood collects within the vessels of the penis it becomes larger and firmer. The veins shut off to keep blood from flowing out and an erection occurs. After **orgasm** has occurred, or after the sexual arousal has passed, the veins reopen and blood flows back into the body and the erection subsides.

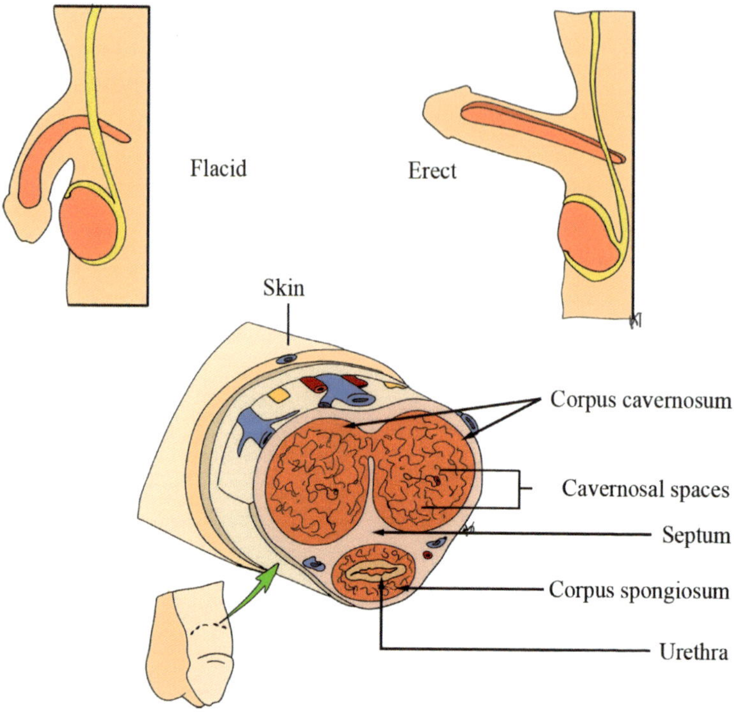

Figure 126. Cross section of penis

Common Conditions and Diseases of the Male Reproductive System

Epididymitis is a swelling and inflammation of the epididymis, the tube that connects the testicle with the vas deferens (Figure 127). The majority of men that develop epididymitis do so because of a **bacterial infection**. Although males of any age can develop epididymitis, it occurs most frequently between the ages of 20 and 39. When children get it, it is usually due to inflammation caused by **trauma** (e.g., sexual abuse) or bacterial infections.

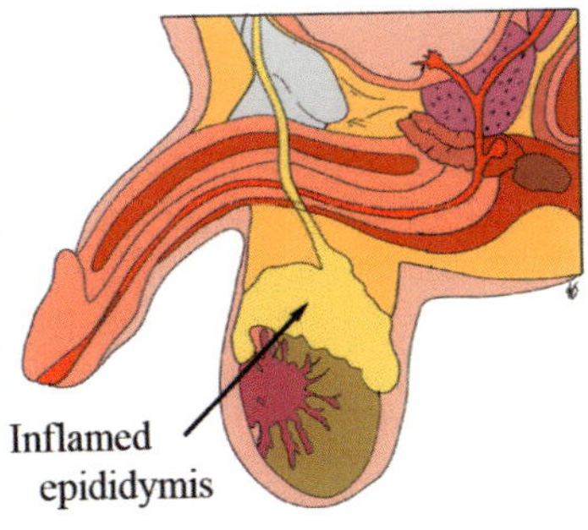

Figure 127. Epididymitis

Epididymitis may begin with a low-grade fever, chills, and a heavy sensation in the testicle. The testicle becomes increasingly sensitive to pressure.

The exact causes of **prostate cancer** are unknown. However, there are a number of contributing factors. These include

- Testosterone: Does not cause prostate cancer but is known to feed its growth;
- Age: Men over age 50 are at risk for prostate cancer, and risk increases with age;
- **Heredity**: If a man's father or an older sibling has had prostate cancer, he is at increased risk. Also, African American men are at increased risk;
- **Genetics**: Genetic flaws are responsible for many cancers and may keep some men from developing a certain enzyme. This enzyme could mount a defense against cells vulnerable to cancer-causing agents in the environment; and
- Diet: Diets associated with lots of animal fats are thought to be more conducive to a man's risk for developing prostate cancer. Diets rich in fruits and vegetables (especially tomato-based products) may decrease the risk.

Chlamydial urethritis is a sexually transmitted disease that involves infection of the urethra (the tube that drains urine from the bladder). It is caused by the bacteria **chlamydia trachomatis**. Chlamydia and **gonorrhea** often occur together. People who are sexually active and those with multiple sexual partners are at highest risk for chlamydia infection. The symptoms can appear similar to those of infection with gonorrhea, but continue even after treatment for gonorrhea has stopped. While the symptoms of chlamydial urethritis vary, they include

- Difficult, painful, or burning sensation during urination;
- Discharge from the penis;
- Redness, swelling, and itching of the opening of the urethra at the tip of the penis; and
- Swelling and tenderness of the testicles.

This concludes a brief overview of the male reproductive system.

Female Reproductive System

Both the anatomy and role of the female reproductive system differ considerably from that of the male. Although both male and female reproductive systems produce gametes (or reproductive cells), they are different in nature in that they have different roles. The female gamete (**ova** or egg) consists of a round cell that is about 0.1 mm in diameter and contains a nucleus. Eggs are haploid; that is, they have half the number of chromosomes as other cells in the body and as such, these female gametes or ova provide only 50% of the necessary genetic material to produce a baby. The male gametes (reproductive cell or sperm) are also haploid. They, too, only contain 50% of the chromosomes necessary to become a baby. During fertilization, the nucleus of an egg cell fuses with the nucleus of a sperm cell to form a new diploid (*di* = two; having two sets of chromosomes) organism or **zygote** (a fertilized egg). The female, however, must also provide a safe and nurturing place where the **embryo/fetus** can develop during the nine months of a typical human **pregnancy**. Let's begin with a discussion of the female reproductive anatomy.

Ovaries

The ovaries are the primary reproductive organs, producing both eggs and hormones. These paired structures are located in the **pelvis**, just to the left and right of the **uterus** (Figure 128). They are suspended between the uterus and pelvic sidewall by folds of peritoneum (*per* = around ; *teinein* = to stretch). A microscopic view of the **ovary** will reveal a collection of sac-like structures called follicles that contain primary oocytes (immature eggs). For the sake of clarity, picture a wasp nest where you can see many small compartments. Each compartment would be similar to a follicle. If you've ever watched the hatching of wasps, you know that they don't all hatch at the same time. The hatching or rupture of eggs from the follicle in a human female is similar in concept. That is, of all the follicles that contain eggs, only a few are chemically selected to be released at **ovulation**. In most instances, only one follicle will end up being "the chosen one" that ruptures and releases an egg into the pelvic cavity. If two follicles rupture, the result could be twins, although this is not the only way in which twins can occur. After the follicle ruptures and the egg is released, the remaining tissue and cells left behind on the surface of the ovary is called the **corpus luteum** (*corpus* = body ; *lutea* = yellow). These cells are yellow in color and produce the hormone called **progesterone**. This essential hormone-producing collection of cells is necessary for maintenance of an early pregnancy. This will be discussed in greater detail later in this chapter.

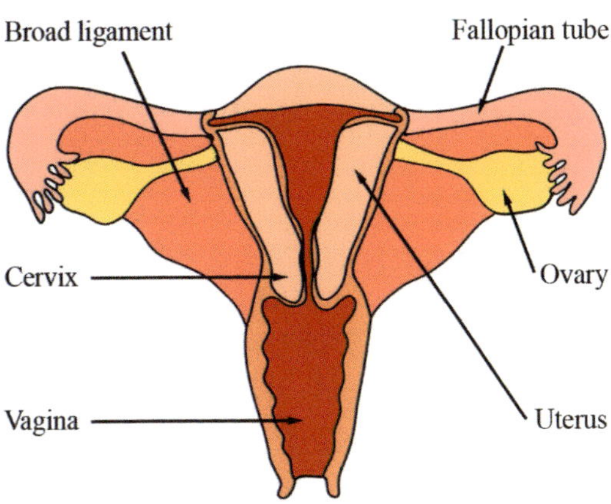

Figure 128. Ovaries and neighboring structures

Uterine or Fallopian Tubes

Far from being simple pipes through which sperm can swim to reach the egg, the fallopian tubes are nourishing, muscular conduits, whose distal (outward) ends form finger-like projections called **fimbria**. The fimbria aid in the capture of the egg that has been released by the nearby ovary. It is within the fallopian tubes that fertilization (the union of the egg and the sperm) occurs (Figure 129). Both the rhythmic movements of the tubal walls (caused by various hormones in the body and most active at the time of ovulation) and the beating of the **cilia** or hair-like structures within the fallopian tubes slowly move the egg toward the uterus. Each of these tubes is about 10 cm (approximately 4 inches) long. The fertilized egg can spend up to three days in the tube before reaching the inside of the uterus. Certain sexually transmitted diseases (specifically, gonorrhea and chlamydia) are notorious for causing tubal scarring and eventual blockage of these delicate structures, resulting in infertility.

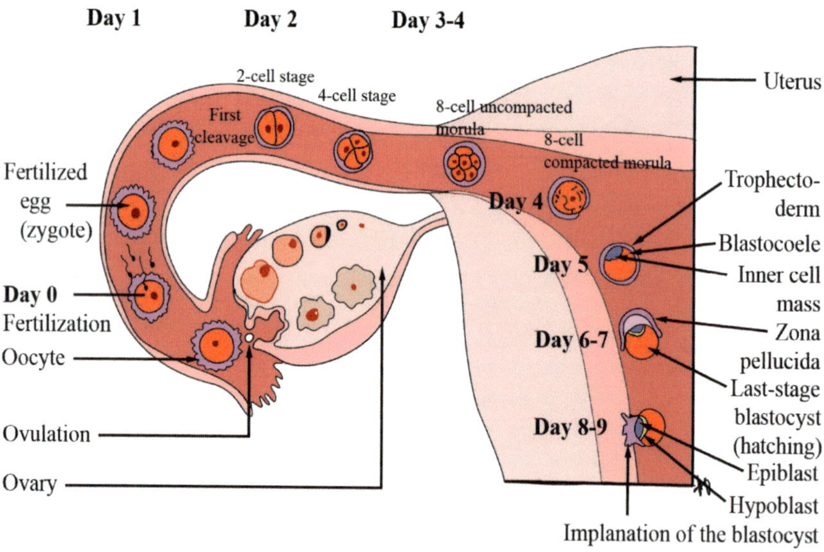

Figure 129. Fallopian tubes and passage of embryo

Uterus

Nestled in the pelvis between the bladder and the rectum, the uterus is a pear-shaped organ about the size of a child's fist. It is hollow and functions as a receptacle to receive, protect, and nourish the fertilized egg.

Suspended in the pelvis by **uterosacral ligaments** (*utero* = uterus ; *sacral* = lower back), its walls consist primarily of involuntary smooth muscle. It is an organ capable of significant increases in size to accommodate a growing fetus.

Figure 130 illustrates the uterus, which is somewhat arbitrarily divided into the **body**, **fundus**, and **cervix**. The cervical portion extends into the vagina and serves as an outlet through which the fetus passes at the time of delivery. There are basically two layers in the uterus: the **endometrium** and the **myometrium**. The innermost layer of the uterus is the endometrium (*endo* = in or within ; *metri* = uterus or womb ; *um* = structure, tissue, or thing). It is the superficial endometrial tissue that is shed every month during a woman's period or **menstrual cycle**. It is this rich vascular layer into which the embryo embeds itself in early pregnancy.

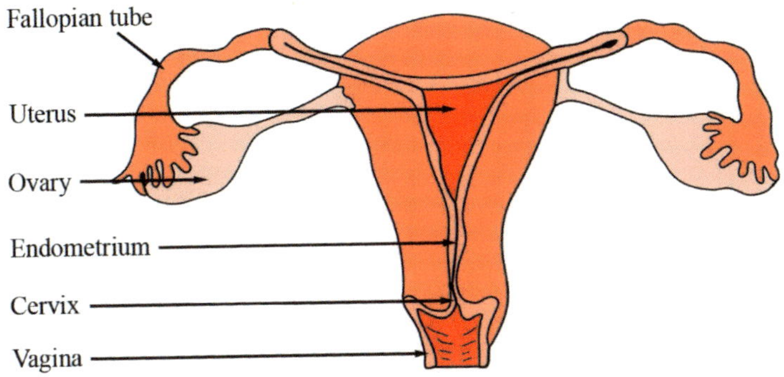

Figure 130. Components of the uterus

The other layer of the uterus is the myometrium (*myo* = muscle ; *metri* = uterus). This is the muscular layer of the uterus that plays a vital role in the process of delivery by producing the repetitive contractions known as **labor**.

Vagina

The vagina extends from the uterus to the exterior of the body (Figure 131). It is a tubular structure 8 to10 cm in length (3 to 4 inches), which provides a passageway for menstrual blood during a woman's monthly period. It is also the organ that receives semen from the male at the time of **intercourse**, and it serves as the birth canal through which the fetus passes at the time of delivery.

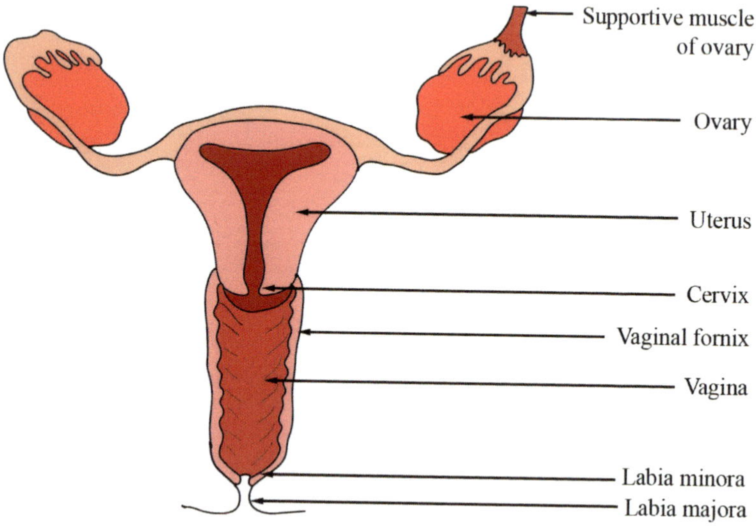

Figure 131. Vagina relative to other pelvic structures

External Genitalia

The external female **genitalia**, also known as the **vulva**, lie at the opening of the vagina. These outer reproductive structures include the vaginal opening, as well as the **labia majora** and **labia minora**, **clitoris**, and the **greater vestibular glands** (Figure 132).

Oogenesis, the Ovarian Cycle, and Reproductive Hormones

Unlike the male, who begins producing gametes (sperm) at puberty and then usually continues for the rest of his life, the female takes the first steps of **oogenesis** (egg production) while still an embryo in her own mother's body (Figure 133). As she develops as an embryo, stem cells

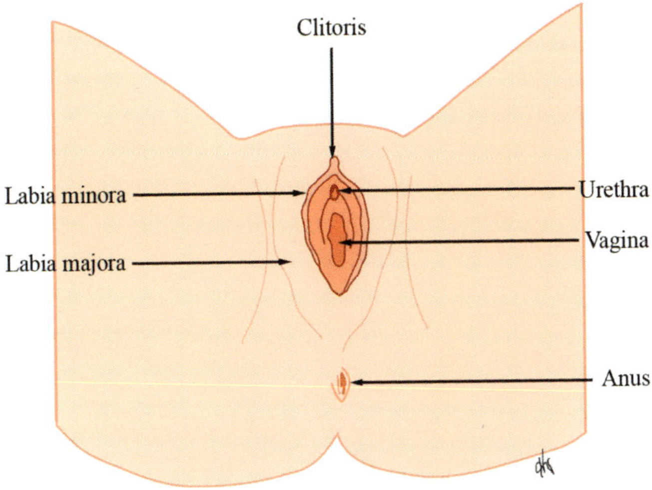

Figure 132. Female external genitalia

destined to produce female gametes (eggs) begin to multiply in number within the ovaries. These oocytes (immature egg cells) are found in the follicles (spherical structures or sacs compared earlier to microscopically small wasp nest compartments) that develop in the ovary with the release of **FSH (follicle stimulating hormone)**. This hormone is released by the pituitary gland to stimulate the ovary to yield an egg-containing follicle.

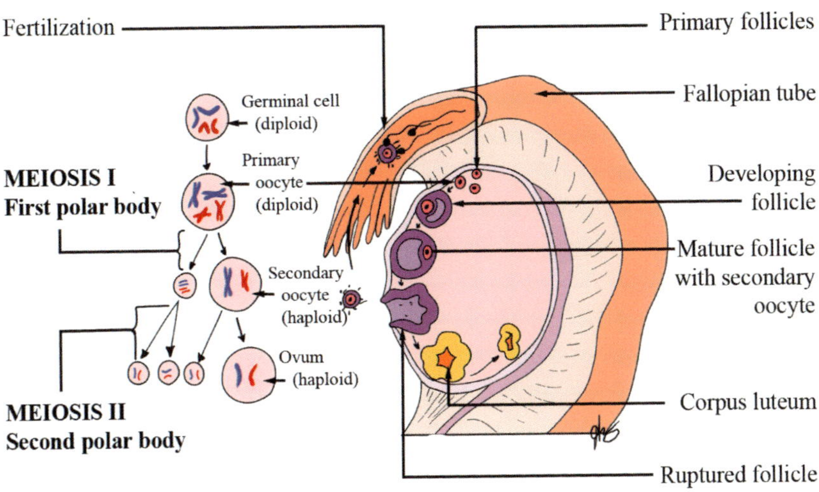

Figure 133. Process of oogenesis

By the time a woman is born, her ovaries contain all the potential eggs she will need during her reproductive lifetime, approximately two million. Further development of the eggs is suspended until puberty, which typically occurs at about the age of 12. It is at this time that the **anterior pituitary**, for reasons no doubt related to the hypothalamic production of gonadtropic hormones, begins to produce and release FSH. This hormone recruits a small number of follicles to begin maturing. Usually only one will have the necessary **microchemical** environment to become the dominant follicle and continue to grow, while the others that may have also been stimulated cease growing. Fewer than 400 to 500 ova will be released in a woman's reproductive lifetime.

As the chosen follicle continues to grow and the fluid around the oocyte increases, it can be seen on **ultrasound** if a **vaginal probe** is used. Prior to rupture of the egg from the follicle, a number of important things must occur. The primary oocyte must replicate (make a copy of) its chromosomes and begin meiosis.

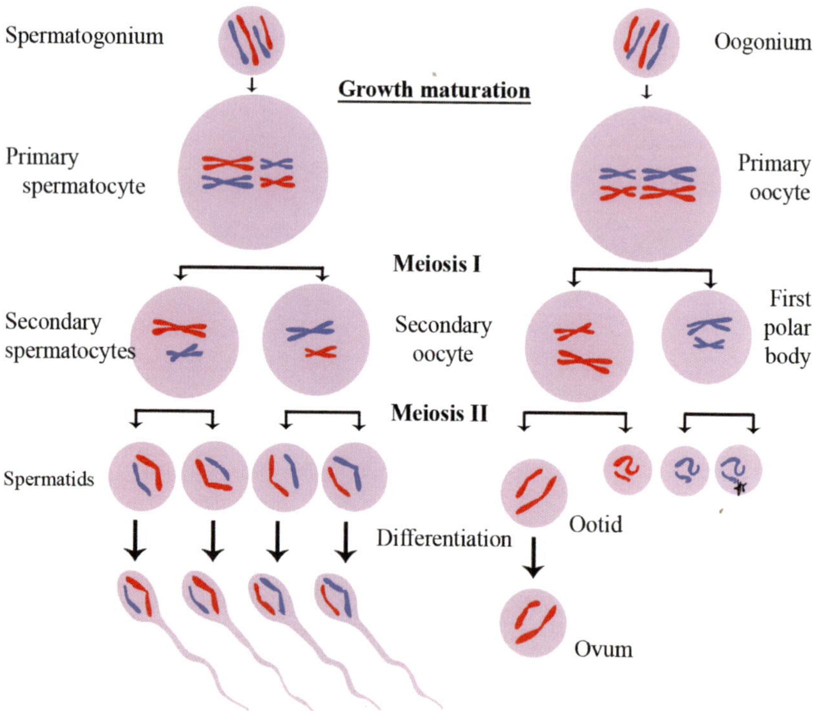

Figure 134. Process of meiosis

To review our discussion of meiosis, remember that the genetic code of a human being is contained within 46 chromosomes (Figure 134). Only half of this number (23) should be present within the cell of a sperm or egg to prepare each for the proper union with the other. The process by which the sperm or egg contain only half of the genetic code necessary to form a complete human being is called meiosis.

By undergoing the process of meiosis in which the number of chromosomes is reduced to 23 total chromosomes in the egg and the same in the sperm, the resulting union between the sperm and the egg can equal 46 chromosomes, the number required for a human being. In other words, the father and the mother each contribute half of the necessary chromosomes to make the baby. Contribution of chromosomes by both parents explains why most children have the looks and characteristics of each parent.

During ovulation the primary oocyte undergoes meiosis and results in formation of two cells that differ from each other in the amount of **cytoplasm** each has. The reason the cytoplasm is unequally divided is to conserve nutrients for the **viability** of the **secondary oocyte** (the cell that holds the bulk of the cytoplasm) and its potential union with the sperm. The other product of the mieosis division contains just a little cytoplasm and is called the **polar body**. While the polar body contains the necessary chromosomes for a union with the sperm, it does not have the necessary nutrients to be viable. Because of this, the polar body is destined to disintegrate. The actual release of the egg through rupture of this fluid-filled follicle requires the timed release of another hormone, **LH (luteinizing hormone**), from the anterior pituitary. The detection of this hormone forms the basis of the currently available ovulation predictor kits now found in drug stores. LH is responsible for producing a change in the follicular cells left behind in the ovary after ovulation. This structure is the corpus luteum. As previously mentioned, the term corpus luteum means "yellow body." If a pregnancy occurs, the corpus luteum provides essential hormones to support the fertilized egg until the **placenta**, another hormone-producing organ, can take over.

If the secondary oocyte is fertilized by a penetrating sperm, the second meiotic division occurs with a resulting ovum, and another polar body is passed off (refer back to Figure 134). The oocyte, like the sperm, has only half the number of chromosomes (the haploid number, 23), but after fertilization has occurred, the diploid number (46) is achieved. The resulting **conceptus** has its full compliment of chromosomes. While all these changes are occurring in the ovary, the lining of the uterus (the endometrium) is going through cyclic alterations brought about by the same hormones that have caused the egg to be released.

The Menstrual Cycle

The female menstrual cycle reflects the hormonal changes initiated by the anterior pituitary and expressed in ovarian hormone production. In general, the entire female menstrual cycle is approximately 28 days long, from the start of one cycle to the start of another, and can be divided into three stages (Figure 135).

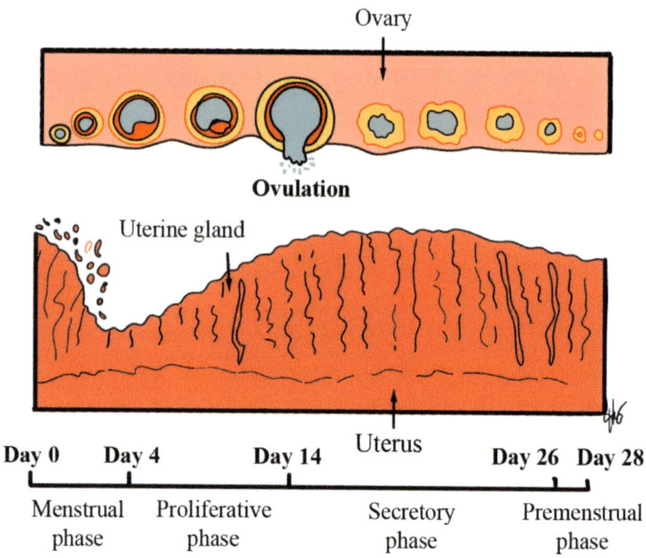

Figure 135. Endometrial changes associated with ovulation

The Menstrual Stage

First is the **menstrual stage**, which is characterized by bleeding from the inside of the uterus as the superficial layer of the endometrial lining is detaching from the inner uterine wall. Bleeding of 3 to 7 days duration is common with 80–100cc (around 6 tablespoons) of blood loss per cycle each month.

The Proliferative Stage

This phase is called the **proliferative stage** because it is during this phase that the lining of the uterus (endometrium) thickens in order to be able to support the fertilized ova should a pregnancy occur. The proliferative stage is produced by the increasing **estrogen** levels associated with the several follicles that are growing in the ovary. As mentioned previously, only one of these follicles is typically "chosen" to ovulate and release an egg. The estrogen produced causes **regeneration** of the layer just shed during **menses** and replenishes the glands and blood supply necessary if an embryo were to arrive. The proliferative phase is quite variable in its length ranging from 7 to 21 days.

The Secretory Stage

The last stage of the menstrual cyclic is the most predictable in length, lasting 14 days. This the **secretory phase**. The relatively high level of progesterone being produced by the corpus luteum is preparing the endometrium for the arrival of a potential conceptus (fertilized egg). Glands in the endometrium are secreting nutrients into the surrounding tissues. If fertilization fails to occur, the corpus luteum (the leftover progesterone-producing cells in the ovary that are the result of the egg being released) begins to degenerate, triggering a falling progesterone level that results once again in sloughing of the superficial endometrial layer and the start of another period.

Pregnancy

If conception does occur, the creation of a new individual begins. In order for fertilization to occur, the sperm must reach the oocyte. This implies that a satisfactory number of sperm have been deposited in the vagina at the time of intercourse and that the fallopian tubes are open and functioning.

Once ovulation has occurred and the egg has been released from the follicle, it will only be viable for about 12 to 24 hours. During this window of opportunity, the sperm must reach it, penetrate the outer layers of the egg, and successfully fertilize it if a pregnancy is to occur. While only one sperm is usually able to penetrate the egg's membrane, many sperm are actually required to be present to assist in the "clearing of an opening" through the egg's surrounding cellular layers. Of the millions of sperm deposited in the vagina, only a few hundred to a few thousand actually reach the area near the egg. Fertilization is complete when the sperm has passed through the egg's outer membrane and has released its genetic material that then combines with that of the egg's to produce a zygote with its full complement of DNA (i.e., 46 chromosomes).

Fertilization, Implantation, and the Embryonic Stage

Fertilization of the egg usually occurs in the fallopian tube, where the conceptus spends about three days making its way to the uterine interior, and here it floats about for another three days before burrowing into the rich endometrium (Figure 136). As it **implants**, it begins to produce a hormone called **human chorionic gonadotropin (HCG)**, which serves as a signal to the corpus luteum that a pregnancy is present and that the corpus luteum needs to continue to make progesterone to support the pregnancy until the placenta can take over. HCG detection serves as the basis of all currently available pregnancy tests. The fertilized ovum is now known as an **embryo**.

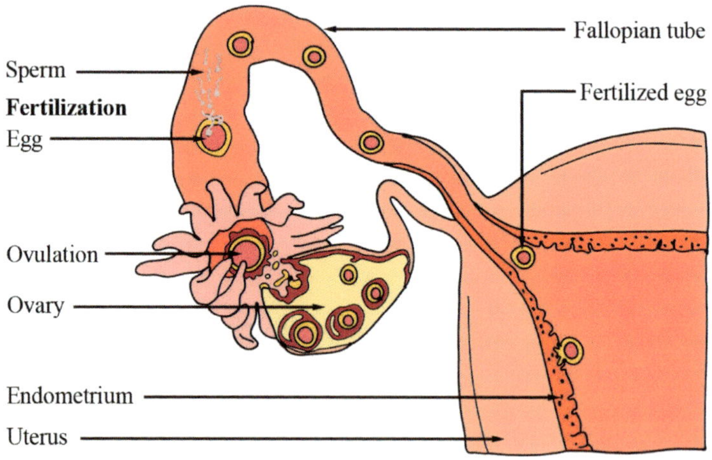

Figure 136. Fertilization

Complex changes at the implantation site produce **trophoblastic tissue**. Trophoblastic tissue cells are the cells of the conceptus that become the placenta and attach the baby to the mother's uterus. These cells provide a fluid-filled protective pouch around the baby in the uterus. They also serve to nourish the baby carrying nutrients from the mother's blood to the baby's blood. These are the cells that are **biopsied** during a **chorionic villus sampling (CVS)** to determine if the baby is genetically normal.

Fetal Stage

The embryonic stage of the pregnancy ends at the ninth week and the fetal stage begins; the embryo is now called the **fetus**. At this point the enlarging placenta (Figure 137) provides nutrients to the fetus and removes wastes products (Figure 138), but it also becomes an endocrine organ by producing estrogen, progesterone, and other vital hormones necessary for the continuing pregnancy.

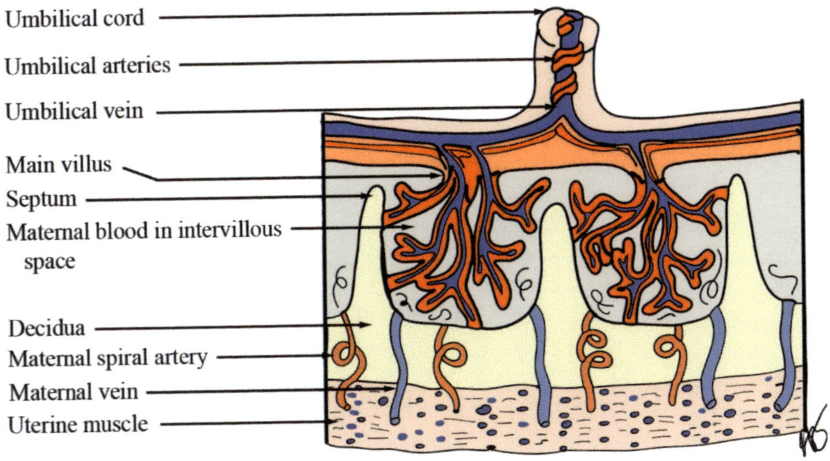

Figure 137. Anatomy of the placenta

Once the fetal stage is reached, the fetus's major organs have been formed and the remaining time is spent growing and completing organ maturation. The mother's body undergoes a number of important and striking adaptations as pregnancy proceeds. As the uterus enlarges, the woman's center of gravity is altered, producing a waddling gait and an increasing **spinal**

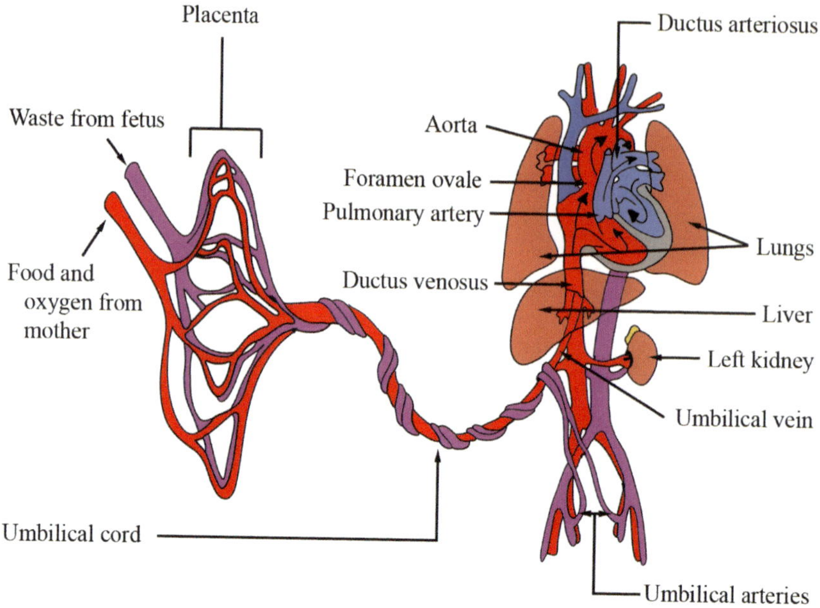

Figure 138. Fetal circulation

lordosis (swayback condition). Among the more important changes are a significant increase in blood volume, elevated pulse rate, shortness of breath, increased urine production, and GI symptoms such as constipation and heartburn.

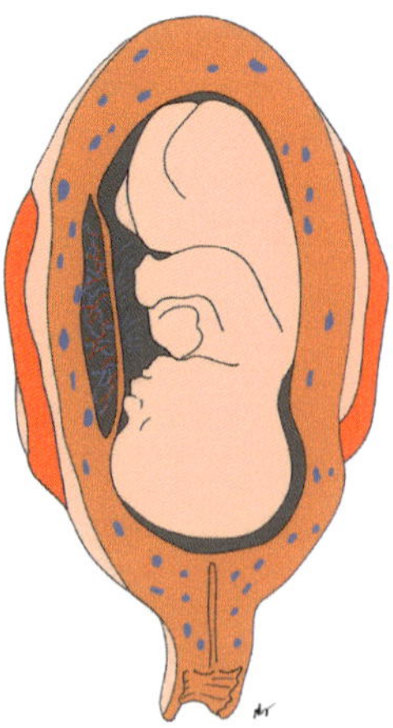

Figure 139. Second trimester fetus

Clinically, pregnancy is divided into three **trimesters**. Though somewhat arbitrary, the first 12 weeks are considered the first trimester; weeks 13 through 27 describe the second trimester (Figure 139); and weeks 28 to 40 make up the third or final trimester. Although 40 weeks is considered full term, a **term pregnancy** is, in fact, any one that reaches 37 to 42 weeks (Figure 140). Thus, any deliveries before 37 weeks are considered **preterm**. **Parturition** or childbirth is the culmination of the nine-month pregnancy. The actual cause of the onset of labor is still poorly understood. It is believed that rising estrogen levels in late pregnancy produce an increase in **oxytocin** (a hormone that produces contractions) receptors in the myometrium (the muscle of the uterine wall).

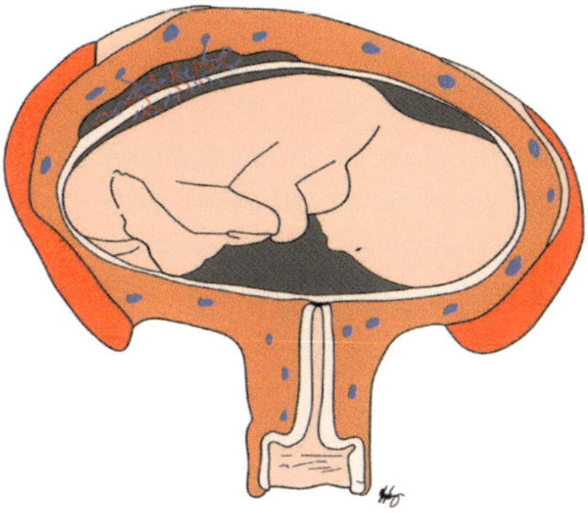

Figure 140. Full term pregnancy

The Process of Labor

The process of labor includes three stages. The **dilation** stage is described as beginning with true painful contractions and ending when the cervix is completely dilated (widened to approximately 10 centimeters, almost 4 inches). The second stage is the **expulsion**, when maternal pushing efforts begin and the fetus passes through the cervix and vagina to the outside. The third and last stage is the **placental** stage, when the placenta (afterbirth) is expelled from the body.

> **Clinical Correlate**
> *Infertility: About 15% of couples will have trouble conceiving. The male is probably the most common culprit with an abnormal semen analysis. In the female, ovulation problems and tubal factors are the leading causes of infertility. Fortunately, ovulation induction medications have been developed, and blocked tubes can be overcome through* ***in vitro fertilization****.*

Menopause

Menopause, the cessation of menses (or a woman's periods) due to falling estrogen levels, is brought on by the slow conclusion of ovulatory function. It appears to a large extent that the onset of menopause is determined genetically, since a woman goes through menopause at about the same age that her mother did. The falling estrogen levels are frequently associated with hot flashes, vaginal dryness, increased risk of **osteoporosis** (weakening of the bones), and the end of reproductive life.

Clinical Correlate

Menopause signals the cessation of reproductive life. The ovary fails, being unable to respond to progressively higher FSH demands from the hypothalamus and the pituitary. The average age of menopause in this country is 50 to 51. It is frequently characterized by hot flashes and vaginal dryness. The presence of menopause puts the woman at increased risk of developing osteoporosis, a weakening of the bones. This is felt to be caused by the inadequate estrogen production.

Common Conditions and Diseases of the Female Reproductive System

An **ectopic pregnancy** occurs when the conceptus is located somewhere other than the uterine cavity (usually the fallopian tubes). Classic presentation is a young female with a positive pregnancy test, pain, and/or bleeding and an empty uterus on ultrasound. It can be treated occasionally with **methyltrexate** but frequently requires surgery. Risk factors include a history of sexually transmitted diseases, particularly chlamydia and gonorrhea, a history of previous tubal surgery, and a history of previous ectopic pregnancy.

There is a strong link between certain types of **human papilloma virus (HPV)** and **cervical cancer.** In fact, for all practical purposes, cervical cancer is a sexually transmitted disease. Because of this association, a vaccine was developed to prevent HPV and reduce the incidence of cervical cancer.

There are many other more-detailed explanations of the female reproductive system. Knowing the essentials of this system will help you become a better coder, medical assistant, or other allied health professional.

Male Reproductive System Glossary

<u>androgen</u> male hormone producing or stimulating male characteristics testosterone

<u>bulbourethral gland</u> (also known as Cowper's glands) one of two glands below the prostate that secretes a fluid to lubricate the inside of the urethra

<u>capacitation</u> ability of a sperm to fertilize an egg once they reach the female genital tract

<u>chlamydia urethritis</u> common sexually transmitted disease that involves an infection of the urethra; commonly found with gonorrhea and other sexually transmitted diseases

<u>Cowper's glands</u> (also known as bulbourethral glands) pair of glands in the urogenital diaphragm that secretes an alkaline, mucus-containing fluid into the spongy urethra

<u>cremaster muscle</u> skeletal muscle that arises from the internal oblique muscle and elevates the testes

<u>diploid</u> 46 chromosomes; enough chromosomes to produce an individual

<u>epididymis</u> tightly coiled tube along the posterior border of each testis where the the sperm mature and are stored

<u>epididymitis</u> swelling and inflammation of the epididymus usually caused by bacterial infection

<u>gamete</u> in the male, the gamete is the sperm that contains half the required chromosomes to have a zygote (the start of a human being); in the female, the gamete is the egg

<u>haploid</u> half the required chromosomes (23) to produce an individual

<u>penis</u> male reproductive organ of mammals used to introduce sperm into the female reproductive tract to insure fertilization

<u>prostate gland</u> part of the male reproductive system that lies below the neck of the bladder and surrounds the superior portion of the urethra and secretes a slightly acid, enzyme-containing fluid into the prostatic urethra; about the size of a chestnut; consists of glandular and muscular tissue; produces a thin, milky, alkaline fluid

that is secreted into the urethra at the time of emission of semen, providing an added medium for the life and motility of sperm

semen — (also known as seminal fluid) combined secretions of the testes, seminal vesicles, prostate, and bulbourethral glands (Cowper's glands) discharged from the male urethra during orgasm

seminal fluid — (also known as semen) mixture of sperm and secretions of the seminal vesicles, prostate and Cowper's glands

seminal vesicles — pair of glands at the base of the urinary bladder that secrete an alkaline fluid rich in fructose into the ejaculatory duct

seminiferous tubules — located in the testes, the specific location of meiosis and subsequent creation of gametes, namely spermatozoa (sperm)

sexually transmitted disease — (also known as STD) infections generally acquired by sexual contact although some of these infections can also be transmitted non-sexually; organisms that cause sexually transmitted diseases may pass from person to person in blood, semen, vaginal and other bodily fluids or from mother to infant during pregnancy or childbirth, or through blood transfusions or shared needles

sperm (o), spermat (o) — sperm; refers to the male reproductive cells

spermatogenesis — formation of sperm cell

STD — (also known as sexually transmitted disease)

testicle — two oval shaped organs that make and store sperm and male sex hormones

testis — (also known as testicle) organ that produces sperm and the male hormones (androgens)

testosterone — primary male hormone produced by in the testes; responsible for secondary male sex characteristics

urethra — three regions: the prostatic portion surrounded by the prostate gland, the membranous in the urogenital diaphragm and the spongy (penile) which runs through the length of the penis; connects the urinary bladder to the genitals for the removal of fluids out of the body. travels through the penis and carries semen as well as urine in males varicocele — enlargement of veins of the spermatic cord; hernia of swollen, twisted veins above the testes

Vas deferens — (also known as ductus deferens) transports sperm through the inguinal canal into the pelvic cavity then loops over and down the back of the urinary bladder and empties into the prostatic urethra

vasectomy — surgical procedure for male sterilization and/or permanent birth control where the Vas deferens of a man is severed, and then tied and sealed to prevent sperm from entering into the seminal stream (ejaculate)

Female Reproductive System Glossary

endometrium — innermost layer of the uterus

follicle stimulating hormone — (also known as FSH) hormone released by the anterior pituitary that stimulates the ovary to produce a follicle containing an egg

fallopian tubes — two tubular, muscular conduits which "scoop up" the egg after it is released from the ovary and provide a location in which the sperm and egg can join

FSH — (also known as follicle stimulating hormone)

HCG — (also known as human chorionic gonadotropin)

human chorionic gonadotropin — (also known as HCG) glycoprotein hormone produced during pregnancy; made by the developing embryo after conception and later by the placenta

LH — (also known as luteinizing hormone)

luteinizing hormone — hormone produced by the anterior pituitary gland that triggers ovulation and development of the corpus luteum

menopause — cessation of menstruation that heralds the end of reproductive life

menstrual cycle — a complex series of hormonal changes that produces endometrial changes in the lining of the uterus to accept a conceptus if pregnancy occurs, and if not, results in a menstrual period

myometrium — smooth muscular portion of the uterine wall is responsible of contractions during labor

oogenesis	production of eggs
ovary/ies	two small almond sized structure which are the source of most female hormones and the source of eggs
oxytocin	hormone released by the posterior pituitary that plays a role in active labor through a production of contractions
PAP smear	(also known as Papanicolaou smear) examination of cervical and vaginal cells for early detection of cervical cancer
pelvic inflammatory disease	(also known as PID) infection and inflammation of the female reproductive organs that can scar the tubes that carry eggs from the ovary to the uterus leading to infertility, ectopic pregnancy, pelvic pain and other problems; the most common preventable cause of infertility; gonorrhea and chlamydia are the most common causes, but other bacteria can also cause PID
PID	(also known as pelvic inflammatory disease)
placenta	hormone producing organ that provides nutrients to the fetus during intrauterine life
polar body	structure produced during oogenesis which contains the necessary chromosomes for union with the sperm, but has inadequate nutrients to remain viable
proliferative stage	portion of the menstrual cycle immediately preceding ovulation where the lining of the endometrium gets thicker under the influence of estrogen
secretory stage	portion of the menstrual cycle immediately following ovulation under the primary influence of progesterone
uterus	pear-shaped structure located in the pelvis which is the source of a woman's menstrual periods and provides a location for the growth of a fetus
vagina	tubular structure about 3 to 4 inches in length which provides a passage way for the release of menstrual blood and receives semen at the time of intercourse
zygote	fertilized egg that contains 46 chromosomes (diploid)

Chapter 9
The Endocrine System

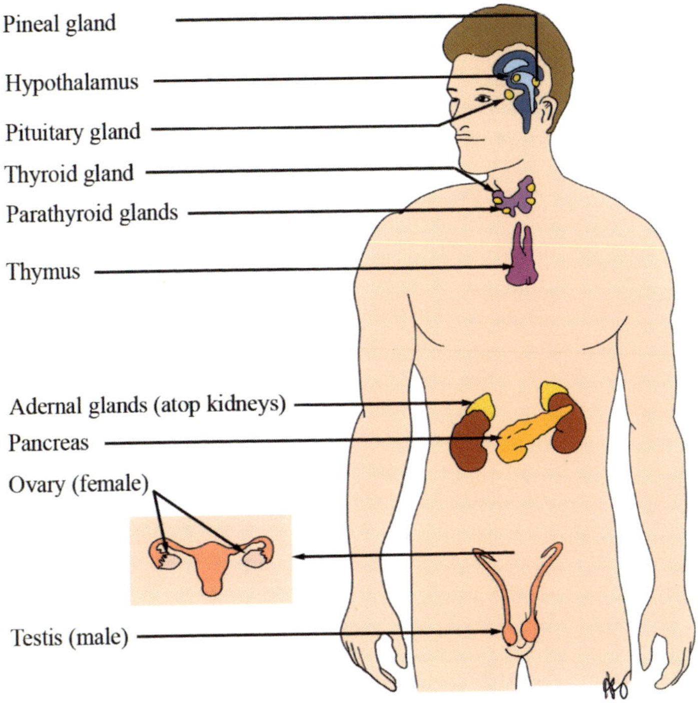

Figure 141. The endocrine system

To orchestrate the complex activities of the body, cells and tissues must communicate with one another. This is accomplished by two systems: the nervous system and the endocrine system. The nervous system sends highly specific messages to different locations, where fast but usually short-lived actions take place. Many of the body's requirements, however, need long-term management (for example, when a young girl is approaching puberty). Control of these slowly evolving processes is best managed by the endocrine system. This chapter will cover some anatomy but will focus primarily on the physiology of this complex system (Figure 141).

The Nature of Hormones

Hormones are chemical messengers released by one tissue and carried through the blood to some distant target tissue, where the hormones produce their effects. While the structure of hormones varies from one to another, the method of action does not. That is, all hormones bind to **receptors** on the target tissues to bring about their effects. Receptors are structures on the surfaces of cells, or within the **cytoplasm** of certain cells, that seem to bind with certain hormones, making that tissue hormone-responsive. For a distant tissue to respond to a particular hormone, that tissue must have receptors for that hormone (Figure 142).

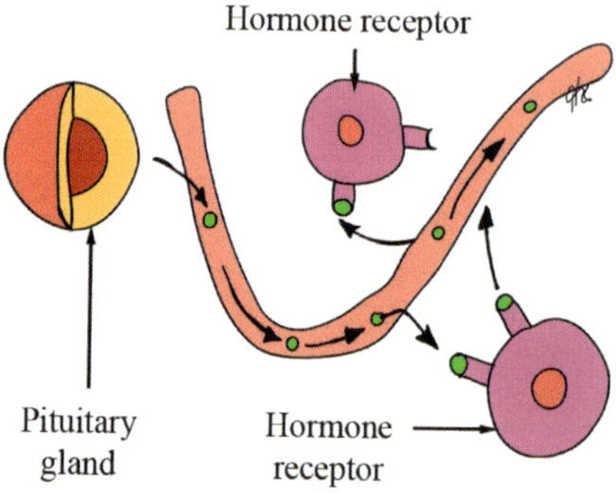

Figure 142. Example of hormone receptors

Picture a sophisticated thermostat for controlling the air in your home. Inside the thermostat there is a temperature sensor. When you decide that your home is too hot, for instance, you can go to the thermostat and lower the temperature. The thermostat kicks in to complete your orders and when it senses that the air has reached your required temperature, the cool air is shut off. In humans, receptors are like sensors on your thermostat. When your brain thinks that some action needs to take place, it gives the command for that action and hormones are released. Like the temperature change that continues to occur in your home until the requested reading is reached, hormones continue to be sent to the receptor until the desired goal is reached in the cell. It is then and only then that they are shut off.

Receptors for these target tissues are located in a variety of places and may be found on the outside or on the inside of the **cell's membrane**, the cytoplasm of the cell or in the nucleus of the cell. The location of the receptor depends on the cell type and the nature of the hormone itself. In some cases, hormones act like they are in a relay race and they may bind to a receptor that produces a "second messenger," which then finishes delivering the chemical signal (Figure 143). Adjustments of hormone levels are based on a negative feedback system that works much like the thermostat in your house.

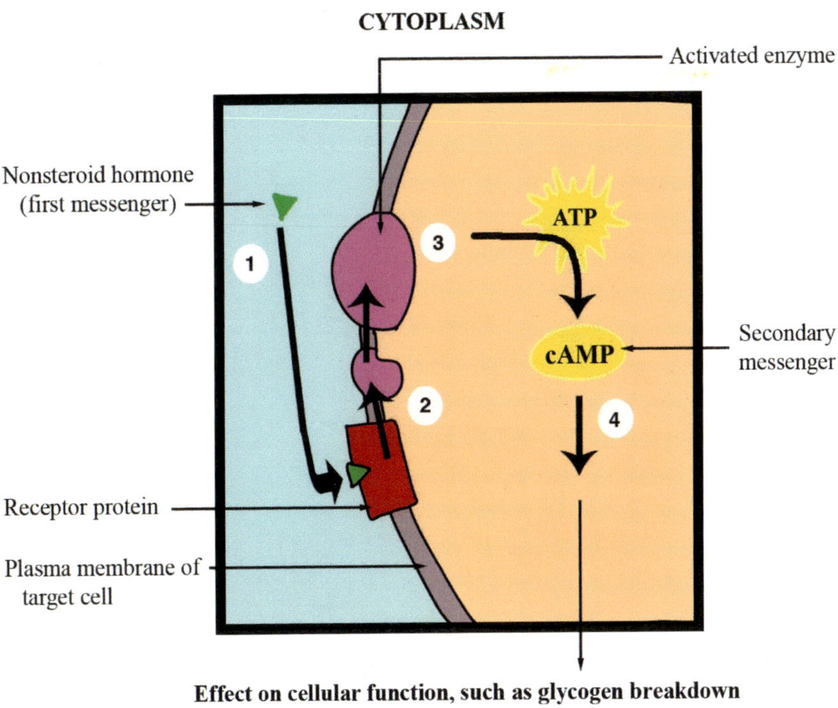

Figure 143. Receptors and second messengers

In humans, a negative feedback system is a self-regulating response to changes experienced by the body, frequently due to external influences. Like the goal of the thermostat, the objective of negative feedback is to restore the system to its previous undisturbed state, or minimize the effects of the initial change. This characteristic of negating the impact of changes defines the concept of negative feedback.

Test Your Knowledge

1. What are receptors?

   ____

   ____

2. Where are receptors found?

   ____

3. What is the objective of a negative feedback system in humans?

   ____

   ____

The Hypothalamus

The highest level of endocrine control through negative feedback is demonstrated by the hypothalamus and the pituitary gland (Figure 144). The hypothalamus is located at the base of the brain near the **optic nerves**. It is often referred to as the **master gland** because it secretes many hormones

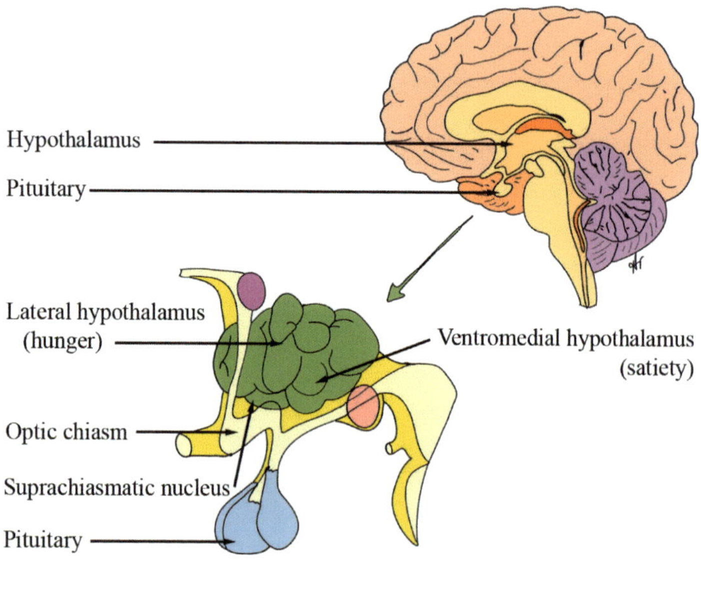

Figure 144. The hypothalamus

that control the actions of other glands. It "bridges the gap" between the central nervous system and the endocrine system by linking the two via the pituitary gland (also known as the **hypophysis** or "under" gland because it is located under the hypothalamus).

The primary function of the hypothalamus is to secrete certain **neurohormones** whose job it is to stimulate or inhibit the secretion of pituitary hormones. It also functions as a typical endocrine gland by secreting **antidiuretic hormone (ADH)**, which influences urine production, and **oxytocin**, which plays a role in milk let-down and labor. Additionally, the hypothalamus controls body temperature, hunger, thirst, fatigue, and **circadian cycles**.

Clinical Correlate

Because the hypothalamus is located at the base of the brain where the optic nerves are, a tumor of the hypothalamus or pituitary can often cause visual problems for a patient.

The Pituitary Gland

The pituitary gland consists of two lobes: the anterior and posterior. It hangs on a stalk beneath the hypothalamus. The pituitary gland secretes nine different hormones. Seven of these come from the anterior pituitary and two from the posterior pituitary. Fundamental differences can be found in the anatomy of these two lobes; most notably, the anterior pituitary is larger (Figure 145).

The anterior pituitary secretes a number of hormones that will be discussed a little later. These hormones include **thyroid stimulating hormone** or **TSH**, **adrenocorticotropic hormone** or **ATCH**, **follicle stimulating hormone** or **FSH**, **luteinizing hormone** or **LH**, **prolactin** or **PRL**, **growth hormone** or **GH**, and **melanocyte-stimulating hormone** or **MSH**. The posterior lobe produces only two hormones, **antidiuretic hormone** or **ADH**, and **oxytocin**. When the hypothalamus communicates with the anterior pituitary, it sends down releasing hormones, whereas when it "talks" to the posterior pituitary, it communicates in a different way, sending **action potentials** down **nerve axons** to the posterior pituitary to deliver its message (Figure 146).

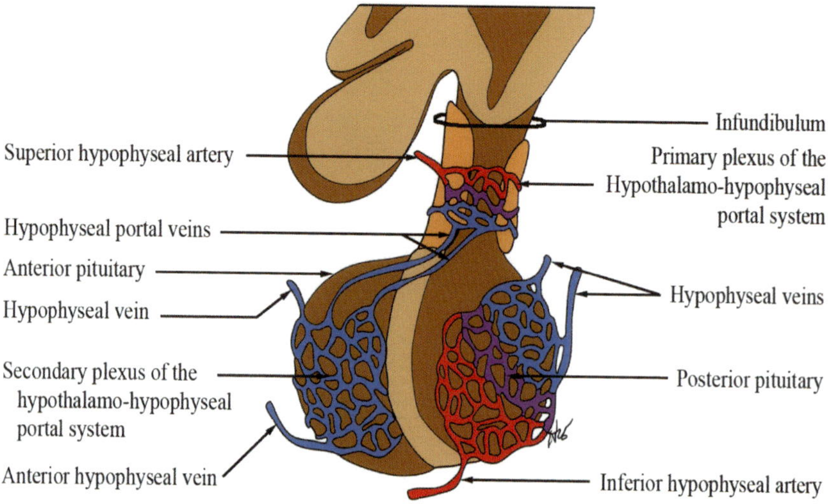

Figure 145. The anterior and posterior lobes of the pituitary

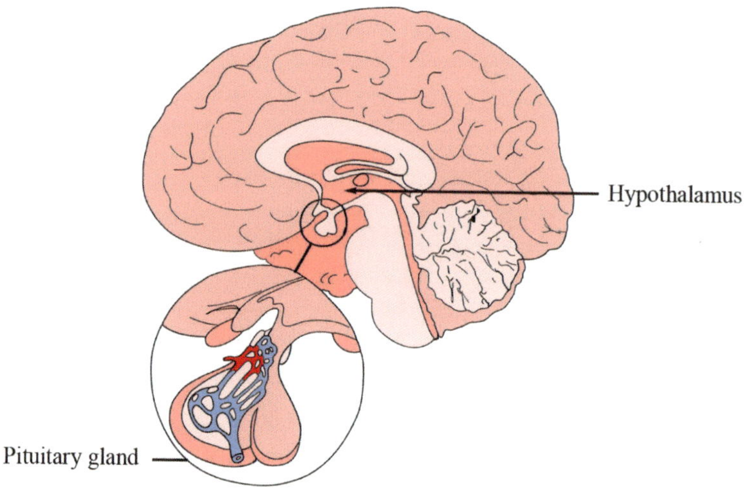

Figure 146. Diagram of the pituitary

As we've already stated, the anterior pituitary gland produces TSH or thyroid stimulating hormone. TSH stimulates the thyroid gland to produce thyroid hormones that regulate the body's metabolic activities, increase heart rate, basal metabolic rate, improve brain development, increase the body's ability to consume oxygen for the production of energy, and stimulate the rate of **protein synthesis** in the body.

Clinical Correlate

You may see a patient who comes in complaining of ***lethargy****, aches, pains, infections,* ***vertigo****, dizziness, loss of interest in activities, depression, and mood swings. Although there are many possible reasons for these symptoms, often, upon checking the amount of thyroid hormones in the blood, you will discover that the patient has either* ***hypo-*** *(under) or* ***hyper-*** *(too much) thyroid. Too much or too little thyroid can usually be corrected, often relieving the patient of these symptoms.*

The principal function of adrenocorticotropic hormone (ACTH) is to stimulate the adrenal glands (*ad* = near ; *ren* = kidney) to secrete hormones called **glucocorticoids**. The glucocorticoids control the body's use of sugar and also assist a person during stress. Disorders in the function of adrenocorticotropic hormone include **Addison's disease** (too little cortisol) and **Cushing's disease** (too much cortisol).

The symptoms of Addison's disease develop over time and may include fatigue, lightheadedness, muscle weakness, fever, weight loss, difficulty in standing up, anxiety, nausea, vomiting, diarrhea, headache, sweating, changes in mood and personality, and joint and muscle pains. Some people crave salty foods.

Patients with Cushing's disease (Figure 147) typically present with symptoms that include rapid weight gain, particularly of the trunk and face (round/moon face). The limbs remain relatively unchanged. You will also typically see growth of fat pads along the collarbone and on the back of the neck (**buffalo hump**). Other symptoms may include excess sweating, dilation of capillaries, and thinning of the skin (which causes easy bruising and dryness, particularly of the hands) and other mucous membranes, which may result in hemorrhage of the affected areas. You will find these red/purple marks on the trunk, buttocks, arms, legs, or breasts. You may also see facial male-pattern hair growth, baldness, and/or hair that is extremely dry and brittle.

Produced by the anterior pituitary gland, follicle stimulating hormone (FSH) is a **gonadotropic** (*gonad/o* = sex glands ; *troph* = development or nourishment ; *ic* = pertaining to) hormone that stimulates the growth of follicles in the ovary and induces the formation of sperm in the testes, whereas luteinizing hormone (LH) has effects on **ovulation** in females (triggering ovulation), and in males LH triggers the production of **testosterone**.

Prolactin has two major functions in females. First, it works together with other hormones to stimulate the development of the ducts in the **mammary glands**. Second, it stimulates the production of milk after childbirth. Prolactin may have no effect on males or might help regulate androgen production. The primary purpose of growth hormone (GH) in childhood is to stimulate bone and tissue growth. Growth hormone also contributes to proper **bone density**.

The single most important effect of antidiuretic hormone is to conserve body water by reducing the loss of water in urine.

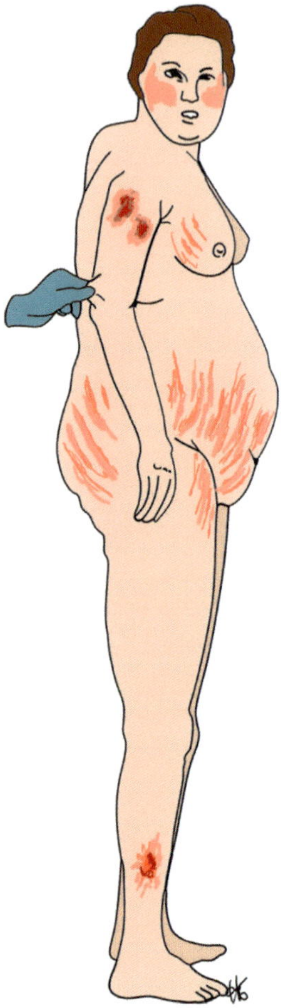

Figure 147.
Stigmata of Cushing's disease

The hormone oxytocin, also secreted by the pituitary gland, has a number of functions including those associated with labor and delivery (facilitates rapid and efficient labor), and in nursing mothers it promotes milk production and letdown. This hormone is considered to be a bonding hormone and also appears to be linked with trust, attachment, and love, with people secreting higher levels of the hormone when they are involved in activities with people they are close to. This hormone is released when mothers nurse their babies, and it is suggested that it also helps the mother bond with her child.

Test Your Knowledge

1. Which gland is considered the master gland and why?

 ____

 ____

 ____

2. Name some of the functions of the hypothalamus.

 ____

 ____

 ____

3. T or F: The posterior pituitary gland is larger than the anterior pituitary gland?

 ____

4. How does the hypothalamus communicate with the anterior and posterior pituitary glands?

 ____

 ____

 ____

5. What hormones are released by the anterior pituitary gland?

 ____

 ____

 ____

 ____

 ____

The Thyroid Gland

This gland (Figure 148) straddles the **trachea** anteriorly, just beneath the "Adams apple." It is highly vascular and like the pituitary, also consists of two lobes that are connected by an **isthmus** (a narrow connection or passage between parts of the body). The purpose of the thyroid gland is to produce hormones that help regulate growth, metabolism, and energy levels, and since nearly all body tissues contain some thyroid receptors, thyroid hormones have far-reaching metabolic effects.

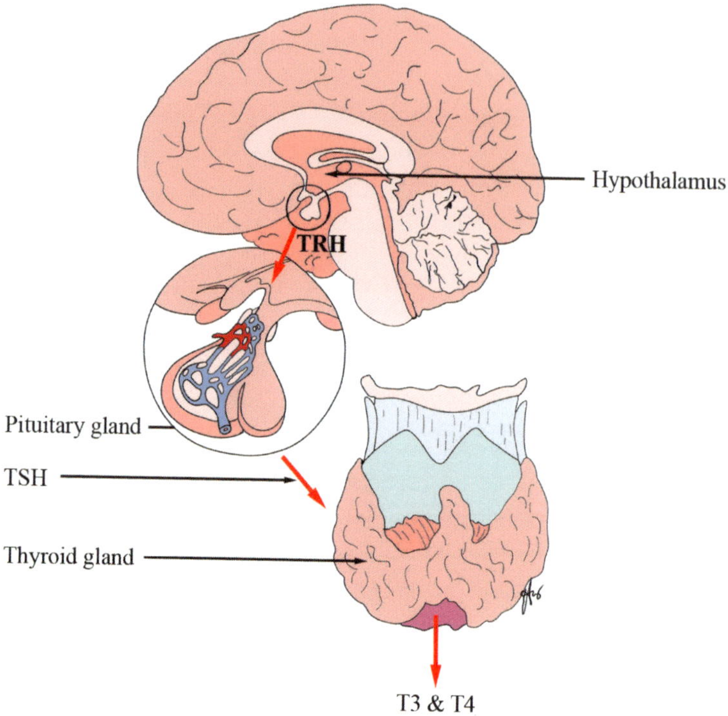

Figure 148. Hypothalamic control of the thyroid gland

Like many hormones, **thyroxin** or **T4**, which makes up over 90% of the thyroid hormones released, is secreted by the gland in response to the arrival of thyroid-stimulating hormone (TSH) from the anterior pituitary. When T4 reaches its target tissues, it binds to receptors to produce increased heat and oxygen consumption.

Clinical Correlate

*Sometimes when a person's thyroid level is low (**hypothyroid** = low thyroid) the patient gains weight. The gland may have an inadequate response to TSH. The person who is hypothyroid, therefore, may experience temperature regulation issues, weight gain, mental fatigue, dry skin, and hair loss, among other things.*

The thyroid gland also secretes **calcitonin**, a hormone that is released to decrease higher-than-normal calcium levels in the blood.

The Parathyroid Gland

Embedded in the substance of the thyroid gland, on its posterior surface, are the parathyroid glands (Figure 149). These glands secrete **parathormone** in response to low calcium levels. Parathormone boosts **osteoclastic** (*osteo* = bone ; *clast* = broken ; *ic* = pertaining to) activity and enhances **renal reabsorption** of calcium, which results in a rise in serum calcium levels. Now think about that. You may wonder why parathormone increases osteoclastic activity. When osteoclastic activity is on the rise in the body, the body "senses" that there could be some destruction of bones. To maintain the **homeostasis** of the body and keep the bones strong when this osteoclastic activity is sensed, the body absorbs more calcium so that this rise in the serum calcium levels can offset the osteoclastic activity.

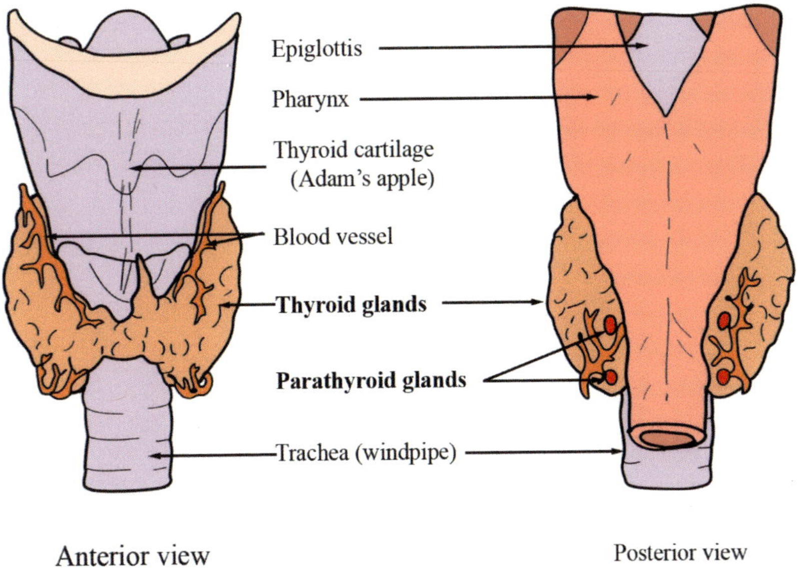

Figure 149. Parathyroid and thyroid glands

Test Your Knowledge

1. Where is the thyroid gland?

 ____

2. What is the purpose of the thyroid gland?

 ____

3. What is the purpose of the parathyroid gland?

____

____

The Adrenal Gland

The adrenal glands are triangular shaped and measure about 1/2 inch in height and 3 inches in length. The two adrenal glands sit atop the upper pole of each **kidney** (Figure 150). Each adrenal gland consists of a **cortex** and the **medulla**. The cortex produces a variety of **steroid** hormones, the most important of which are the mineralocorticoids (MCs), the glucocorticoids, and small quantities of androgens. These three hormones will be briefly discussed.

The **mineralocorticoids** are important in the maintenance of the **electrolyte balance** of the body's fluid, specifically the salt and potassium levels. Anyone who has ever ingested a lot of salty foods like popcorn or chips has experienced feeling bloated a few hours later. This full feeling oc-

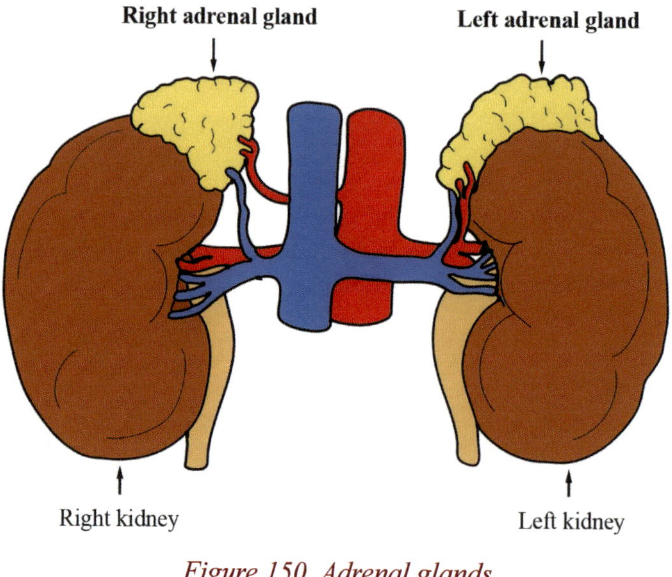

Figure 150. Adrenal glands

curred as a result of the sodium ingested and excessive water absorption. Too much fluid in the body and in the blood can lead to an increase in blood pressure.

A reduction in salt intake tends to lower blood pressure. This effect seems to be greatest in those who already have high blood pressure, the obese and the elderly. In contrast, reduced blood pressure is linked to increased potassium levels, which tend to increase the elimination of sodium and can lower blood pressure.

Aldosterone, the primary mineralocorticoid, is secreted when blood pressure falls, or blood volume contracts. It produces retention of sodium by reducing the loss of sodium by the kidneys and at the same time it lowers the potassium levels. Since water follows sodium, the blood volume increases and blood pressure returns to normal. As their name implies, the glucocorticoids are intimately involved in **glucose** regulation. In the liver, the rate of glucose synthesis is enhanced when glucocorticoids go to work. Through the action of glucocorticoids in the body's fatty tissues, fatty acids are released and converted to energy (thus sparing glucose).

The overall effect is to raise serum glucose levels. Glucose is used as an energy product by most cells but in order to get inside the cells, the presence of **insulin** is required.

Clinical Correlate

A practical application of this information occurs when a diabetic is admitted to the hospital with a severe allergic reaction to something and is treated with oral or ***intravenous*** *(intra* = inside ; *venous* = vessels*) steroids. The person's glucose levels must be carefully monitored since the steroids can adversely affect the patient's glucose level and may require a change in the insulin dosage.*

Small quantities of androgens (the male sex hormone) are produced in both males and females in the adrenal cortex (located on the superior pole [on top of] the kidney). In the female, many of the androgens are converted to **estrogens** in the body's **peripheral** tissues.

The adrenal medulla that is controlled to a large extent by the **sympathetic nervous system**. (The primary action of the sympathetic nervous system is to mobilize the body's resources under stress to make the **fight-or-flight response** work and to constantly be active at the most basic levels to maintain homeostasis.) About 75% of the work of the medulla is to produce **epinephrine (adrenaline)** and **norepinephrine (noradrenaline)**. Receptors for epinephrine and norepinephrine are found in a variety of locations such as muscle, fat, cardiac, and liver cells, and they prepare the body for action by increasing the availability of glucose and ATP, should muscular activity be required. When a person feels threatened—for example, running into a bear on a lonely path—his body immediately reacts to prepare him to either fight the bear or run (flight).

The Pancreas

A long and somewhat **nodular** organ, the pancreas is located just beneath the stomach and just lateral to the duodenum (Figure 151). The pancreas has both **exocrine** and **endocrine** functions. As an exocrine gland, the

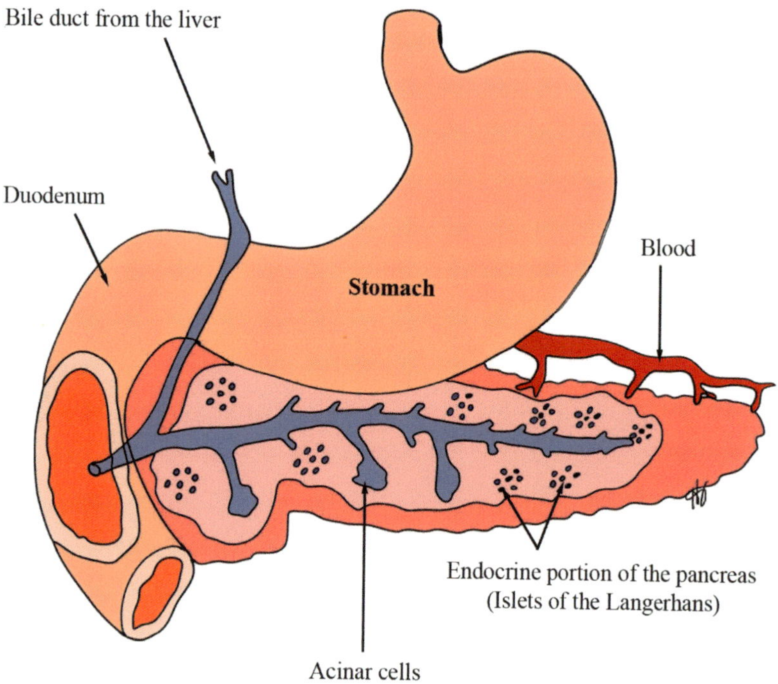

Figure 151. The pancreas

pancreas releases digestive juices through the **pancreatic duct** and into the duodenum. Here the digestive juices have two jobs: (1) to help neutralize the high acid content of the **chyme**, (the creamy-like substance that forms as the result of food being digested), that is arriving there from the stomach, and (2) to provide juices that break down food content so that it can be absorbed. Ninety-nine percent of the pancreas is involved in the exocrine function.

The function of an endocrine gland is to pass secretions directly into the bloodstream. The endocrine function of the pancreas is housed in the **alpha** and **beta** cells of the **islets of Langerhans** found scattered throughout the organ. Alpha cells release **glucagon** directly into the bloodstream. (Glucagon is a hormone that produces an increase in blood sugar levels, thus opposing the action of insulin.) Beta cells make and release insulin, a hormone that tends to lower the level of glucose in the blood by allowing glucose to pass into cells. Through opposing actions, both of these hormones (glucagons and insulin) are responsible for regulating glucose levels. Insulin is released when glucose levels get too high, and glucagon is released when the levels get too low. Nearly all of the body's cells have receptors for insulin. Notable exceptions to this rule are neurons, red cells, and certain cells of the kidneys and digestive tract.

When not enough glucose is available, most cells turn to fatty acid and proteins as their secondary fuels.

> **Clinical Correlate**
> *The Atkins diet works on the principle that by lowering the* ***carbohydrate*** *intake (reducing the amount of glucose available from carbs) the body seeks its energy from fatty acids, resulting in the utilization of fat and, consequently, weight loss.*

The Pineal Gland

This small gland is located deep in the center of the brain, between the two hemispheres. Its shape resembles a tiny pine cone (from the Latin word *pinealis*: *pinea* = pine cone), and although the function of this gland is not completely understood, it is felt to have some function is assisting with sleep in that it secretes **melatonin**, a hormone that helps control sleep and wake cycles.

Test Your Knowledge

1. What is the purpose of the adrenal glands?

____

____

2. T or F: The pancreas has both exocrine and endocrine functions.

____

3. What is the difference between an endocrine and an exocrine gland?

____

____

____

4. What is the function of the pineal gland?

____

____

Other Hormone-Producing Organs

Several other organ systems and tissues function like endocrine glands, but typically we don't think of them when we consider the endocrine system. These include the heart, which releases **ANP (atrial natriuretic peptide)** when it senses a rise in blood pressure or volume. ANP tends to facilitate sodium loss as well as water loss in the kidneys. The digestive tract accomplishes much of its local control through local hormones. The kidneys release several hormones including **calcitriol** (secreted when calcium levels are low), **erythropoietin** (increases red cell production in the bone marrow in response to low oxygen levels), and **renin** (released in response to drops in blood pressure or volume). Other hormone-producing organs are the male and female gonads, which produce several hormones that maintain secondary sex characteristics and facilitate the maturation and release of sperm and eggs.

Common Conditions and Diseases of the Endocrine System

Diabetes is a disease characterized by higher than normal glucose (sugar) levels in the bloodstream. There are a variety of types including:

- **Type 1** (sometimes called **juvenile onset diabetes**);
- **Type 2** or **adult onset diabetes**; and
- **Gestational** or **pregnancy-related diabetes**.

Type 1 diabetes is a chronic condition in which the pancreas produces little or no insulin, a hormone needed to allow sugar (glucose) to enter cells to produce energy. Type 2 diabetes, which is far more common, occurs when the body becomes resistant to the effects of insulin or doesn't make enough insulin. Each type is managed differently.

Insulin is almost always required in Type 1, whereas Type 2 diabetes often can be managed with diet, exercise, and oral medications. Pregnancy-related diabetes is managed primarily with diet and insulin as needed. Diabetes is characterized by either a decrease in insulin in the body or an increase in insulin resistance. Symptoms include fatigue, excessive thirst, weight loss, frequent urination, and increased appetite.

Hyperthyroidism is a condition where too much thyroid hormone is released. It can be **asymptomatic**, but frequently produces:

- Fatigue
- **Goiter** (a swelling in the neck)
- Elevated pulse rate
- Heat intolerance
- Nervousness
- Increased blood pressure

A common cause of hyperthyroidism is **Graves' disease** (where the immune system mistakenly attacks the thyroid gland and causes it to overproduce the hormone thyroxine. This higher thyroxine level can greatly increase the body's metabolic rate, which may affect the patient in numerous ways, from moods to physical appearance).

Infertility is a remarkably common condition that in many cases has an endocrine basis.

Endocrine System Glossary

<u>ACTH</u> (also known as adrenocorticotrophic hormone) hormone produced and released by the pituitary gland, stimulates secretion of glucocorticoids such as cortisol

<u>adenohypophysis</u> glandular, anterior lobe of the pituitary gland; the anterior pituitary regulates several physiological processes including stress, growth, & reproduction

<u>ADH</u> (also known as antidiuretic hormone or vasopressin) released by the posterior pituitary in response to diminished blood volume or hypotension by decreasing urine formation; influences the absorption of water by kidney tubules in response to changes in blood pressure and blood volume

<u>adrenal cortex</u> outer portion of adrenal gland which consists of 3 zones: outer = zona glomerulosa, thin zone = zona fasciculata (a thin - middle zone), and the inner zone = zona reticularis; produces ADH which reduces the amount of urine made

<u>adrenals</u> two glands located on top of the kidney which produce gluco- and mineralocorticoids responsible for a wide range of physiologic effects

<u>adrenocorticotropic</u> hormone produced and secreted by anterior pituitary basophils and chromophobes; stimulates the release of steroid hormones from the adrenal cortex

<u>aldosterone</u> regulates sodium and potassium levels between the blood and the kidneys, increased sodium absorption by the kidneys regulates the blood volume, blood pressure and blood pH

<u>alpha cells</u> located in the pancreas and constitute one of the endocrine functions of the pancreas; produce the hormone glucagon

<u>antidiuretic hormone</u> (also known as ADH or vasopressin) influences the absorption of water by kidney tubules in response to changes in blood pressure and blood volume

<u>beta cells</u> produces the hormone insulin used to control blood sugar; part of the endocrine function of the pancreas (like alpha cells)

<u>calcitonin</u> important in the regulation of blood calcium levels

<u>corticosteroids</u> more than two dozen steroid hormones produced in the adrenal cortex, responsible for the use of sugar, and in assisting a person during periods of stress

<u>cortisol</u> anti-inflammatory; also has a role in glucose regulation and the ability of the body to respond to stress

<u>Cushing's syndrome</u> condition that may be caused by an increase in cortisol secretion and characterized by a external physical changes including humpback, abdominal stria, moon facies, development of diabetes and increased weight

<u>effector</u> any cell, tissue, gland or organ that is stimulated by a neuron or hormone

<u>endocrine pancreas</u> consists of small groups of cells scattered among the exocrine cells; produces glucagon and insulin from alpha and beta cells respectively; the bulk of the pancreas is used to provide digestive juices which is its "exocrine function"

<u>epinephrine</u> (also known as adrenaline) has a variety of actions including increased heart rate and blood pressure; responsible for the fight or flight mechanism

<u>estrogen</u> primary female hormone; contributes to the development of secondary sex characteristics such as breasts, a widened pelvis, and increased amounts of body fat in the buttock, thigh and hip region essential part of a woman's reproductive process; regulates the menstrual cycle and prepares the uterus for pregnancy by enriching and thickening the endometrium

<u>exocrine pancreas</u> majority of the pancreatic substance; produces digestive juices that are secreted into the small bowel (duodenum)

<u>exophthalmos</u> condition in which one or both eyeballs protrude because of hyper thyroid function

<u>follicle stimulating hormone</u> (also known as FSH)

<u>FSH</u> (also known as follicle stimulating hormone or follitropin) released from the anterior pituitary where it travels through the blood to the ovary and stimulates follicle production and estrogen

galactorrhea	production of milk from the breast of a woman that is not lactating; usually signifies an excess of prolactin
GH	(also known as growth hormone or somatotropin) produced by pituitary gland; acts on various tissues to stimulate their growth
glucagon	hormone produced by the alpha cells in the pancreas and results in an increase in glucose levels in the blood (the opposite effect of insulin)
glycosuria	glucose in the urine
gonadotropins	follicle-stimulating hormone and luteinizing hormone; regulate the activities of the gonads in both males and females
Grave's disease	autoimmune condition resulting in excessive thyroid hormone production resulting in a characteristic array of signs and symptoms including exophthalmos, tachycardia and possible weight-loss
growth hormone	(also known as GH) stimulates cell growth and replication by accelerating the rate of protein synthesis
HGH	(also known as human growth hormone)
hirsutism	condition characterized by excessive hair growth or growth of hair in unusual places; can be associated with elevated testosterone levels
human growth hormone	(also known as HGH) protein-based peptide hormone stimulating growth, cell reproduction and regeneration in humans
humoral	denotes travel through the blood
hyperglycemia	medical term for high blood sugar
hypersecretion	excessive secretion of a hormone; underweight/thin (high metabolic rate)
hyposecretion	under secretion of a hormone
hypothalamus	together with the pituitary this gland regulates essentially all the body's hormones and is considered the master gland; bridges the gap between the nervous system and the endocrine system
insulin	hormone released by the beta cells of the endocrine pancreas; lowers blood glucose levels by increasing the rate of glucose uptake and utilization by most body cells

<u>islets of Langerhans</u> irregular clusters of endocrine cells scattered throughout the tissue of the pancreas that secrete insulin and glucagon; also known as islands of Langerhans

<u>LH</u> (also known as luteinizing hormones)

<u>luteinizing hormones</u> (also known as LH) produced by pituitary gland; acts on the ovary in females to stimulate the production of estrogens and induce ovulation and on the testis to stimulate the production of testosterone in males

<u>mineralocorticoids</u> released by the adrenal gland; steroid hormones that affect the electrolyte composition of body fluids

<u>MSH</u> melanocyte stimulating hormones produced by pituitary gland; stimulates skin tone

<u>norepinephrine</u> another adrenal hormone much like epinephrine which readies the body to deal with stress

<u>pancreas</u> lies within the abdominopelvic cavity in the J-shaped loop between the stomach and the small intestine; has both exocrine and endocrine functions; the vast majority of the gland is used for its exocrine functions; it's alpha and beta cells produce insulin and glucagon which regulate glucose levels in the blood

<u>parathormone</u> (also known as PTH) parathyroid produces PTH in response to low blood calcium levels by enhancing the renal absorption of calcium

<u>parathyroid gland</u> small glands embedded in the thyroid gland which are important to regulate calcium levels

<u>pituitary gland</u> (also known as the "master" gland or hypophysis) located in the sella tursica of the sphenoid bone; small, pea-like gland that together with the hypothalamus regulates the majority of the endocrine function of the human body

<u>PRL</u> (also known as prolactin)

<u>progesterone</u> produced in the ovary; responsible for changes in the uterine lining in the event that a pregnancy occurs; it is the drop in progesterone when a pregnancy does not occur that produces menses (a period)

<u>prolactin</u> (also known as PRL) produced by pituitary gland; activates milk let down during lactation

<u>PTH</u> (also known as parathormone)

<u>receptors</u> structures responsible for recognizing hormones; can be located on the cell surface or in the cell's cytoplasm

<u>target cell</u> cells that are sensitive to a particular hormone or stimulation

<u>testosterone</u> predominant male hormone responsible for secondary male characteristics

<u>thyroid gland</u> gland located in the neck that has primarily metabolic effects

<u>thyroid stimulating hormone</u> (also known as TSH) produced by pituitary gland; acts on the thyroid gland to signal the production of thyroxin

<u>thyroxine</u> secreted by the thyroid gland, occurring naturally as l-thyroxine; chief function is to increase the rate of cell metabolism

<u>TSH</u> (also known as thyroid stimulating hormone)

Chapter 10
The Nervous System

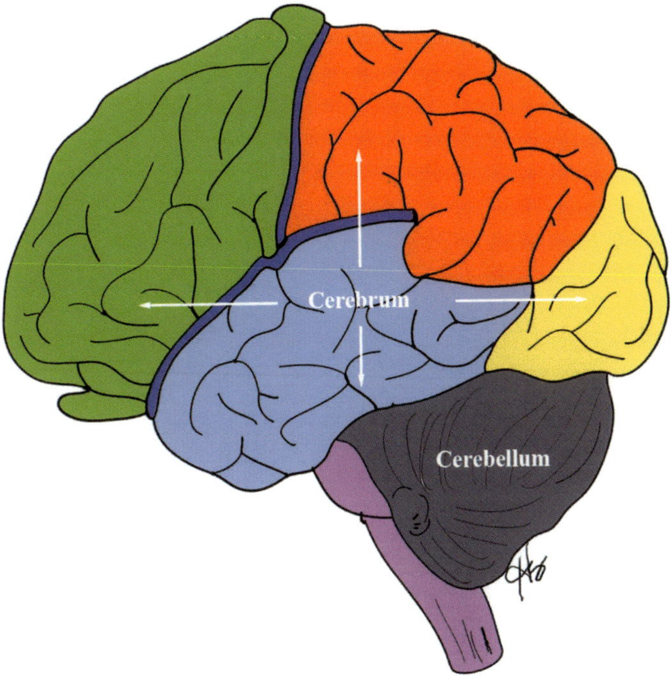

Figure 152. The "CEO" of the nervous system

How do you remember how to get to your classroom or the directions to a place downtown? Why does your heart beat without you ever thinking about it? Where does creativity come from? The brain and the nervous system are in charge of these things and a lot more (Figure 152). With billions of neurons that receive, analyze, and store information about internal and external conditions, your brain is the control center, the "mainframe computer," of your body.

As the most complex of all of the body systems, the brain serves as the control center and electrochemical wiring network so that your body can continue to function even when you're asleep. Your brain is the source of conscious and unconscious thoughts, moods, and emotions and is the key to **homeostasis** (*home/o* from the Greek meaning "always the same" ; *stasis* from the Greek word histasthai meaning "standing"), meaning keeping the body at the same levels to achieve optimal health. The brain plays such an important role in homeostasis because it detects, interprets, and responds to changes in internal and external input.

For example, the brain is ultimately responsible for your sight and your feelings (emotions) about what you see. The brain accomplishes its job by combining countless bits of information and generating responses to that data.

When the brain reacts to the **stimuli** it receives (thoughts, sounds, emotions, etc.), it sends out **electrochemical impulses** through nerves to the appropriate organs and organ systems (such as muscles and glands) to make them react.

To learn how the nervous system functions, it's important to learn how the nervous system is put together. The nervous system can be divided into several connected systems that function together. Let's start with a simple division:

1. The **central nervous system** (**CNS**), which includes the brain and spinal cord; and
2. The **peripheral nervous system** (**PNS**), which connects the brain's orders to the rest of the body allowing for taste, smell, sight, hearing, and balance.

The nervous system can be divided, somewhat arbitrarily, in several other ways. This chapter will explain the roles of the different parts of the brain and how both the peripheral and central nervous system work to keep you alive, well, and functioning.

The Central Nervous System

There are major divisions of the brain that govern the nervous functions of the body. These include

- The cerebrum;
- The brain stem;
- The cerebellum; and
- The **diencephalon** (the hypothalamus and the thalamus).

The Cerebrum

The cerebrum makes up 85% of the brain's weight and is the biggest part of the brain (Figure 153). The cerebrum is split into left and right, folded and grooved **hemispheres** (halves) at a **fissure** (deep groove). The two hemispheres communicate with each other through the **corpus callosum**, a bundle of fibers between them. The cerebrum is the "thinking part" of the brain and it controls voluntary muscles, language, conscious thought, hearing, **somatosensory functions** (sense of touch), memory, personality development, and vision.

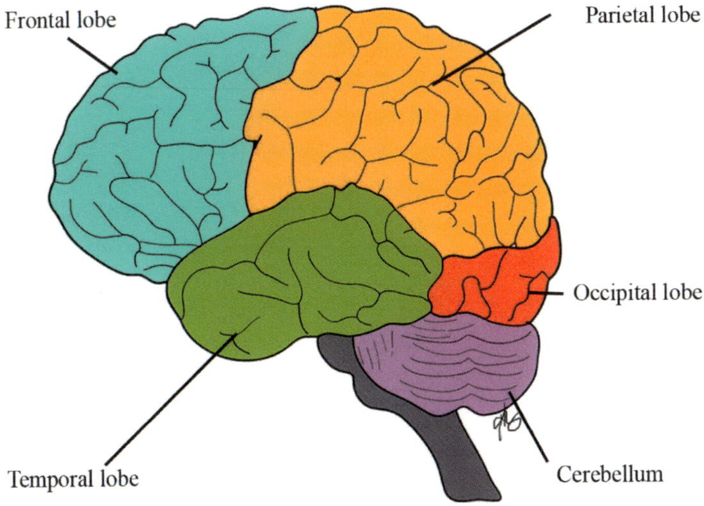

Figure 153. The cerebrum

When you're thinking and reasoning about how to solve a personal issue or trying to figure out how to get the money to stay in school, you're using your cerebrum. Both **short-term memory** (what you wore yesterday) and **long-term memory** (the name of that girl you used to know in high school) live in the cerebrum.

Perhaps you've heard someone say that they were all "right brained" (meaning they were the creative type) or that they were all "left brained" (book worm, logical type). The right side of the brain appears to contribute to abstract and creative thought. Whether or not this is actually true is debatable. What we do know is that the right half (hemisphere) of the cerebrum controls the muscles and glands on the left side of your body and the left hemisphere controls the muscles and glands on the right side of your body.

You will often hear the terms gray matter and white matter thrown around a lot. Don't be confused. **Gray matter** refers to areas that are made up predominately of **neuronal cell bodies**, whereas **white matter** refers to areas consisting of (usually) **myelinated axons**. The gray matter in the **spinal cord**, when seen in cross section, has a butterfly-like shape and is surrounded by white matter. If you were to **dissect** a brain, you'd see that the outermost layer of the brain (the **cerebral cortex**) is composed of gray matter (unmyelinated or noninsulated nerve cell bodies). Continuing your dissection you'd see that underneath the cerebral cortex is the white matter (myelinated or insulated axons). You'd also notice that the cortex looks like a bunch of folds and grooves, sort of like lots of towels stuffed into a suitcase without being properly folded. These folds and grooves are important because they allow more gray matter to fit into the skull.

The Brain Stem

The brain stem is similar to a tree trunk and looks like a long tube coming out of the bottom of the brain. Specifically, the brain stem sits posterior to the cerebrum and adjacent to the cerebellum and connects the cerebrum and cerebellum to the spinal cord, which runs down your neck and back. The brain stem (Figure 154) is in charge of most of the automatic functions your body needs to stay alive. These would include basic attention levels, arousal, breathing air, digesting food, circulating blood, and overall consciousness.

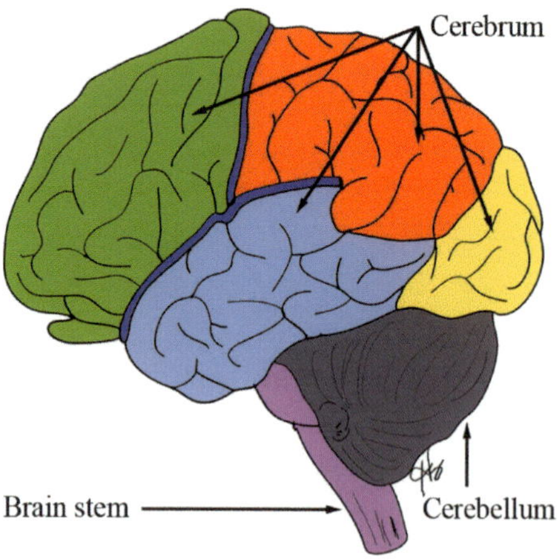

Figure 154.
Brain stem and higher level structures

There are three important anatomic features of the **brain stem**: the **midbrain**, the pons, and the **medulla** (Figure 155).

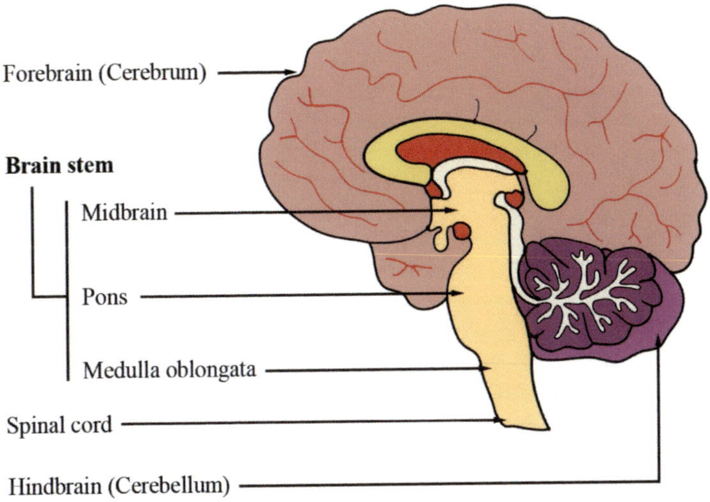

Figure 155. The brain stem structures and pons and medulla

The Midbrain

The midbrain consists of ascending and descending nerve tracts and houses the **reticular system**, an essential component for regulating many involuntary functions.

The Pons

The pons (Latin for "bridge"), is located in the brain stem above (superior to) the medulla and in front of (anterior) to the cerebellum. The pons relays signals from the cerebrum to the cerebellum and is primarily responsible for sleep, respiration, swallowing, bladder control, hearing, and equilibrium.

The Medulla

The medulla oblongata (or simply medulla) is located in the lower half of the brain stem inferior to (below) the pons and is anterior to (in front of) the cerebellum.

The medulla deals with **autonomic** (automatic) functions such as breathing, heart rate, and blood pressure and contains the cardiac, respiratory, vomiting, and **vasomotor centers** (and is anterior to the cerebellum).

The Cerebellum

The cerebellum is located at the rear of the brain and below the cerebrum (refer back to Figure 155). It controls balance, posture, and coordination of muscle movements and helps one to stand upright, do yoga, catch a ball in the air, and many other functions. Although the cerebellum is only one-eighth the size of the cerebrum, it is similar in that it also has right and left hemispheres that control opposite sides of the body and are covered by gray matter and surface folds. Whereas the **vermis** is a narrow structure that connects the hemispheres with one another, it is the pons that links the hemispheres of the cerebellum and higher brain centers with the spinal cord.

The Spinal Cord

The spinal cord is a long, cylindrical, cable-like structure that is a continuation of the brain stem. It passes through the **vertebral canal**, which is a tunnel formed on all sides by bone called **vertebrae** but extends down the body only as far as the space between the first and second lumbar vertebrae. There it terminates in a fibrous extension known as the **filum terminale**. The spinal cord carries messages between the CNS and the rest of the body and has three major functions:

- It serves as a conduit for motor information, which travels down the spinal cord and signals movement to the arms, legs, etc.
- It serves as a conduit for sensory information, which travels up the spinal cord when something is felt, seen, heard, tasted, or smelled; and
- It serves as a center for coordinating certain reflexes.

The spinal cord is remarkably organized and consists of cell bodies and axons of neurons. These are the structures that carry information up and down the cord (Figure 156).

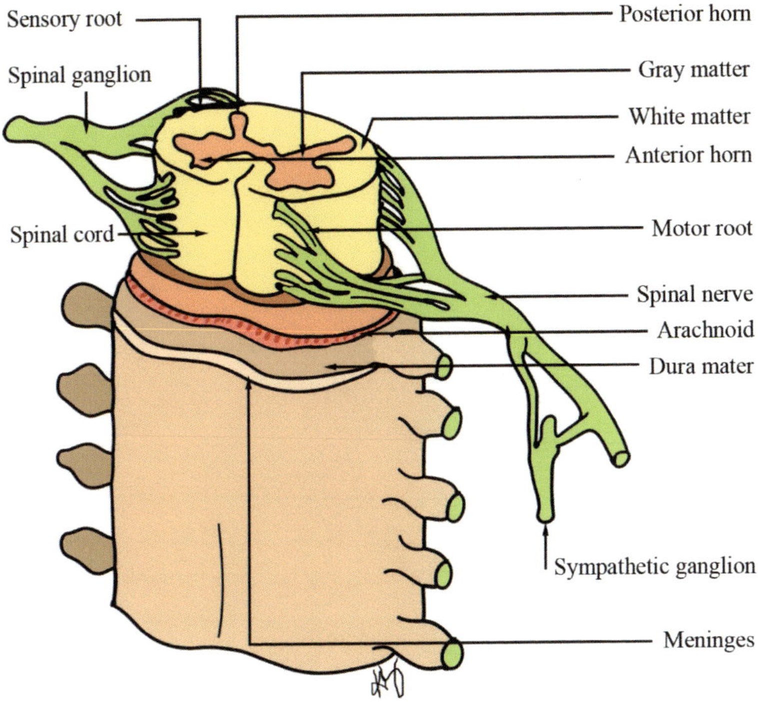

Figure 156. Cross sectional anatomy of spinal cord

The sensory neurons and axons tend to be located in the posterior portions of the cord, whereas the motor ones are more anterior. The spinal cord is made up of 31 segments that are identified by a letter and number (e.g., C3, L4, and so on) based on where the nerves exit the cord. Each segment has an associated dorsal and ventral root ganglion, or mass of nerve tissue (Figure 157). The **dorsal ganglia** (on the back side, like a dorsal fin) bring incoming sensory information to the cord, and the **ventral ganglia** (on the front side) carry outgoing motor commands. The two ganglia join outside the cord to form the **spinal nerve**, which is referred to as "mixed," since it carries both motor and sensory fibers.

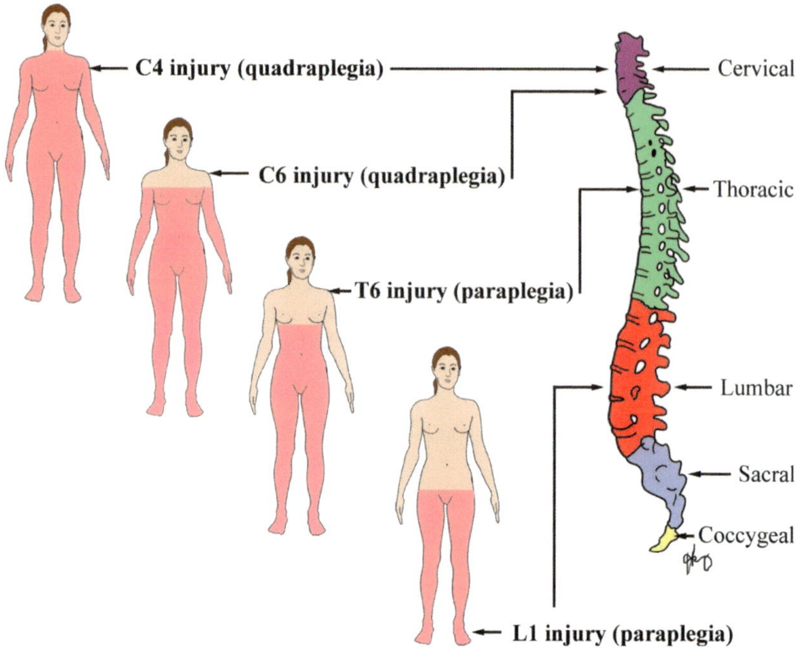

Figure 157. Cord injuries and vertebral column

Clinical Correlate

The gross and microscopic anatomy of the spinal cord has been so well studied that the location of a spinal cord injury can usually be accurately predicted from the patient's specific motor or sensory deficits. Suppose someone is in a car accident and receives an injury at level C3 (meaning the third cervical segment). The chances are that this patient will be totally paralyzed and possibly need the assistance of a respirator.

Test Your Knowledge

1. What functions does the cerebrum perform?

____

____

____

2. What do the terms gray matter and white matter mean?

____

____

____

3. What is the brain stem in charge of?

____

____

4. What is the function of the cerebellum?

____

____

5. What does the pons do?

____

____

6. What is the function of the medulla?

____

____

7. What is the basic overall function of the spinal cord?

____

____

____

Other Structures in the Brain

Hypothalamus

The hypothalamus is a small cone-shaped structure located below the thalamus and just above the brain stem. It links the nervous system to the endocrine system via the pituitary gland (hypophysis). The hypothalamus regulates homeostasis through its impact on **visceral** (organ-related) activities, food and fluid intake, sleep and wake patterns, sex drive, and emotional states. The hypothalamus is the body's inner thermostat and will help keep body temperature at a normal level of about 98.6° Fahrenheit or 37° Celsius.

Thalamus

The thalamus is a paired symmetrical structure found on either side of the midline situated between the cerebral cortex and lower brain centers. Considered a relay and preprocessing station for the many nerve impulses that pass through it to the appropriate brain areas that need the information, the function of the thalamus includes relaying sensation, spatial sense, and motor signals to the cerebral cortex, along with the regulation of consciousness, sleep, and alertness.

Pituitary Gland

About the size of a pea and located at the base of the brain where it attaches to the hypothalamus, the pituitary gland's job is to produce and release hormones that control growth as well as a variety of other functions (see Chapter 9: The Endocrine System).

Test Your Knowledge

1. Describe the job of the pituitary gland.

   ____

   ____

2. What does the hypothalamus do?

   ____

   ____

   ____

3. What is the job of the thalamus?

____

____

____

The Meninges

The primary function of the meninges and of the **cerebrospinal fluid** is to protect the central nervous system. The meninges consists of three connective tissue layers whose job it is to protect the brain and spinal cord (with the help of cerebrospinal fluid) by enveloping the central nervous system. The cerebrospinal fluid is produced by the **choroid plexus**, a tissue containing blood capillaries and **ependymal cells**. This specialized tissue is found in the brain's **ventricles**, which are channels in the brain that communicate with the cord and allow circulation of this fluid. Much can be learned about the CNS in certain clinical conditions by sampling this fluid and sending it to the laboratory for evaluation. This is accomplished by performing a **spinal tap**.

The outermost layer of the meninges is the **dura mater**. It forms partitions in the skull that prevent the brain from excessive movement. The middle or **arachnoid** layer, so named because it resembles a spider web, acts as a cushion between the dura mater and the **pia mater**. It is porous and allows cerebrospinal fluid to flow through it to bathe the brain and spinal cord in nutrients. The innermost layer is the pia mater, which gets it name from a Latin term meaning "tender mother." It is the delicate innermost layer of the meninges that closely envelops the entire surface of the brain and supplies blood to the superficial areas of the cortex. It also supports larger blood vessels passing over the surface of the brain running down into the fissures of the cortex.

Another protective substance, cerebrospinal fluid, surrounds the brain and spinal cord. The brain floats within the cerebrospinal fluid, which prevents it from being crushed under its own weight and cushions against shocks from walking, jumping, and running.

So the brain is your mainframe computer, but it needs lots of nerves, the spinal cord, and the vertebrae that protect it to truly function. Together, the spinal cord and the brain are known as the central nervous system.

Neurons

The nervous system is made up of millions of **neurons**, which are the functional unit of the nervous system. Neurons (Figure 158) are electrically excitable microscopic cells that transmit electric signals like an electric wire. They have tiny branches, called **dendrites**, coming off of them that allow them to connect to many other neurons (Figure 159).

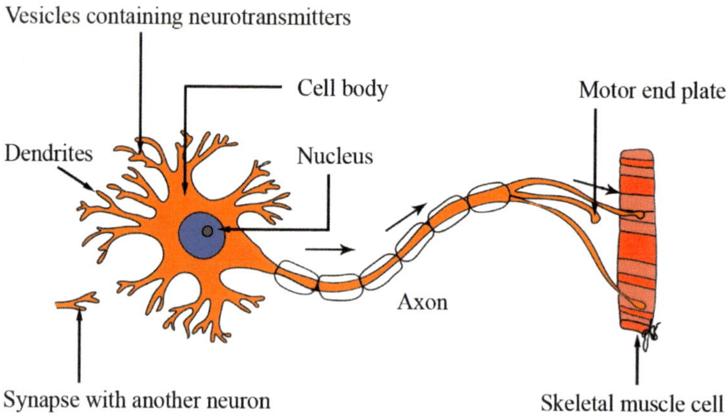

Figure 158. Anatomy of a neuron

A neuron has three parts. These include

- The **cell body**, which contains the **nucleus**, **mitochondria**, and other organelles typical of **eukaryotic cells**;
- The **axon**, which conducts messages away from the cell body;
- The dendrites, which are short branches that extend from the neuron and receive information from other neurons. These messages are transmitted to the cell body, where the neuron's main genetic information can be found. The axon sends messages to other neurons; the dendrites receive messages from other neurons.

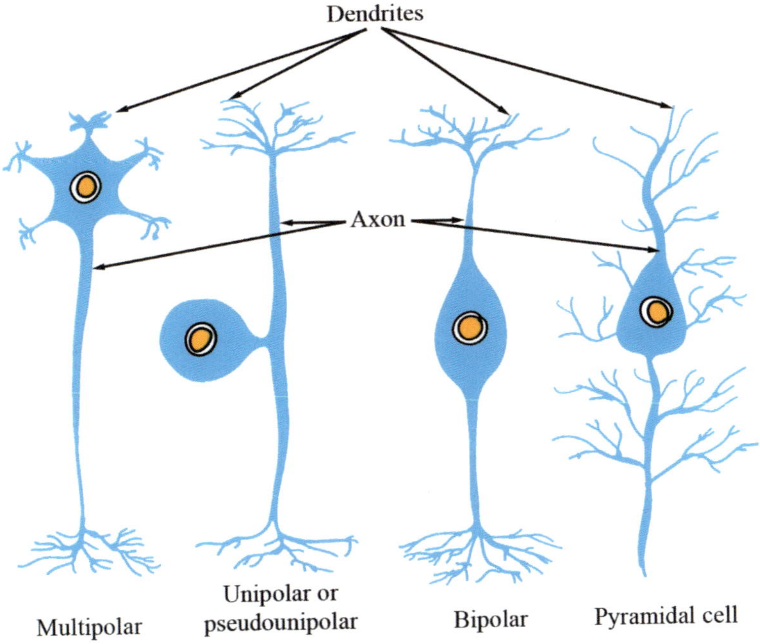

Figure 159. Types of neurons and examples of dendrites

For our nerves to work, neurons need to talk to each other via connections. This form of communication is known as **signaling**. But the communication needs to occur both within the cell and between other cells. **Intracellular** signaling involves the communication inside the cell and **intercellular** signaling involves the communication between cells.

There is also communication that occurs from one neuron to the next. This kind of messaging occurs with a bridge called a **synapse** and through a process called **neurotransmission**. Neurotransmission (*transmissio* = passage, crossing; from *transmitto* = send, let through), also called **synaptic transmission**, is movement within synapses caused by the spread of nerve impulses. Nerve impulses are sent along the entire length of an axon similar to the way electricity travels through your home via the wires that have been set up to carry it.

To make the nerve impulses travel faster, some axons are partially coated with **myelin sheaths**. Myelin is an insulating layer made up of protein and fatty substances that forms around nerves, including those in the brain and spinal cord.

Clinical Correlate

Since the purpose of the myelin sheath is to allow rapid and efficient transmission of impulses along the nerve cells, damage to the myelin can slow down the impulses. This can cause diseases like ***multiple sclerosis****.*

Test Your Knowledge

1. Name the layers of the meninges.

___

___

___

2. What are the basic parts of a neuron?

___

___

___

3. What is neurotransmission?

___

___

How Neurons Work

Neurons send rapid signals along their lengths to communicate with other cells by generating an **action potential**. These action potentials are produced when a neuron is adequately stimulated, which means that it reached its threshold. The neurons send action potentials in only one direction.

Let's break down this concept to make it easier to understand.

Reaching a threshold can be compared to firing a loaded gun. When enough pressure is applied to the trigger, the hammer is released and a shot is fired. Cells in general, but particularly neurons, work to maintain a slightly negative voltage potential across their membranes. They accomplish this by keeping the ion composition inside their cells considerably different from that on the outside of the cell. Through the use of potassium gates and sodium/potassium exchange pumps mounted in the cell membrane, cells keep a higher concentration of potassium on the inside than outside and relatively less sodium on the inside than on the outside.

It is these ion differences that help establish the cell's resting membrane potential. When a neuron receives adequate stimulation, as in the case of light falling on the sensory neurons of the retina, a transient (brief) change in the cell's membrane permeability occurs leading to a loss of the negative resting potential (depolarization) and an action potential occurs and spreads across the membrane of the cell that has become stimulated. If, however, the stimulation is inadequate, no action potential is created and only a graded potential is produced, which does not spread across the entire cell (Figure 160). The communication from cell to cell is always accomplished through the use of action potentials. The action potential is typically transmitted down the cell's axon. The axon may be "insulated" (myelinated) or uninsulated (un-myelinated).

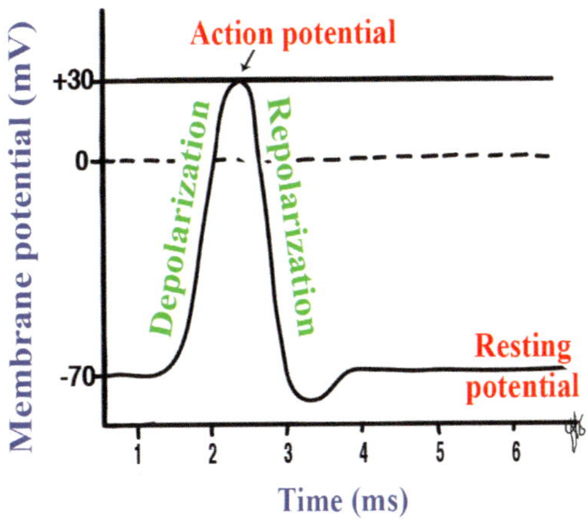

Figure 160. Electrical changes associated with action potential

Once the end of the axon is reached, one or more synapses are encountered (Figure 161). (As a reminder, a synapse is the specialized structure that passes the information along to the next neuron.) The synaptic knob doesn't actually touch the next cell but instead releases a neurotransmitter that crosses the narrow gap between the two cells and may or may not produce an action potential in that next cell. A variety of neurotransmitters exist including acetylcholine, dopamine, epinephrine, and a host of others. Most are rapidly removed or broken down once released. Neuroglia (also called glia), on the other hand, serve as a supporting cast to the neurons. They are non-neuronal cells, meaning they are not actual neurons.

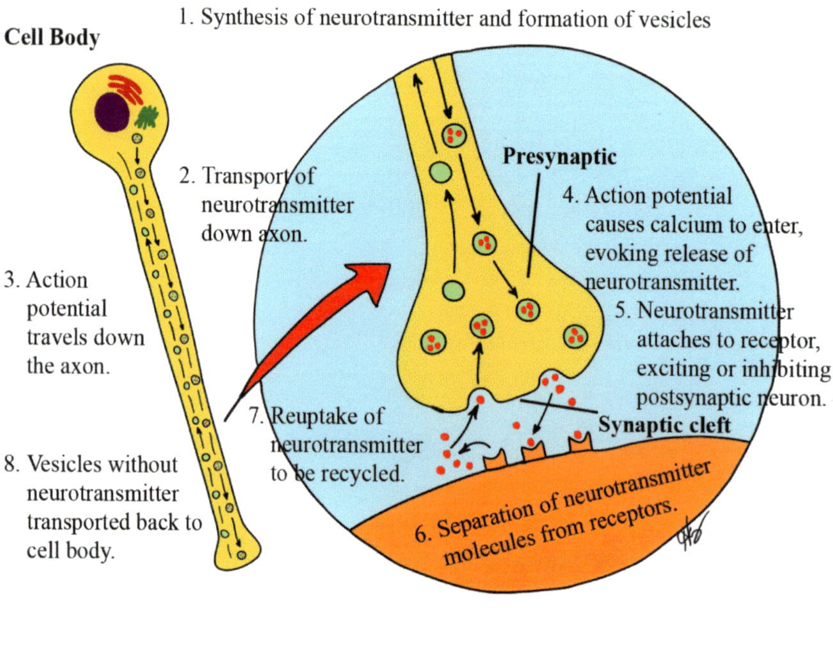

Figure 161. Neuron synaptic action

The term *neuroglia* comes from the Greek words *neuro* = nerve ; *glia* = glue, and as such neuroglia are commonly known as the "glue" of the nervous system. Not only do the glial cells surround neurons and hold them in place, they also supply nutrients and oxygen to neurons, insulate them from one another, destroy disease-producing microorganisms, remove dead neurons, and control neurotransmission. Overall they maintain homeostasis for the nervous system in many ways including the formation of myelin, and by providing support and protection for the neurons.

There are four recognized types of neuroglia in the CNS:

- **Astrocytes**—the most numerous of the neuroglia, which play a vital role in maintaining the blood–brain barrier;
- **Oligodendrocytes**—which are responsible for providing the insulation or myelin for the neuron axons;
- **Microglia**—the most uncommon of the neuroglia, which function as **phagocytes** to destroy disease-producing microorganisms; and
- **Ependymal cells**—which make cerebrospinal fluid, in which the brain and cord float.

Test Your Knowledge

1. What is an action potential?

____

____

____

2. What is the major role of neuroglia?

____

____

____

Peripheral Nervous System

In general, the sensory receptors, the nerves that connect them to the central nervous system (CNS) and the nerves that link the CNS to the body's muscles make up the peripheral nervous system (PNS).

The peripheral nervous system can be divided into three major parts:

1. The **somatic** (voluntary) **nervous system** (SNS), which interacts with the outside world;
2. The **autonomic** (involuntary) **nervous system** (ANS), which seeks to maintain homeostasis internally; and
3. The **enteric nervous system** (ENS), part of the peripheral nervous system (PNS), which directly controls the gastrointestinal system. It will not be discussed in this text.

Somatic (Voluntary) Nervous System

The somatic nervous system serves all sensory organs, (nose, eyes, ears, tongue, and skin) as well as all the skeletal muscles used for voluntary movement (e.g., walking, smiling, shaking hands). The word *somatic* comes from the Greek word *soma* = body ; *ic* = pertaining to, and is meant here to describe nerves that act on the body as opposed to the viscera (internal organs not under voluntary control). Since SNS has two basic functions, movement and sensory, there are two mechanisms that it uses to carry these impulses. To move muscles voluntarily, the somatic nervous system carries impulses from the brain to the muscle to be moved. It does this through the **efferent neurons**, which, as the name implies (*efferent* from the Latin *ex* = out ; *ferre* = to carry), carry impulses from the brain to the voluntary muscles.

In its sensory capacity the somatic nervous system also carries impulses from the sensory organ to the brain via **afferent neurons** (*afferent* is from the Latin *ad* = to ; *ferre* meaning to carry). Notice the difference here. To make the muscle move, the brain must tell it to move by sending an impulse from the brain to the muscle. But with the senses, the organ (like the nose or the tongue) receives the signal and then sends it to the brain so that the brain can identify what it is that one is smelling or tasting.

Neurons in the somatic nervous system have a direct line from the brain or spinal cord to the muscle or sense organ. There are no intermediate cells or synapses, no detours or stops along the way. There are 12 pairs of **cranial nerves** (Figure 162) that connect the brain to many of its sensory organs as well as direct motor activities using the motor branches of many of these same nerves.

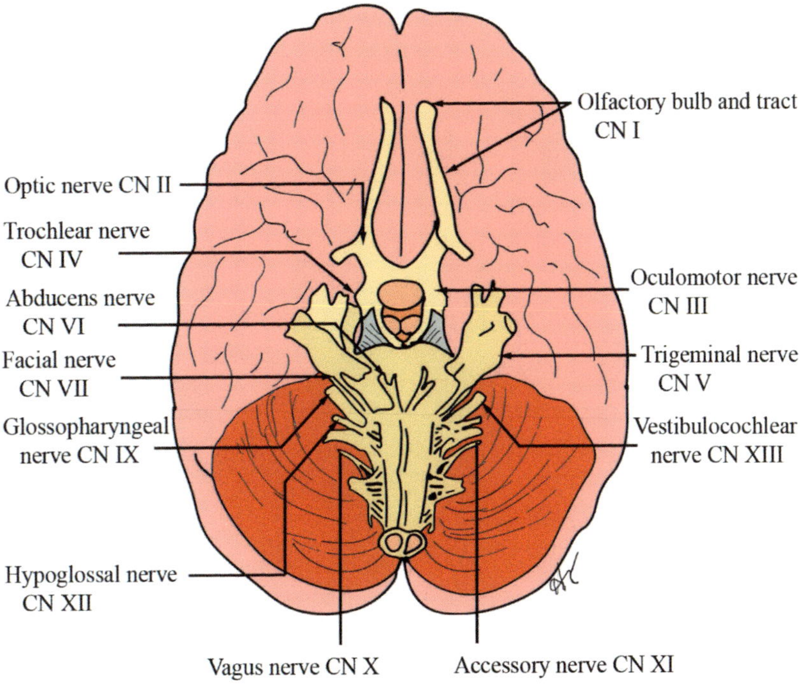

Figure 162. Cranial nerves

There are 31 pairs of **spinal nerves** that emerge from various places along the spinal cord. Each spinal nerve has a dorsal root and a ventral root. The dorsal root contains afferent (sensory) fibers that transmit information to the spinal cord from the sensory receptors. The ventral root contains efferent (motor) fibers that carry messages from the spinal cord to the effectors.

Figure 163 shows a segment of the somatic motor system. The cell body is located in either the brain or spinal cord and projects directly to a skeletal muscle.

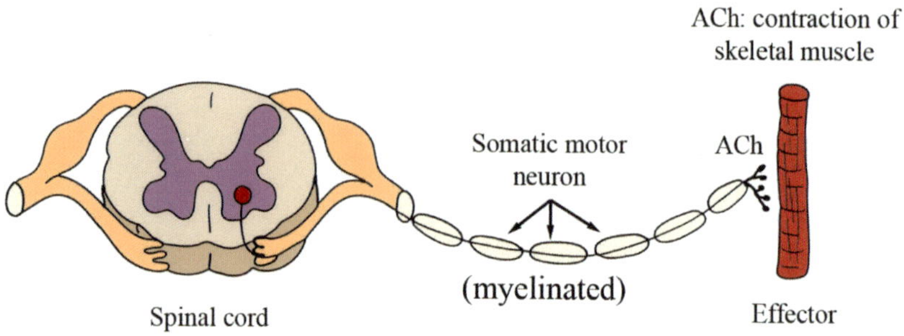

Figure 163. Somatic motor neuron

Autonomic Nervous System

The ANS is the counterpart to the somatic nervous system, and it controls smooth muscle of the viscera (internal organs) and glands to maintain internal homeostasis. As its name implies, this system works automatically and without conscious control. To work properly, the autonomic nervous system includes these basic things:

- Receptors within viscera (internal organs);
- The afferent nerves that relay the information to the CNS (from the organ to the brain); and
- The efferent nerves (from the brain back to the organ) that relay the action back to the effectors such as smooth muscle, cardiac muscle, and glands.

Examples of autonomic control are breathing and the movement of food through the digestive tract during sleep (Figures 164 and 164). It is the efferent portion of the autonomic system that is divided into **sympathetic** and **parasympathetic divisions**.

1. The sympathetic nervous division prepares the body for action in the case of a stressful or dangerous situation. The effects are widespread throughout the body and tend to be relatively long lasting such as increased blood pressure, breathing rate, and blood flow to muscles. This is known as the fight or flight reaction and it occurs when one senses danger or an impending accident.

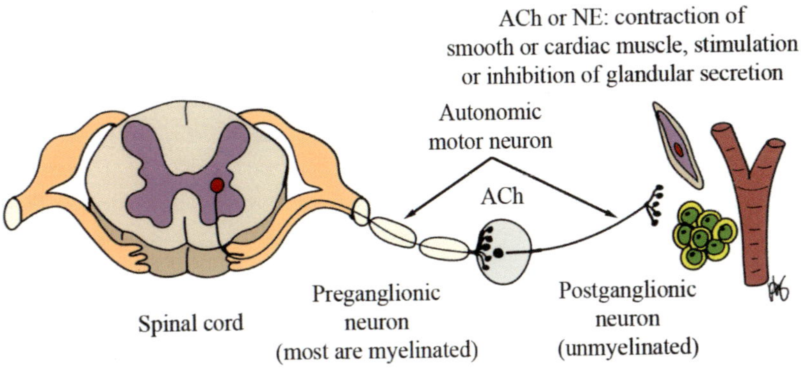

Figure 164. Autonomic motor neuron

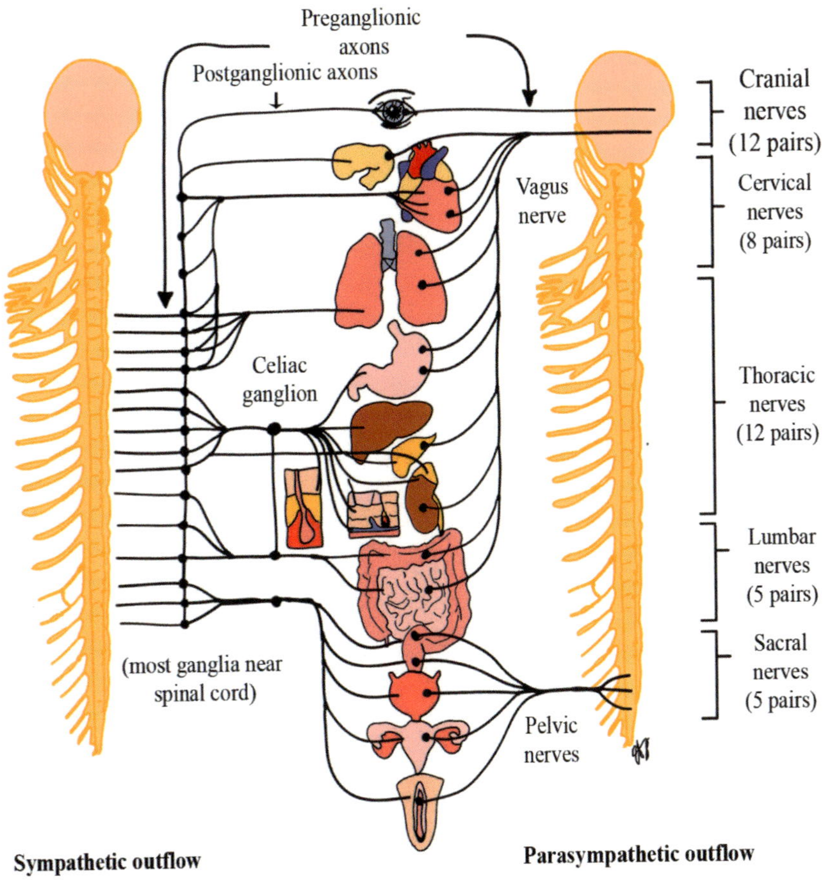

Figure 165. Autonomic nervous system

2. The parasympathetic nervous division restores the body to its resting state after a danger or stressor has passed and has a calming effect on the individual by slowing the heartbeat and breathing rate, and promoting digestion and elimination.

It is the action of both the parasympathetic and sympathetic nervous divisions on different parts of the body that cause the autonomic nervous system to be called a **neuroendocrine** (nerve and blood) system. Most of the action of the autonomic nervous system is below the level of conscious awareness. Figure 165 illustrates the general organization of the autonomic nervous system. In the autonomic nervous system two neurons carry messages between the gland and the brain. This differs from the somatic nervous system, which has only one neuron between the central nervous system and the target organ.

Test Your Knowledge

1. What are the three divisions of the peripheral nervous system?

____

____

____

2. What is the somatic nervous system responsible for?

____

____

3. What is the autonomic nervous system responsible for?

____

____

4. What is the enteric nervous system responsible for?

____

____

____

Common Conditions and Diseases of the Nervous System

Multiple sclerosis is an **autoimmune disease** that affects the brain and spinal cord. For reasons not fully understood, an inflammation develops specifically affecting the insulating myelin sheath that covers the axons of some nerves. This usually results in degeneration of the affected nerves as the disease progresses. Females are affected more often than males. There are drugs that can delay progression, but there is no cure at the present time.

Parkinson's disease affects one in twenty Americans over the age of 65. It is the result of a decrease in dopamine-producing cells in the **substantia nigra**, a structure at the base of the brain. Affected patients have trouble making smooth muscular movements and their balance is also impaired. Eventually, walking becomes challenging and falls become common. The possibility of a cure lies in the advances in stem cell research.

Meningitis is a swelling and inflammation of the meninges (the fibrous connective tissue that surrounds the central nervous system). It may have a bacterial or viral origin. When it is caused by bacteria, it is a true emergency that can result in death or significant neurologic dysfunction. It can present with a change in the patient's mental status and/or a stiff neck. Selection of the right antibiotics can often result in a cure.

Alzheimer's disease is a progressive, fatal disease that was first described in 1906. It is the most common form of dementia. Characteristic plaques and tangles of nervous tissue can be seen in radiologic studies of the brain, and it is believed they cause disruption of nerve cells. At the present time, there is no cure.

Nervous System Glossary

acetylcholine — common nervous system neurotransmitter in both the peripheral nervous system (PNS) and central nervous system (CNS)

Alzheimer's disease — progressive, fatal disease which is the most common form of dementia in this country; characterized by plaques and tangles of nervous tissue which disrupts nerve cell function

astrocytes — the most numerous of the various neuroglia which play a vital role in maintaining the blood brain barrier

autonomic nervous system — (also known as ANS) controls the smooth muscle of the internal organs (viscera) and glands to maintain internal homeostasis; works automatically without conscious control

brainstem — region of the brain that serves as a relay between the cerebrum, cerebellum, and spinal cord; responsible for breathing, heart rate, and body temperature and a variety of other tasks

central nervous system — (also known as CNS) consists of the brain and spinal cord

cerebellum — portion of the brain located below the occipital lobes of the cerebrum; responsible for control and coordination of skeletal muscles

cerebral cortex — outer layer of the cerebrum consisting of gray matter; responsible for higher mental funtions

cerebral palsy — (also known as CP) movement disorder, usually spastic in nature, that is present at birth and often, but not always, associated with varying degrees of mental retardation

cerebrospinal fluid — plasma-like clear fluid circulating in and around the brain and spinal cord;provides protection to the brain and spinal cord

cerebrum — largest portion of the brain; also called cerebral cortex

CNS — (also known as central nervous system)

CP — (also known as cerebral palsy)

cranial nerves	12 pairs of nerves arising directly from the brain; only the first and the second pair emerge from the cerebrum; the remaining 10 pairs emerge from the brainstem; I = olfactory, II = optic, III = oculomotor, IV = trochlear, V = trigeminal, VI = abducens, VII = facial, VIII = vestibulocochlear, IX = glossopharyngeal, X = vagus, XI = accessory, XII = hypoglossal
CSF	plasma-like clear fluid circulating in and around the brain and spinal cord; provides protection to the brain and spinal cord
ependymal cells	one of four types of neuroglia in the CNS; makes cerebral spinal fluid in which the brain and cord "float"
frontal lobe	anterior section of each cerebral hemisphere responsible for voluntary muscle movement and personality
glia/neuroglia	non excitable supporting cells of nervous tissue
hypothalamus	bridges the gap between the nervous and endocrine systems and as such is considered to be the "master gland"
meninges	three membranes that cover the brain and spinal cord, consisting of the dura mater = outermost layer, arachnoid = middle layer, and pia mater = inner layer; primary function is to protect the nervous system
meningitis	inflammation of the meninges; cause is usually viral or bacterial in origin
microglia	one of four types of neuroglia; most common of all neuroglia; functions as phagocytes that destroy disease producing organisms
MS	(also known as multiple sclerosis)
multiple sclerosis	(also known as MS) autoimmune disease of the central nervous system characterized by the demyelination (deterioration of the myelin sheath) of nerve fibers, with episodes of neurological dysfunction (exacerbation) followed by recovery (remission)
neurons	nerve cells
neurotransmitters	chemical that allows one cell to communicate with another through passage of a chemical across a narrow gap between the cells
occiptial lobe	portion posterior to the parietal and temporal lobes, responsible for vision

<u>ogliodendrocytes</u> type of neuroglia in the CNS that act as insulation; help to form myelin sheaths for neuronal axons

<u>parasympathetic nervous system</u> division of the ANS that is most active under resting conditions; it counter balances the effects of the sympathetic system by restoring the body to a restful state after a stressful experience

<u>parietal lobe</u> portion posterior to the frontal lobe, responsible for sensations such as pain, temperature and touch

<u>Parkinson's disease</u> condition of slowly progressive degeneration of an area of the brainstem resulting in decrease of dopamine; affected patients have trouble making smooth muscular movements and their balance is sometimes impaired

<u>spinal cord</u> nerve pathways connecting the brain to the peripheral nervous system

<u>spinal nerves</u> 31 pairs of nerves arising from the spinal cord

<u>sympathetic nervous system</u> division of the ANS concerned primarily with preparing the body in stressful or emergency situations

<u>temporal lobe</u> portion that lies below the frontal lobe, responsible for a variety of functions most importantly an understanding of speech and expression

<u>thalamus</u> two gray matter nuclei deep within the brain; responsible for relaying sensory information to the cortex

<u>ventricles</u> series of interconnected cavities within the cerebral hemispheres and brainstem filled with cerebrospinal fluid

Chapter 11
The Senses

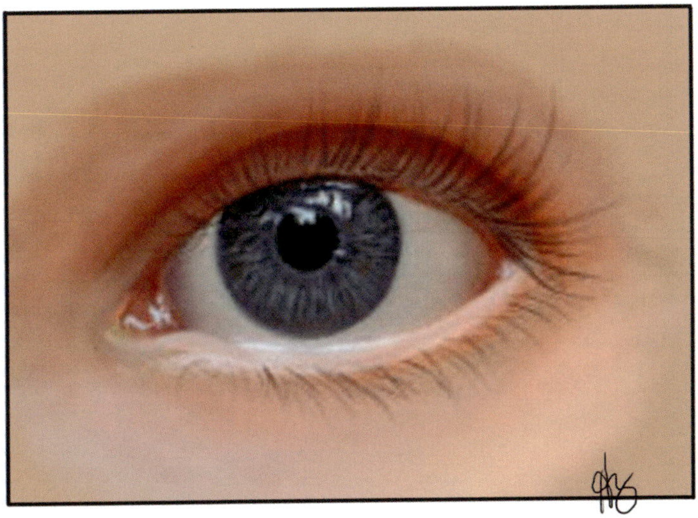

Figure 166. The human eye

As critical as touch, taste, and smell are to the richness of our everyday life, students who are pursuing certification or associate degrees in health-related fields are not likely to be frequently involved with issues surrounding these senses. Thus, we will limit our detailed discussion to vision and hearing.

Vision

Our most dominant and, arguably, most refined sense is the sense of vision. Through our eyes we enjoy a world of shapes and hues. The eye (Figure 166) is a delicate sensory organ housed and protected by the bony orbit in the skull and surrounded by muscles and fat pads to provide some degree of cushioning.

Each of our eyes allows us to see a slightly different view of the world. We are able to judge both distance and depth. Depth perception allows us to see in three dimensions and allows us to know when to come to a stop while driving a car or where to pour lemonade into a glass. It also enables us to work in very definitive ways to fix a clock, sew by hand, paint detailed pictures, or even perform surgery. Further, the coordinated efforts between our eyes, brain, and hands allow us to catch balls in flight, pick up small objects, and perform other fine motor tasks. Depth perception requires that both eyes work together, have normal or near normal vision, and be aligned to face in the same direction. Sometimes, when vision is impaired, glasses or contact lenses may be needed to obtain normal 20/20 vision. (The term 20/20 *vision* means that one can see at 20 feet the same as most other people can see at 20 feet. If you have 20/50 vision, it means that what you can see at 20 feet, others can see at 50 feet.) Both eyes see independently of each other, and each sends its own images to the brain for processing. The ability of the brain to blend these two similar images is called **fusion**. Fusion permits the brain to blend separate images from each eye into one image. Babies do not have a high level of fusion, an important milestone not completely developed until somewhere between the ages of 5 and 9.

To understand this better, let's take a closer look at the structure of the eye from outside in and see how it works.

Our eyelashes and eyelids protect our eyeballs. In the wind, your eyes shut quickly when something tries to fly inside, so that your eyelashes and eyelids can help trap and prevent unwanted debris from entering your eye. When you squint in the sun or when you first wake up, the eyelids are helping to block excess light. The eyelids also help distribute tears evenly during blinking and help lubricate the eye's surface.

The eyelids are composed of several layers, the outermost of which is the skin. The skin is followed by a layer of muscle and more supportive tissue, and finally by the innermost **conjunctiva**. The eyelid muscles help open and close the eyelids while giving them tone and shape.

The conjunctiva on the inside of the eyelids is continuous with the conjunctiva on the surface of the eyeball. It is a thin, transparent **mucous**

membrane that covers the inner surface of the eyelid and the white exposed part of the eyeball (the **sclera**), making blinking and eye movements comfortable (Figure 167). The sclera is the tough, white outer layer of the eyeball to which skeletal muscles are attached, allowing the eyeball to move in the desired direction (Figure 168).

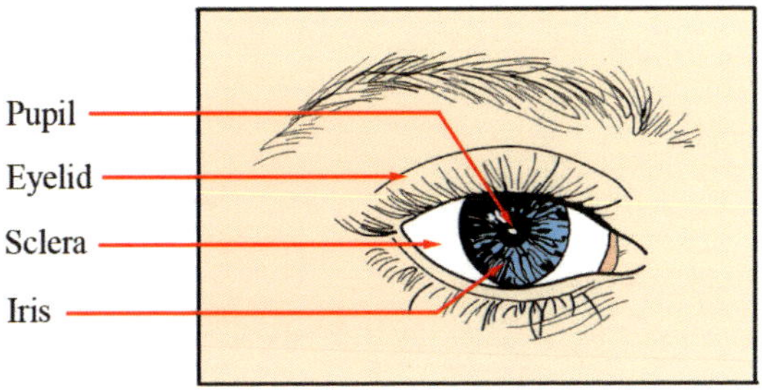

Figure 167. External anatomy of the eye

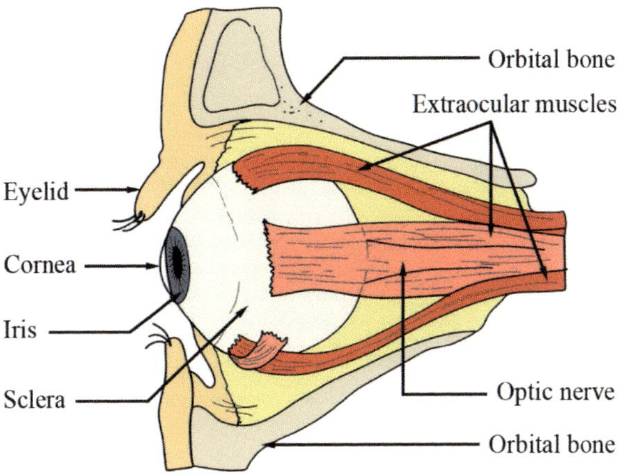

Figure 168. Sclera and attached eye muscles

The **cornea** is a clear, round window in the front of the eyeball through which light travels to enter the eye. Its purposes include protection of the eye and bending and refracting light so that images can focus on the **retina**.

The **iris** is the colored part of the eye that acts like an aperture in a camera, opening and closing to regulate the amount of light that enters the eye. The cornea and **lens** invert the image arriving through the **pupil** (the black part of the eye, which is the opening regulated by the iris) and focus it on the retina at the back of the eye (Figure 169). The cornea performs about 70% of the necessary bending of light rays, while the lens performs the other 30%.

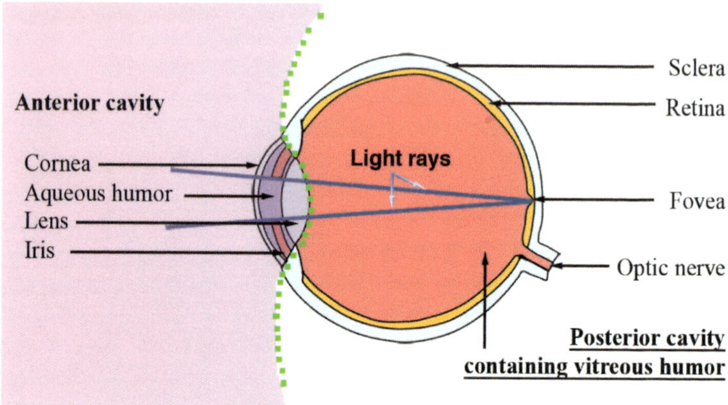

Figure 169. Cross section of human eye

Clinical Correlate

***Cataracts** are formed when the proteins that make up the lens continue to grow with age. This makes the lens larger, cloudier, and yellowish brown in color and forms what we know as a cataract. Additionally, when the lens ages and becomes thicker it cannot change its shape as easily as it did in the person's youth. Nearby objects become more difficult to see without the help of reading glasses.*

The processing of visual information actually starts in the retina; thus, the retina is actually part of the brain in that sense. The retina is the light-sensitive layer that receives images made of light rays and transfers these into electrical signals to the brain to be "seen." There are light-sensitive receptors inside the retina known as **rods** and **cones**. Cones are color sensitive; you can remember this because the words color and cone both start with the letter "c."

Cones facilitate daytime vision and are most responsive to the color red. Rods are used primarily for night vision and are most sensitive to the color green. Rods and cones are not evenly distributed on the retina. The cones are concentrated primarily in the center of the retina (the **fovea**), and are less concentrated toward the edge or periphery of the retina. The rods are just the opposite. They are not even present in the fovea, but increase in concentration nearer to the periphery of the retina. The nerves of the retina exit the eyeball at the **optic disc**, also called the "blind spot." At this exit site there are no cones or rods, just axons carrying information from the eye to the brain (Figure 170). These axons make up the **optic nerve** (**cranial nerve II**) that exits from each retina. Many of the nerves arriving from the left eye cross to the right side of the brain, and nerves from the right eye cross over to the left side of the brain. This crossing over of the optic nerve from each eye forms an X-shaped pathway called the **optic chiasm**.

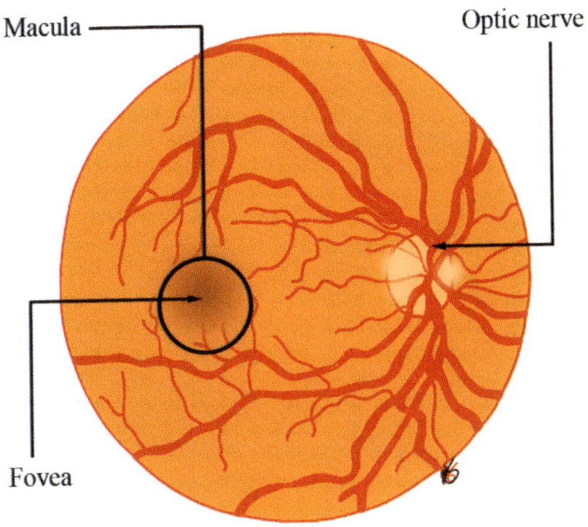

Figure 170. View of the posterior wall of the eyeball showing the blind spot where the optic nerve exits the eye

To explain how you see in a little more detail, note that the optic nerve is the cable that carries information from the eye to the brain in the form of electrical signals. Specifically, nerve fibers from the retina come together in a bundle to form the optic nerve and travel toward the **visual cortex** found in each hemisphere of the brain, eventually reaching the posterior (back area) of the cerebrum where the visual cortex is located (Figure 171).

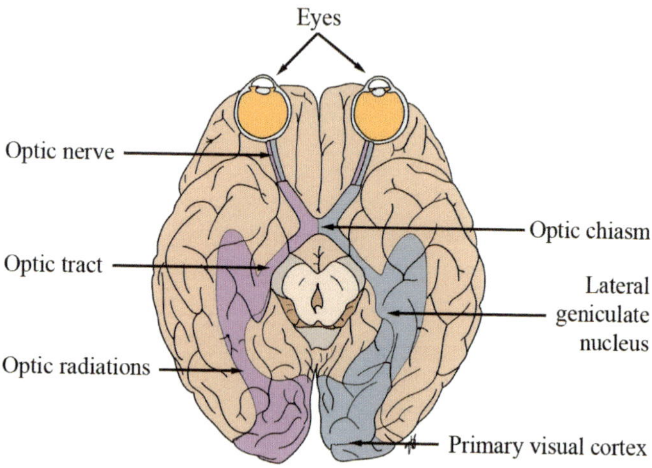

Figure 171. Pathway of optic nerves

The eye contains two fluid-filled cavities, the anterior and posterior. The **anterior cavity** can be divided into two parts or chambers: the **anterior chamber** and the **posterior chamber**. These anterior and posterior chambers are filled with **aqueous humor**, a watery-like liquid, and are separated by the iris (Figure 172). The large posterior cavity is filled with **vitreous humor**.

Aqueous humor is a clear, slightly alkaline liquid. It resembles blood plasma in composition and is formed from the blood by filtration, secretion, and diffusion through the **ciliary body**, a muscular structure located behind the iris that controls the curvature of the lens but contains less protein and glucose than blood and more lactic and ascorbic acid than blood plasma. The purpose of the aqueous humor is to provide nutrients to eye tissues that lack a direct blood supply (such as the lens) and to remove

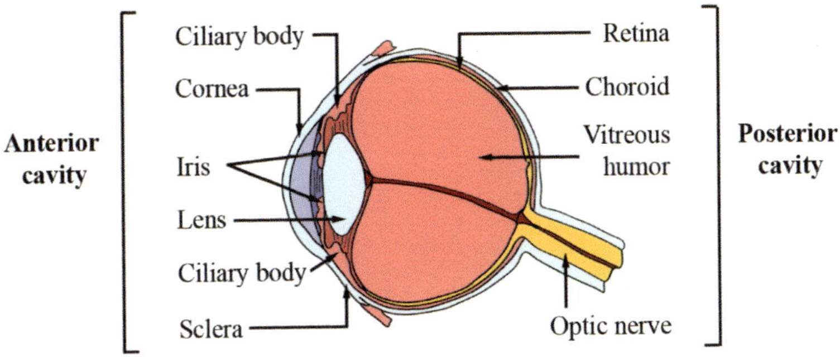

Figure 172. Cross section of human eye demonstrating anterior and posterior cavities

waste products. Aqueous pressure is responsible for the **intraocular pressure** that keeps the eyeball (globe) properly formed.

The vitreous humor that is contained in the posterior cavity of the eye is composed of 99% water in a firm, jellylike consistency that helps the eye hold its shape. The other 1% is a mixture of collagen, proteins, salts, and sugars.

The choroid is the vascular connective tissue of the human eye located between the retina and the sclera whose main purpose is to send oxygen and other nutrients to the retina (refer back to Figure 172).

Hearing and Equilibrium

Whether it is the loud report of a gunshot or the subtle melody of a waltz, the auditory system helps us process these sounds and appreciate them. The ear (Figure 173) is composed of three regions:

- The **outer ear**, which is visible on each side of the head;
- The **middle ear**, which consists of three tiny bones and which turns sound waves into physical movement; and
- The **inner ear**, which contains the sensory receptors that transmit the mechanical movements of sound waves into nerve impulses that are forwarded to the brain in the **auditory/vestibular nerve** (cranial nerve).

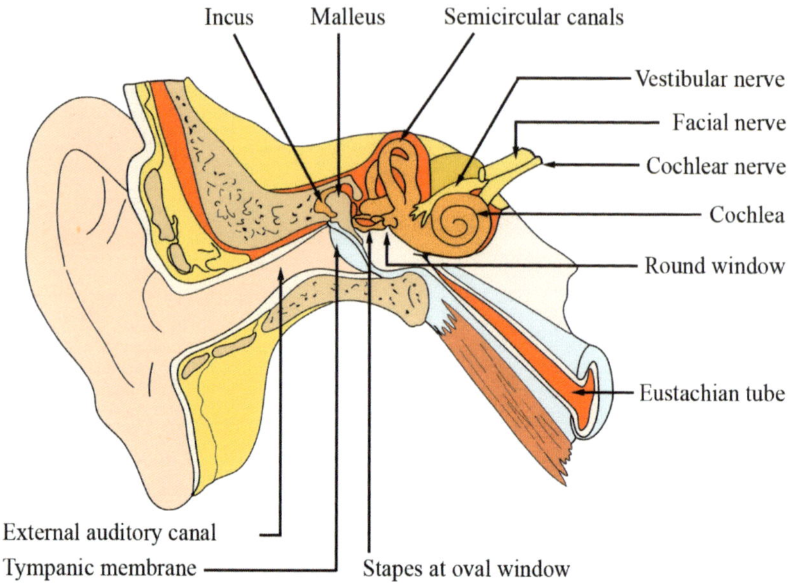

Figure 173. Anatomy of the human ear

External Ear

The outer ear is composed of the **pinna** (from the Latin word meaning "wing") visible on the side of the head, and the **external auditory meatus** (ear canal) that extends from the pinna to the **tympanic membrane**.

The basic job of the pinna is to gather sound waves and direct them to the tympanic membrane. The twists and folds of the pinna enhance the frequency (pitch) of sounds and also help one to determine where the sound is coming from. Sounds that come from the front and side tend to be louder than those coming from behind simply because the shape of the external ear allows them to go directly into the ear canal (external auditory meatus), whereas sounds from behind tend to be slightly reduced.

The external auditory meatus or ear canal is about one inch in length (2.5 cm) and has a diameter about the size of a pencil eraser. **Cerumen** (or ear wax) is produced by glands that are found in the outer half of the ear canal, and it serves to moisturize and protect the skin of the inner ear and to trap dust and particles before they reach the eardrum. The external auditory meatus ends at the tympanic membrane. The tympanic membrane (abbreviated TM and commonly referred to as the eardrum) is a thin membrane that separates the external ear from the middle ear. Sounds travel down the external auditory meatus (ear canal) and strike the TM, causing it to vibrate. These vibrations are then transmitted to the tiny bones called ossicles inside the middle ear.

Middle Ear

The middle ear is that portion of the ear internal to the eardrum and external to the oval window of the **cochlea**, a spiral-shaped, fluid-filled structure in the inner ear. Basically, the job of the middle ear is to amplify sound waves that have come off of the tympanic membrane (found in the external ear) through the movement of tiny bones (ossicles) and onto the oval window of the inner ear. When the sound waves reach the inner ear, those sound waves, which had previously been turned into mechanical movement, are once again changed back into waves. These fluid waves actually affect the sensory receptors of hearing. The sound is transmitted through the ossicles (Figure 174). The first of these bones is called the **malleus** (from the Latin word meaning "hammer"). The malleus is attached on one

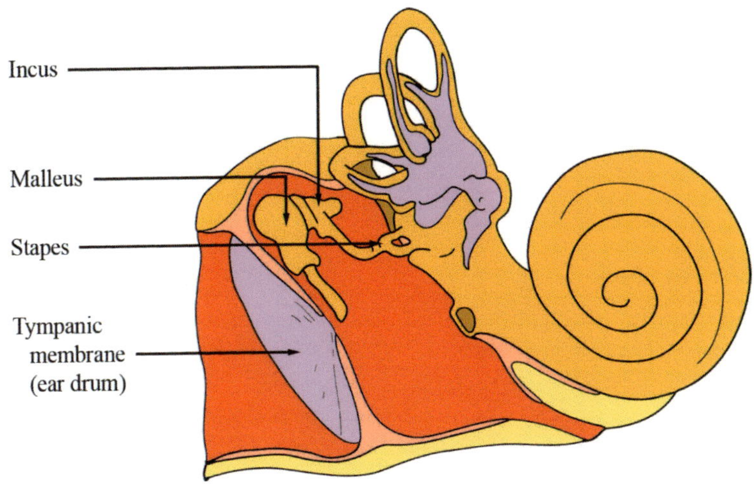

Figure 174. Middle ear showing malleus, incus and stapes

side to the inside surface of the TM and on its other side to the **incus** (from the Latin word meaning "anvil," based on its shape), and finally to the innermost bone, the **stapes** (from the Latin word for "stirrup," because of its shape). Sound sets this whole structure into movement. The vibration of the footplate of the stapes trembles within the oval window opening of the cochlea, transferring sound energy to the fluids and tissues of the cochlea.

The Inner Ear

Because the cochlea (Figure 175) is filled with a watery liquid, it moves in response to the vibrations coming from the middle ear via the oval window. As this fluid moves, receptors consisting of hair cells are stimulated when arriving fluid waves cause them to rub against an overlying membrane. These hair cells are set in motion, and they convert that motion to electrical signals that are communicated via neurotransmitters to many thousands of nerve cells. All of this happens in the **organ of Corti** (Figure 176), a complex structure located within the cochlea that is responsible for allowing us to hear the full range of sounds that we are sensitive to. The organ of Corti is considered to be the body's microphone, and it sends action potentials along the auditory portion of the eighth cranial nerve and on to the brain (Figure 177).

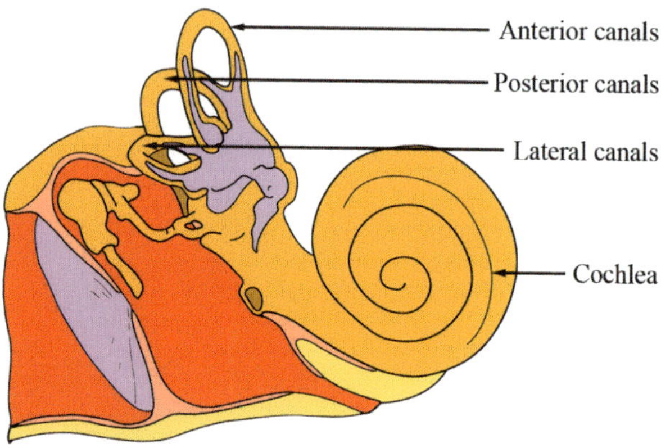

Figure 175. Inner ear showing semicircular canals and the cochlea

In addition to the cochlea, the inner ear also contains the three semicircular canals (Figure 178) that provide us with information regarding the position of our head in space and help us maintain balance. Gravity and ac-

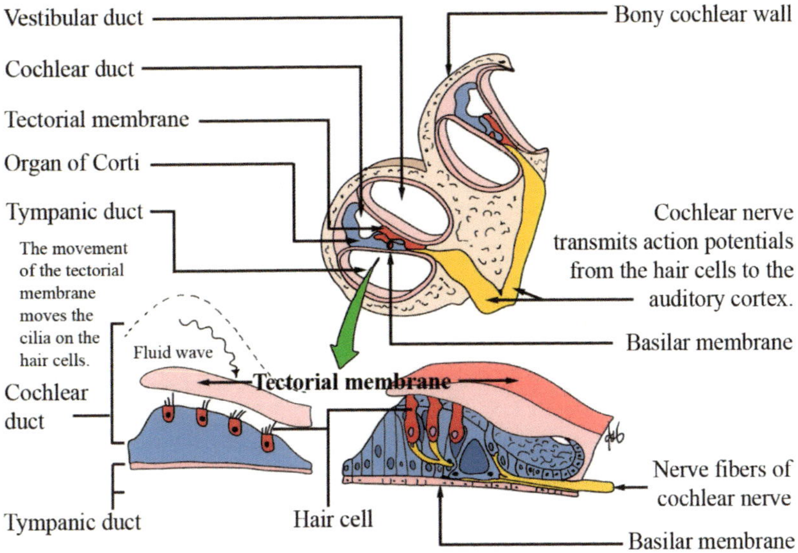

Figure 176. Detailed anatomy of the organ of Corti

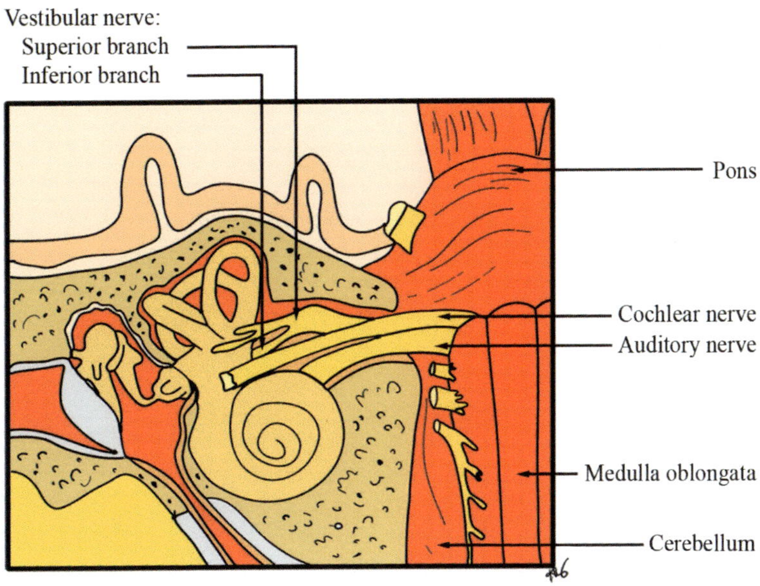

Figure 177. Distribution of the inner ear nerves

celeration stimulate hair cell receptors found inside the semicircular canals by producing motion in the liquid in which they are housed. Specifically, small suspended particles called otoliths are displaced by gravity or acceleration and cause the hair cells to sway, inducing the receptors to fire action potentials.

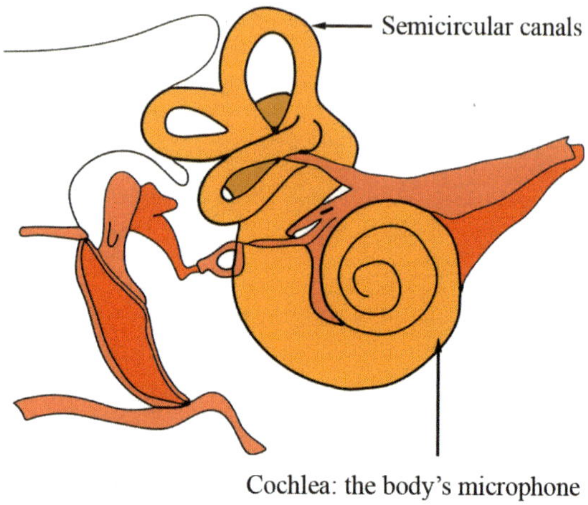

Figure 178. The organ of Corti: the balance organ

Test Your Knowledge

1. What are the three basic parts of the ear?

___

___

___

2. Where is the tympanic membrane found?

___

___

3. Where are the ossicles found and how many ossicles are there?

___

___

4. What is the Organ of Corti commonly known as, and where is it found?

___

___

5. What parts of the ear help us with balance, and where are these structures located?

___

___

Common Conditions and Diseases of the Eye and Ear

Glaucoma - a disorder in which the optic nerve can be injured by excessive fluid pressure in the eye. If untreated, it can result in permanent damage.

Color Blindness refers to a diminished ability to perceive certain colors. There is usually a strong genetic contribution. It is much more common in males than females since it is carried in the "X" chromosomes.

Tinnitis - a ringing or noise in the ear not associated with external sounds. It may be transient (brief) as in exposure to a loud gunshot or permanent.

Vertigo refers to dizziness or a sensation of motion even while still. There are a variety of causes and treatment depends on which of several causes are present.

Our Sense of Smell

The Olfactory Sense (*olfacere* = to smell; *ory* = pertaining to)

Our sense of smell, the olfactory sense, allows us to detect aromas of Thanksgiving dinner as well as the subtle scent of a woman's perfume. Smell, like taste, is a form of chemoreception (a physiological response to a chemical) and is far less sensitive in humans than in other creatures, like dogs, but nevertheless, provides us with a full range of sensory experience. While the sense of smell is able to detect a variety of scents, it frequently adapts rapidly, a phenomenon known as sensory adaptation. That is to say, you become less and less aware of the particular smell, the longer you are exposed to it.

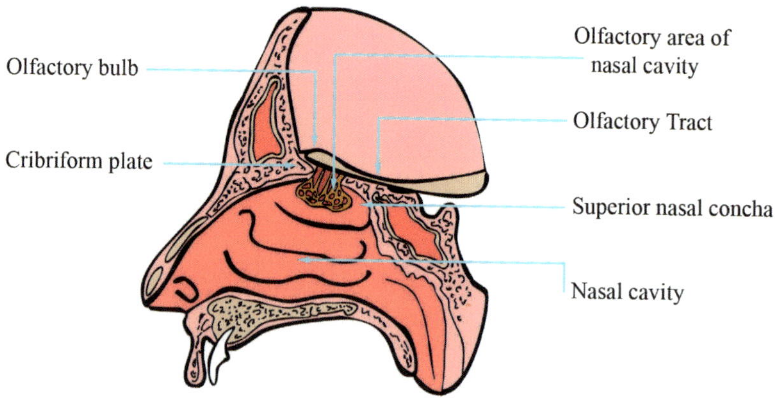

Figure 179. The olfactory sense

Smell begins when an inhalation of air is brought in through the nose. Smells carried in that air next come into contact with what are called sensory receptors within the cribiform plate, a sieve-like region in the human skull (and part of the ethmoid bone) which separates the nasal cavity from the brain (Figure 179).

Our understanding of how airborne odorants produce stimulation of these receptors is somewhat limited. There are a variety of theories that attempt to explain how airborne molecules are detected and how they produce action potentials that the brain interprets as smells. (As you may recall, action potentials were explained in the chapter on The Nervous System and basically refer to *How Neurons Work.*) What is known is that these molecules dissolve in the mucus that covers these scent receptors in the superior nasal concha (a shell-shaped spongy bone in the nasal passage) (Figure 179).

These olfactory receptors send information via axons that make up the first cranial nerve. This nerve extends to the brain where the various olfactory inputs are pieced together and the perception of a particular smell is resolved.

Our Sense of Taste

The Gustatory Sense (*gustare* = the sense of taste; *ory* = pertaining to)

Taste refers to the ability to detect the flavor of substances such as food, certain minerals, and poisons, but it only contributes partially to the sensation and flavor of food in the mouth — other factors include smell, texture, temperature, and spiciness.

Your tongue and the roof of your mouth (at least when you are a child) are covered with a multitude of taste buds that allow us the ability to perceive a wide range of taste sensations.

As food begins to be broken down by chemicals present in saliva, receptors in our taste buds begin to be stimulated resulting in action potentials (see Chapter 10: The Nervous System for a complete discussion of action potentials). These action potentials send information to the brain regarding the flavors we are currently tasting.

Taste buds are not randomly located over the tongue, but are grouped together in anatomically distinct areas based on their principal sensitivities. Those that primarily detect bitter sensations are located in one area, sour or sweet in another, and salty in yet another (Figure 180). The sour sensation is located on the sides of the tongue, while bitter is on the back of the tongue and sweet and salty are located on the tip of the tongue. A fifth sensation called "umami" has also been identified. Umami, a word borrowed from the Japanese culture, denotes a strong "meaty" taste often associated with the effects of MSG and certain other amino acids. The "distribution" of taste buds is a bit misleading since all taste buds contain receptors for

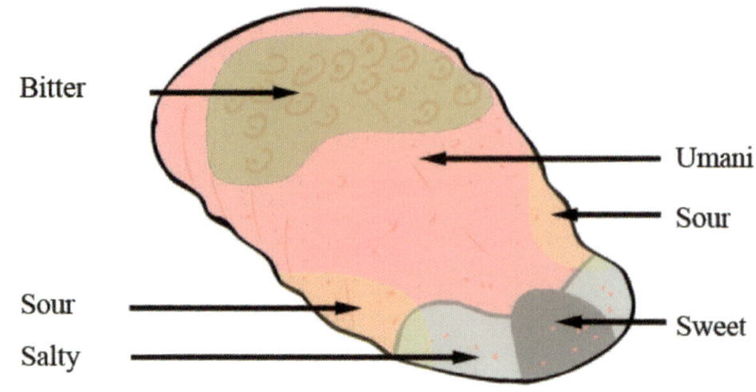

Figure 180. The tongue with areas of taste sensation

all five basic taste sensations. What is important to note here is that sensitivity to certain tastes are more prevalent on taste buds located in certain areas (Figure 181).

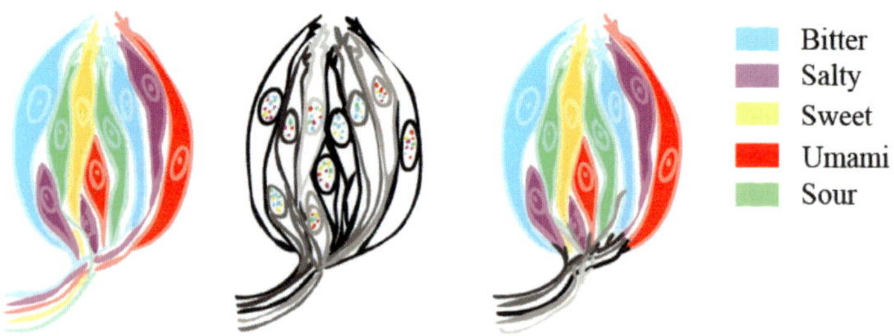

Figure 181. The taste bud

Once a substance is ingested, taste information is transmitted to the brain from the taste bud receptors and travels along several cranial nerves including the facial, glossopharyngeal, and vagus nerves.

Sense of Touch

The Somatosensory System (*somat/o* = body; *sensus* = sensation of feeling; *ory* = pertaining to)

The sense of touch allows us to distinguish between sandpaper, the soft skin of a newborn baby, and the relative comfort of a well-fitting pair of shoes. It also helps us identify the location of our limbs in space. This phenomenon is called proprioception (*proprio* = one's own; *cept* = to receive or take in; *tion* = the condition of).

Although touch receptors that feel pressure, pain, and temperature are not evenly distributed throughout the body, they are found all over the body's various surfaces and are located in the skin layer known as the dermis (Figure 182). The uneven distribution of touch receptors is readily apparent when one considers the difference in sensitivity in areas such as the back and the fingertips.

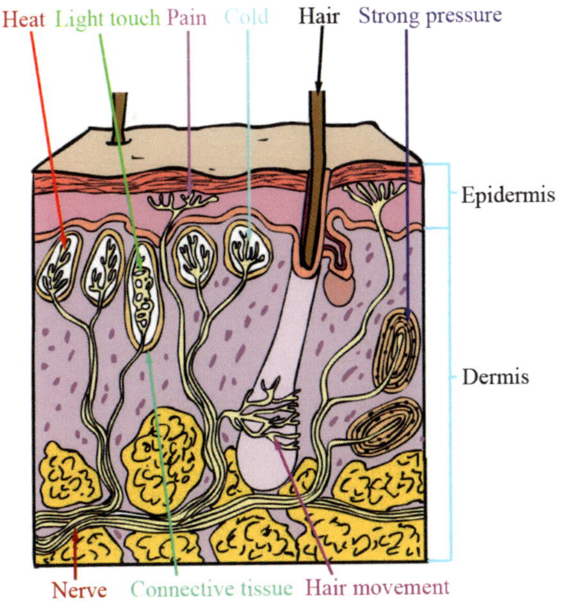

Figure 182. Touch receptors within the dermis

Four basic types of receptors have been identified. These include the mechanoreceptors (mechanical pressure or distortion), thermoreceptors (temperature), nociceptors (pain) and chemoreceptors (chemical stimuli). Mechanoreceptors are any sensory nerve endings that respond to mechanical stimuli, such as touch, pressure, sound, and muscular contractions. There are three types of mechanoreceptors. Free nerve endings inform the brain about pain and are located over the entire body. Pacinian corpuscles detect pressure, telling the brain when a limb has moved. Meissner corpuscles are grouped on the skin of the fingertips, lips, orifices of the body, and the nipples and are stimulated when touched.

Thermoreceptors are nerve endings that are sensitive to heat or a rise in body temperature. There are two types of thermoreceptors, the end-bulb of Krause, which detects cold, and Ruffini's end organ, which detects heat.

Nociceptors are groups of cells that act as receptors for painful stimuli and allow us to feel needle pricks or pinches and even mosquito bites.

Chemoreceptors are specialized sensory end organs adapted for excitation by chemical substances (e.g., gustatory and olfactory receptors) or specialized sense organs of the carotid body and are sensitive to various chemical changes in the bloodstream.

Proprioception is our "body sense" that enables us to unconsciously monitor the position of our body.

These various receptors rarely, if ever, act alone, but instead work in concert to provide us with a full range of sensory experience. Because of their wide distribution on the body's surface, touch receptors do not travel on a specific nerve track as did the smell receptors.

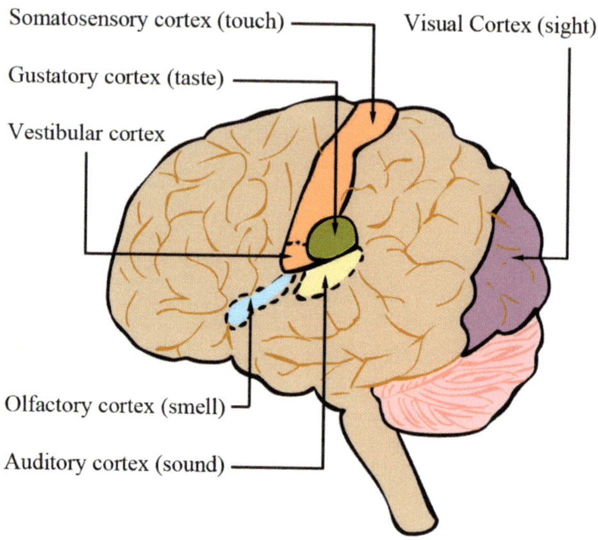

Figure 183. The brain with areas of senses

Senses Glossary

accommodation	process whereby the eyes make adjustments for seeing objects at various distances
audition	sense or act of hearing
auditory nerve	nerve that carries sound information from the coclea to the brain
auditory ossicles	three small bones found in the middle ear; transmit the sound waves from the eardrum to the inner ear by vibration
blind spot	the point at which the optic nerve leaves the eye, creating a "blind" spot because no receptor cells are located there
cataract	clouding of the lens resulting in difficulty reading; may be congenital (present at birth) or caused by trauma (injury) or disease; however, the formation of most cataracts is associated with aging
cerumen	(also known as earwax) secreted by ceruminous glands that line the auditory canal; purpose is to prevent dust and other small structures from getting to the eardrum
cochlea	coiled, bony, fluid-filled tube in the inner ear through which sound waves are turned into fluid waves and then transmitted to the brain
cochleovestibular	refers to hearing as well as balance; pertaining to the cochlea and the vestibule of the ear
cones	retinal receptors that are concentrated near the center of the retina and that function in daylight or in well-lit conditions; detect fine details and give rise to color sensations
convergence	simultaneous inward movement of both eyes (toward each other), usually in an effort to maintain single binocular vision as an abject comes nearer
deafness	the complete or partial loss of the ability to hear
diplopia	(also known as double vision) perception of two images of a single object
epistaxis	nosebleed

eustachian tubes	(also known as the auditory tubes) narrow tubes which lead from the middle ear to the nasopharynx, equalize the air pressure in the middle ear with that of the outside atmosphere
exophthalmos	condition in which one or both eyeballs protrude because of a thyroid dysfunction
farsightedness	condition in which far away objects are seen more clearly than near objects because the image of near objects is focused behind the retina
fovea	central focus point in the retina, around which the eye's cones cluster; the most sensitive part of the retina consisting entirely of cones for detailed color vision
frequency	number of complete wavelengths that pass a point in a given time
glaucoma	characterized by increased intraocular pressure, if untreated this pressure damages the optic nerve and causes the loss of peripheral vision and eventually blindness
hue	dimension of color that is determined by the wavelength of light; what we know as the color spectrum
incus	one of the auditory ossicles; also known as the anvil
inner ear	innermost part of the ear, containing the cochlea, semicircular canals and vestibular sacs
intensity	amount of energy in a light or sound wave, which we perceive as brightness or loudness, as determined by the wave's amplitude
iris	ring of muscle tissue that forms the colored portion of the eye around the pupil and controls the size of the pupil opening
lens	transparent structure behind the pupil that changes shape to help focus images on the retina
malleus	(also known as the hammer) one of the auditory ossicles
nearsightedness	condition in which nearby objects are seen more clearly than distant objects because distant objects focus in front of the retina
opthalmoscope	instrument for studying the interior of the eyeball
optic nerve	the nerve that carries neural impulses from the eye to the brain; also known as the cranial nerve II

otitis	any inflammation of the ear
photophobia	extreme sensitivity to light
pitch	tone's experienced highness or lowness; depends on frequency
pupil	adjustable opening in the center of the eye through which light enters
retina	light-sensitive inner surface of the eye, containing the receptor rods and cones plus layers of neurons that begin the processing of visual information
rods	retinal receptors that detect black, white and grey; necessary for peripheral and twilight vision, when cones don't respond
stapes	one of the auditory ossicles; also known as the stirrup
tinnitus	ringing, buzzing, or roaring sound in the ears
tympanic membrane	(also known as the eardrum) located between the outer and middle ear
vertigo	sense of whirling, dizziness and the loss of balance
vestibular sense	sense of body movement and position, including sense of balance
wavelength	distance from the peak of one light or sound wave to the peak of the next

Index

A

B

C

M

N

O

P

T

U

About the Author

Prior to writing Anatomy and Physiology for Allied Health Professions, Dr. Brady completed his Ph.D. in Psychology at Texas Tech University. He subsequently joined the Navy as an officer and became one of the nation's leading experts on human underwater performance. It was during that time that he decided to attend medical school. He resigned his position with the Navy, returned to Texas Tech, graduated from medical school with honors and was awarded membership into the prestigious Alpha Omega Alpha. From there, Dr. Brady began his residency in OB/GYN at one of the busiest and well known programs in the country, University of California, Irvine Medical Center. Upon completing of his residency, he was lured by Baylor Hospital to enter private practice in Waxahachie, Texas where he served as Chief of Staff there for several years.

Dr. Brady practiced OB/GYN for 15 years. He has taught Anatomy and Physiology on the college level, and has now turned to writing, consulting, providing medical retroactive billing and coding services, and performing medical case reviews. He has two grown children and now resides in Dallas, Texas enjoying fishing, golf, and carpentry.

CPSIA information can be obtained
at www.ICGtesting.com
Printed in the USA
LVIC042255110413
328711LV00001B
* 9 7 8 1 9 3 7 8 1 6 0 1 8 *